SATOKO AND NADA 2

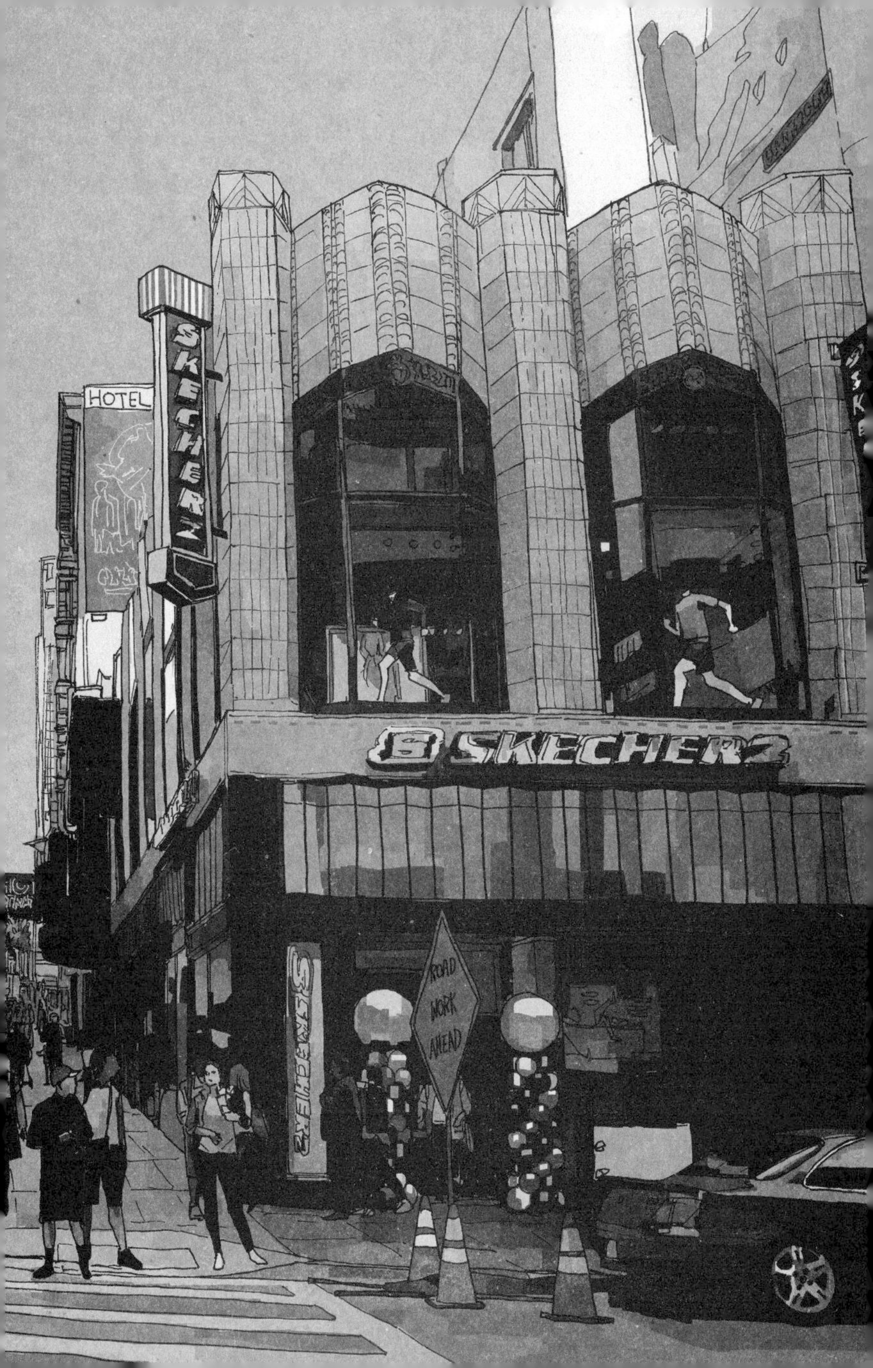
HOTEL
SKECHERS
SKECHERS
ROAD WORK AHEAD
SKECHERS

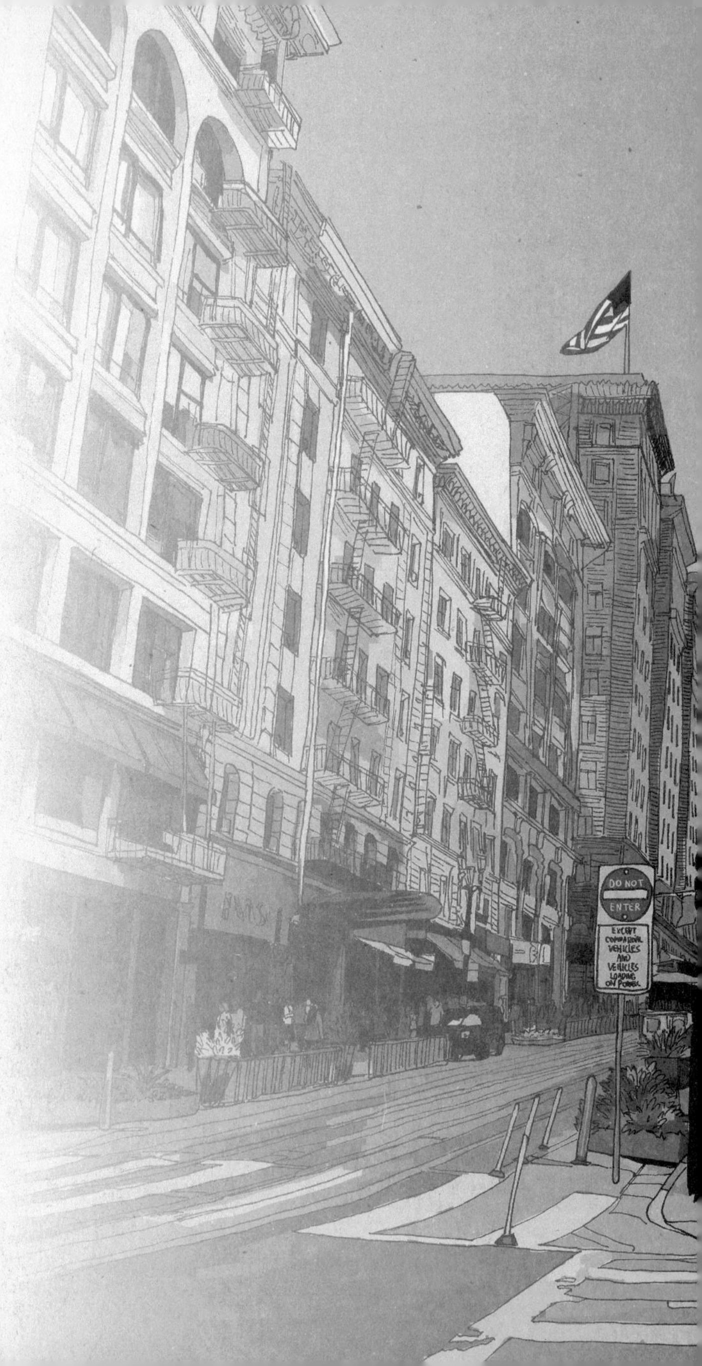
DO NOT
ENTER

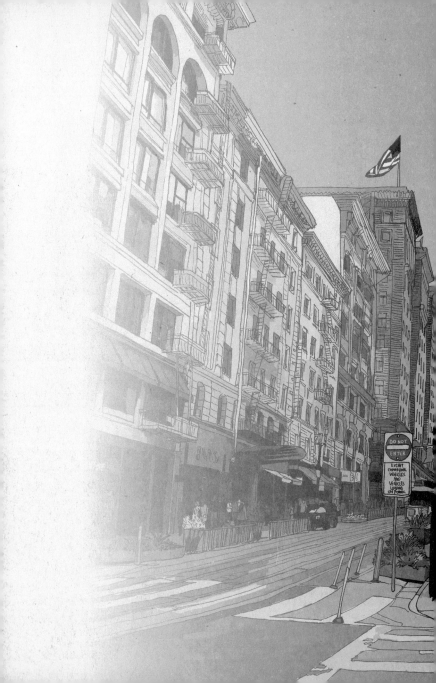

HEROINE

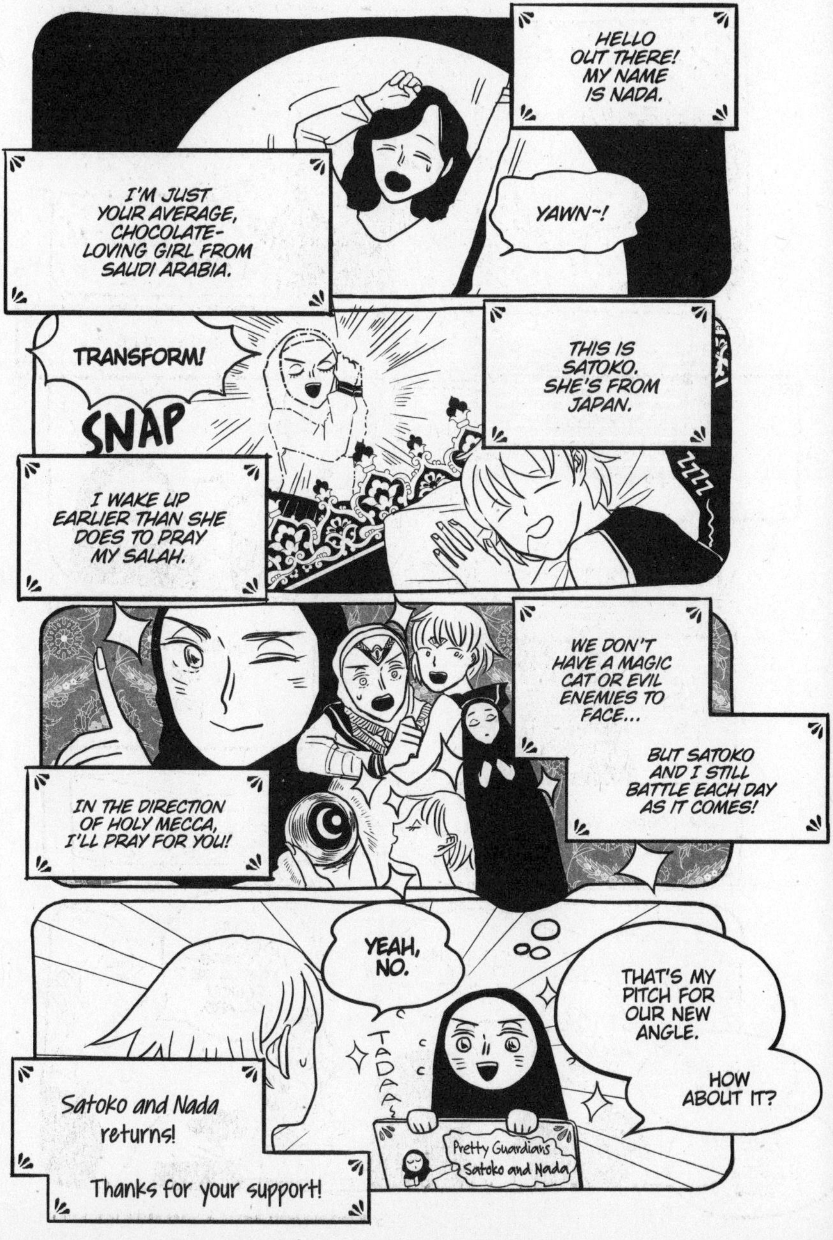
HELLO OUT THERE! MY NAME IS NADA.
I'M JUST YOUR AVERAGE, CHOCOLATE-LOVING GIRL FROM SAUDI ARABIA.
YAWN~!
THIS IS SATOKO. SHE'S FROM JAPAN.
ZZZZ
TRANSFORM!
SNAP
I WAKE UP EARLIER THAN SHE DOES TO PRAY MY SALAH.
WE DON'T HAVE A MAGIC CAT OR EVIL ENEMIES TO FACE...
BUT SATOKO AND I STILL BATTLE EACH DAY AS IT COMES!
IN THE DIRECTION OF HOLY MECCA, I'LL PRAY FOR YOU!
THAT'S MY PITCH FOR OUR NEW ANGLE.
HOW ABOUT IT?
YEAH, NO.
TADAA
Pretty Guardians Satoko and Nada
Satoko and Nada returns!
Thanks for your support!

YOGURT TIME

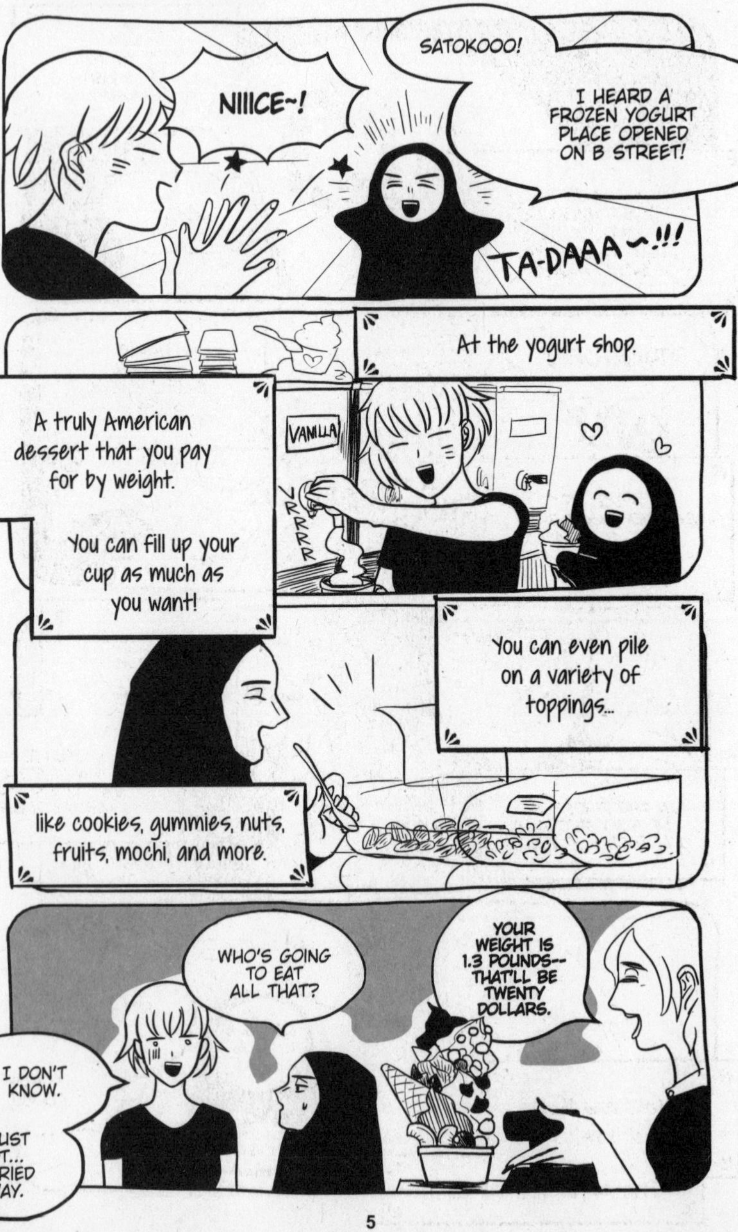

SATOKOOO!
I HEARD A FROZEN YOGURT PLACE OPENED ON B STREET!
TA-DAAA~!!!
NIIICE~!
At the yogurt shop.
A truly American dessert that you pay for by weight.
You can fill up your cup as much as you want!
VANILLA
VRRRR
You can even pile on a variety of toppings...
like cookies, gummies, nuts, fruits, mochi, and more.
YOUR WEIGHT IS 1.3 POUNDS-- THAT'LL BE TWENTY DOLLARS.
WHO'S GOING TO EAT ALL THAT?
I DON'T KNOW.
I JUST GOT... CARRIED AWAY.

SWEET GENTLEMEN

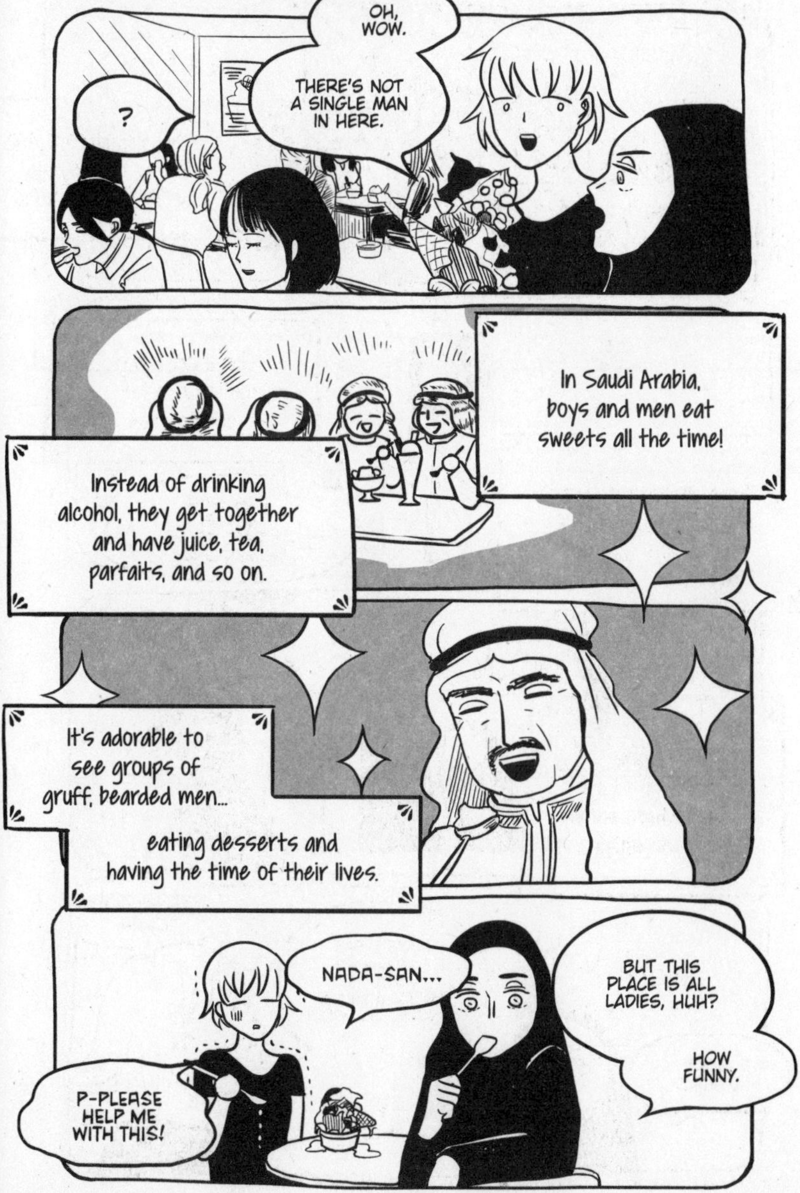
OH, WOW.
THERE'S NOT A SINGLE MAN IN HERE.
?
In Saudi Arabia, boys and men eat sweets all the time!
Instead of drinking alcohol, they get together and have juice, tea, parfaits, and so on.
It's adorable to see groups of gruff, bearded men...
eating desserts and having the time of their lives.
BUT THIS PLACE IS ALL LADIES, HUH?
HOW FUNNY.
NADA-SAN...
P-PLEASE HELP ME WITH THIS!

SINGLE SECTION

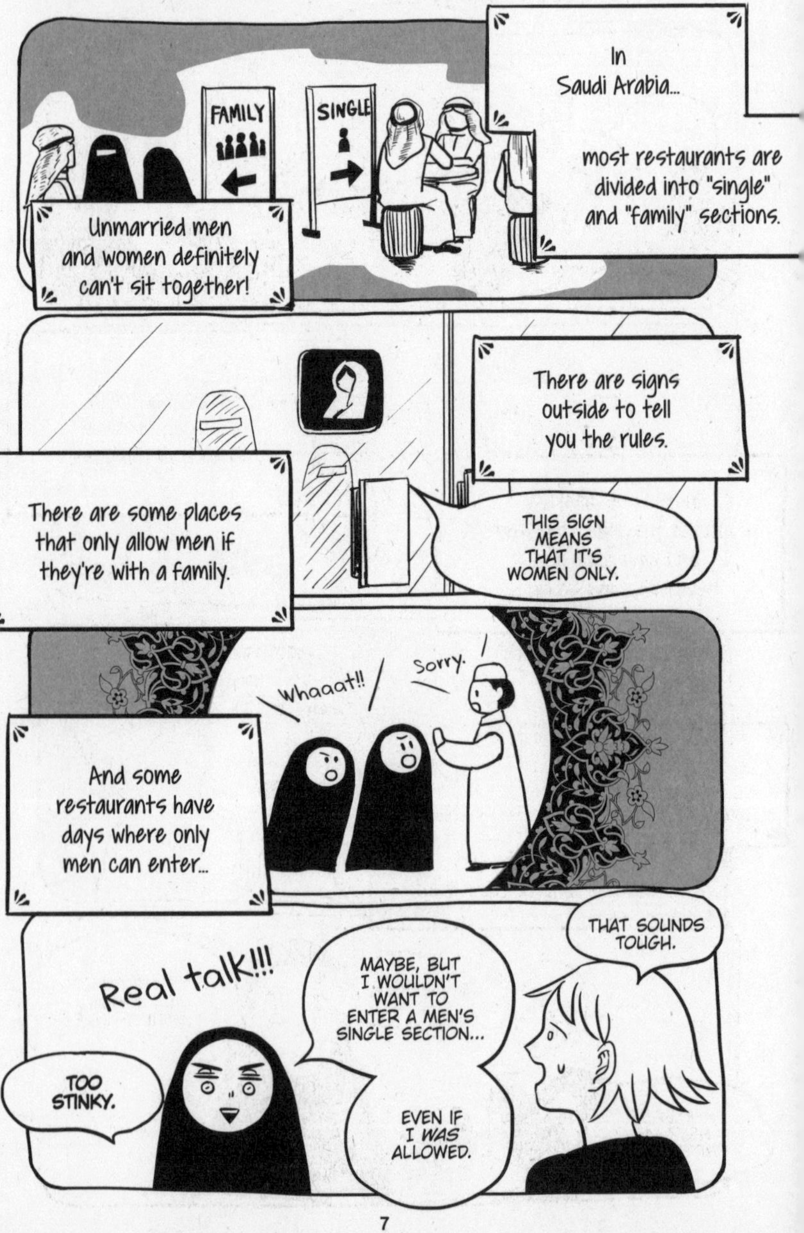

In Saudi Arabia...
most restaurants are divided into "single" and "family" sections.
SINGLE
FAMILY
Unmarried men and women definitely can't sit together!
There are signs outside to tell you the rules.
THIS SIGN MEANS THAT IT'S WOMEN ONLY.
There are some places that only allow men if they're with a family.
Sorry.
Whaaat!!
And some restaurants have days where only men can enter...
THAT SOUNDS TOUGH.
MAYBE, BUT I WOULDN'T WANT TO ENTER A MEN'S SINGLE SECTION...
Real talk!!!
EVEN IF I WAS ALLOWED.
TOO STINKY.

INDIRECT CHAT

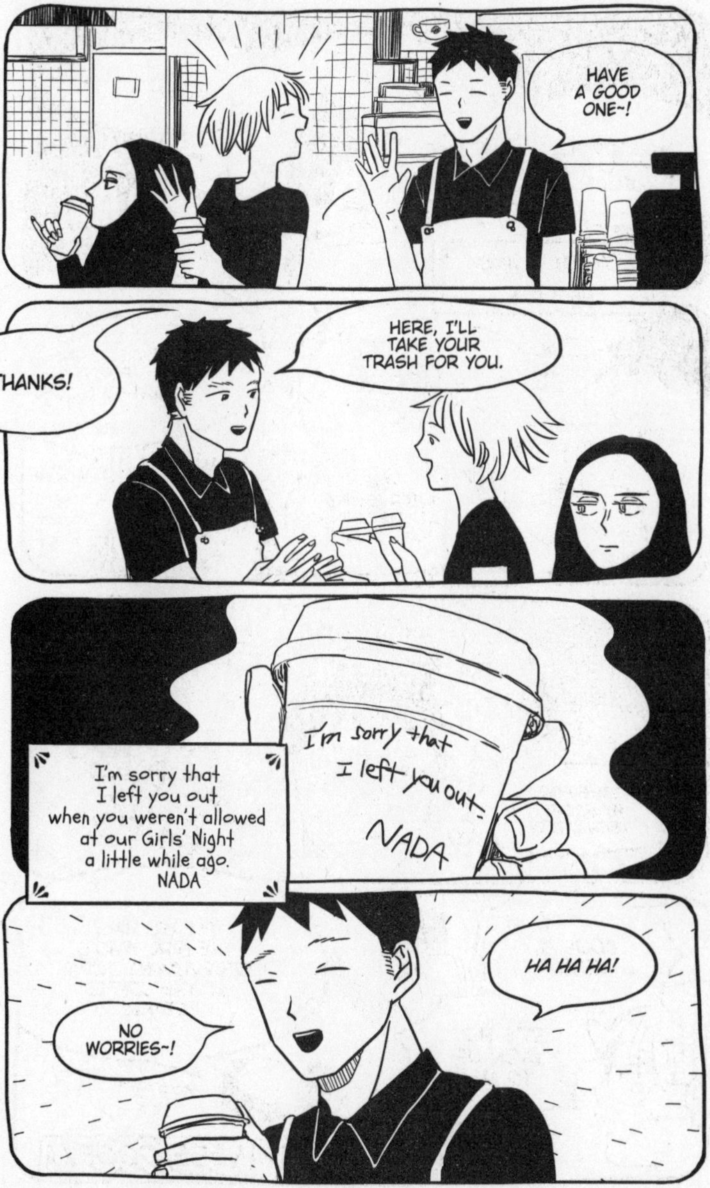
HAVE A GOOD ONE~!
HERE, I'LL TAKE YOUR TRASH FOR YOU.
THANKS!
I'm sorry that I left you out. NADA
I'm sorry that I left you out when you weren't allowed at our Girls' Night a little while ago. NADA
HA HA HA!
NO WORRIES~!

PART-TIME JOB

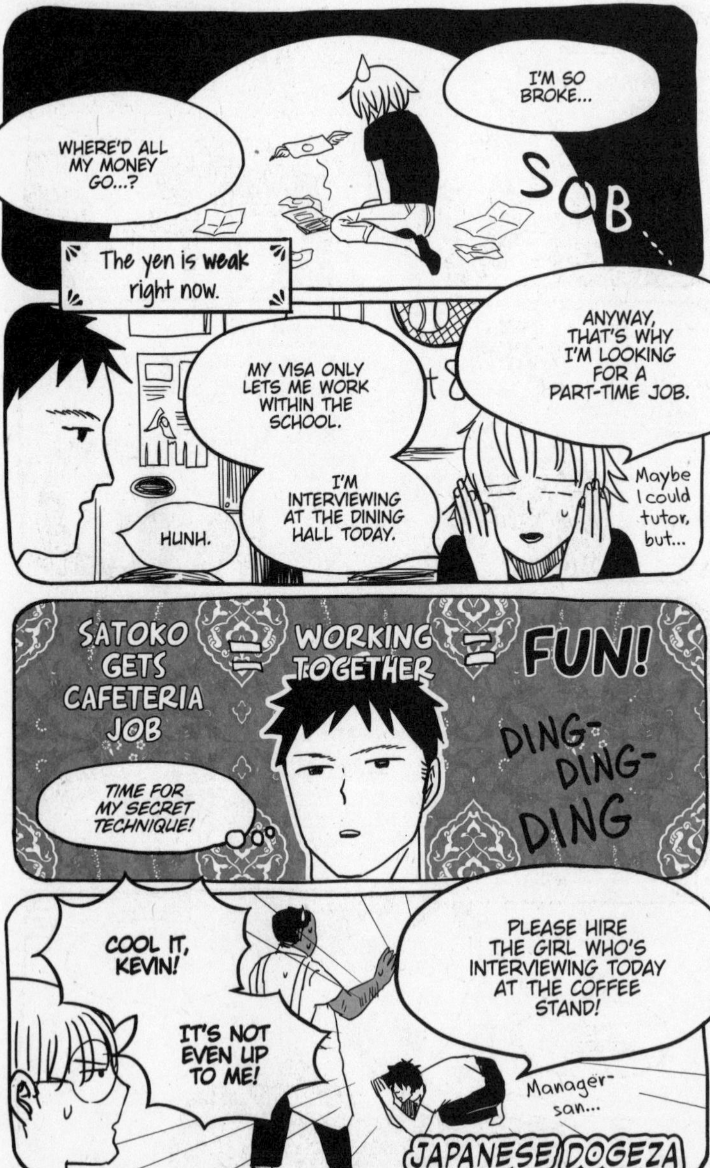
I'M SO BROKE...
SOB...
WHERE'D ALL MY MONEY GO...?
The yen is weak right now.
ANYWAY, THAT'S WHY I'M LOOKING FOR A PART-TIME JOB.
Maybe I could tutor, but...
MY VISA ONLY LETS ME WORK WITHIN THE SCHOOL.
I'M INTERVIEWING AT THE DINING HALL TODAY.
HUNH.
FUN!
WORKING TOGETHER
SATOKO GETS CAFETERIA JOB
DING-DING-DING
TIME FOR MY SECRET TECHNIQUE!
PLEASE HIRE THE GIRL WHO'S INTERVIEWING TODAY AT THE COFFEE STAND!
Manager-san...
JAPANESE DOGEZA
COOL IT, KEVIN!
IT'S NOT EVEN UP TO ME!

INTERVIEW

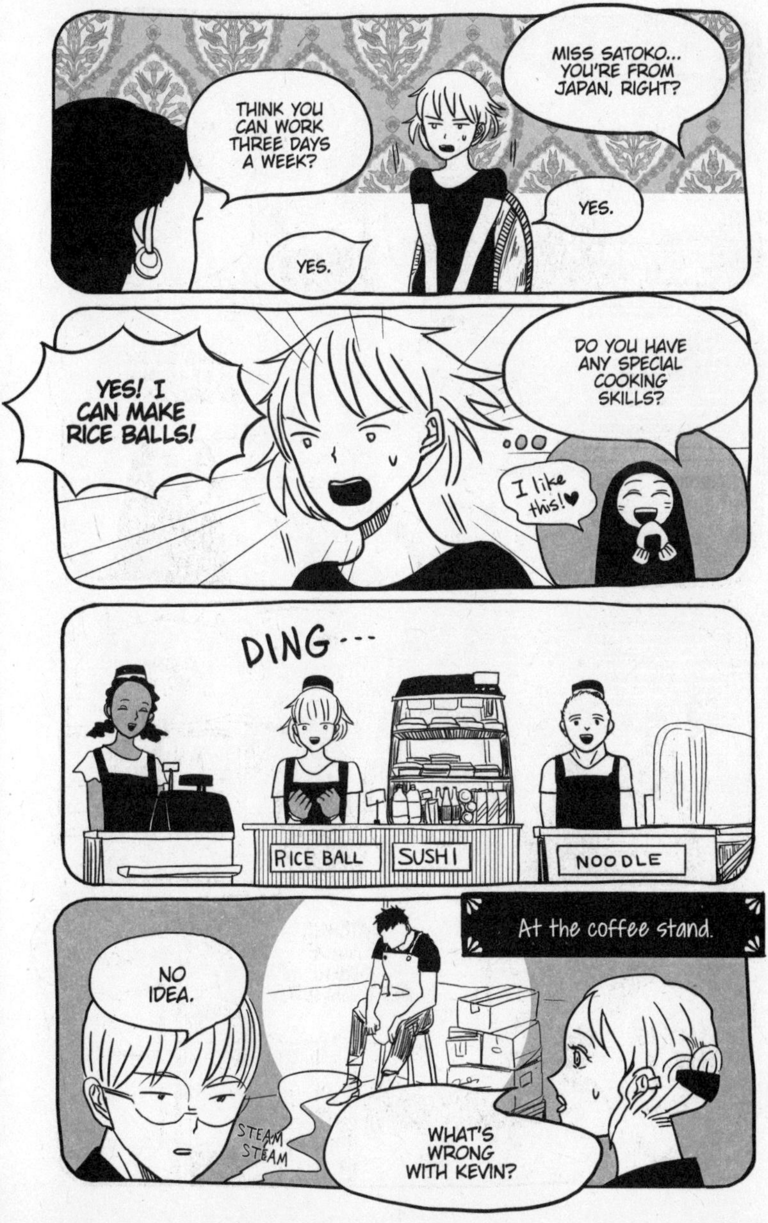
MISS SATOKO... YOU'RE FROM JAPAN, RIGHT?
THINK YOU CAN WORK THREE DAYS A WEEK?
YES.
YES.
DO YOU HAVE ANY SPECIAL COOKING SKILLS?
YES! I CAN MAKE RICE BALLS!
I like this!♥
DING...
NOODLE
SUSHI
RICE BALL
At the coffee stand.
WHAT'S WRONG WITH KEVIN?
NO IDEA.
STEAM STEAM

FIRST DAY

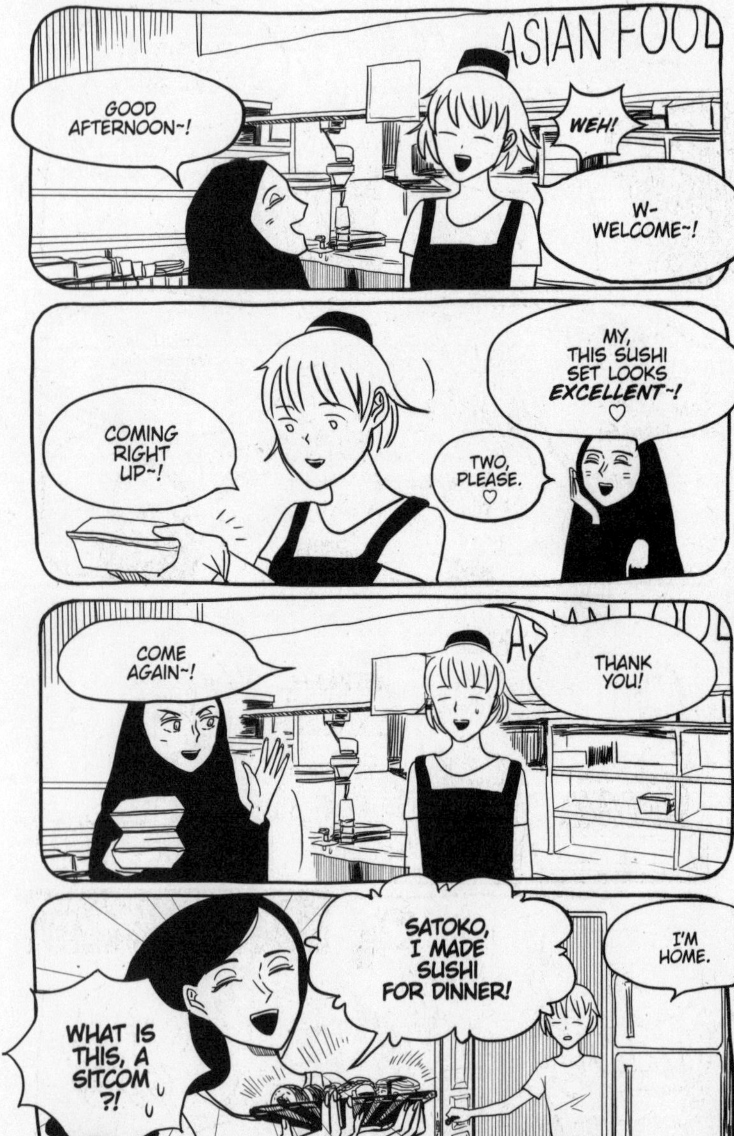

WEH!
W- WELCOME~!
GOOD AFTERNOON~!
MY, THIS SUSHI SET LOOKS EXCELLENT~! ♡
TWO, PLEASE. ♡
COMING RIGHT UP~!
THANK YOU!
COME AGAIN~!
I'M HOME.
SATOKO, I MADE SUSHI FOR DINNER!
WHAT IS THIS, A SITCOM?!

USED TO IT

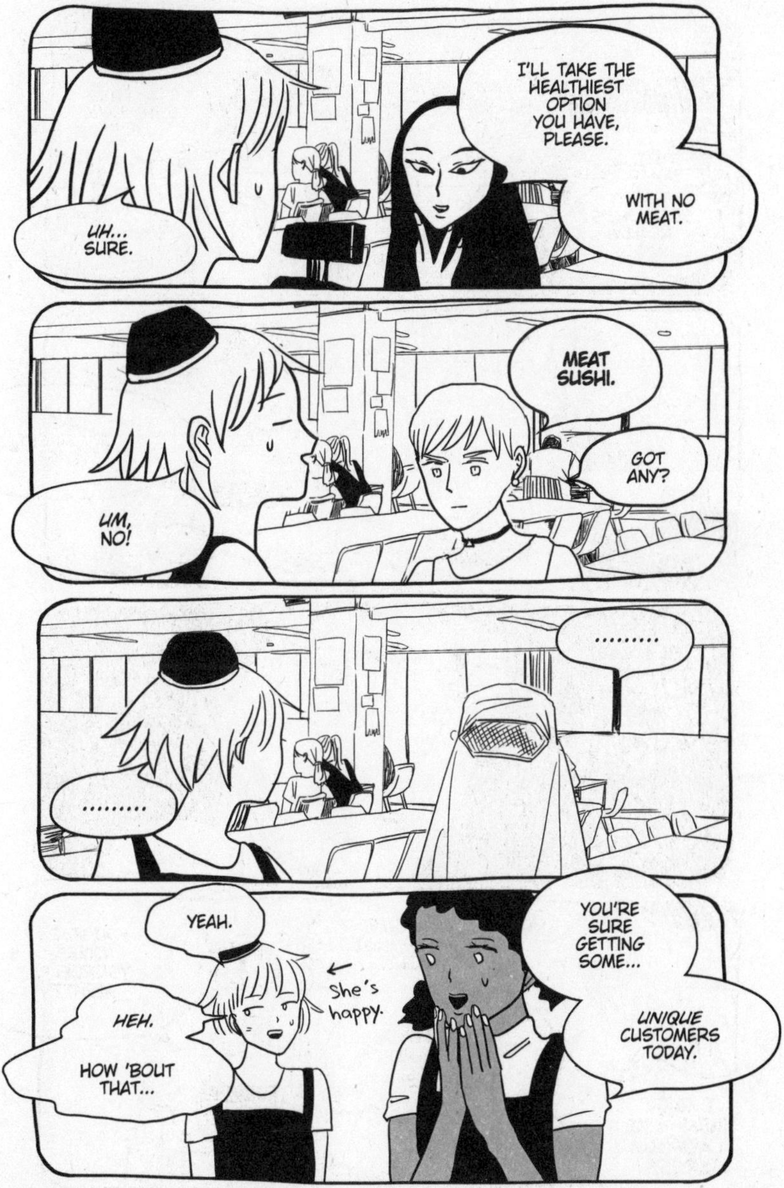

I'LL TAKE THE HEALTHIEST OPTION YOU HAVE, PLEASE.
WITH NO MEAT.
UH... SURE.
MEAT SUSHI.
GOT ANY?
UM, NO!
....
....
YOU'RE SURE GETTING SOME...
UNIQUE CUSTOMERS TODAY.
YEAH.
She's happy.
HEH.
HOW 'BOUT THAT...

ARMPITS

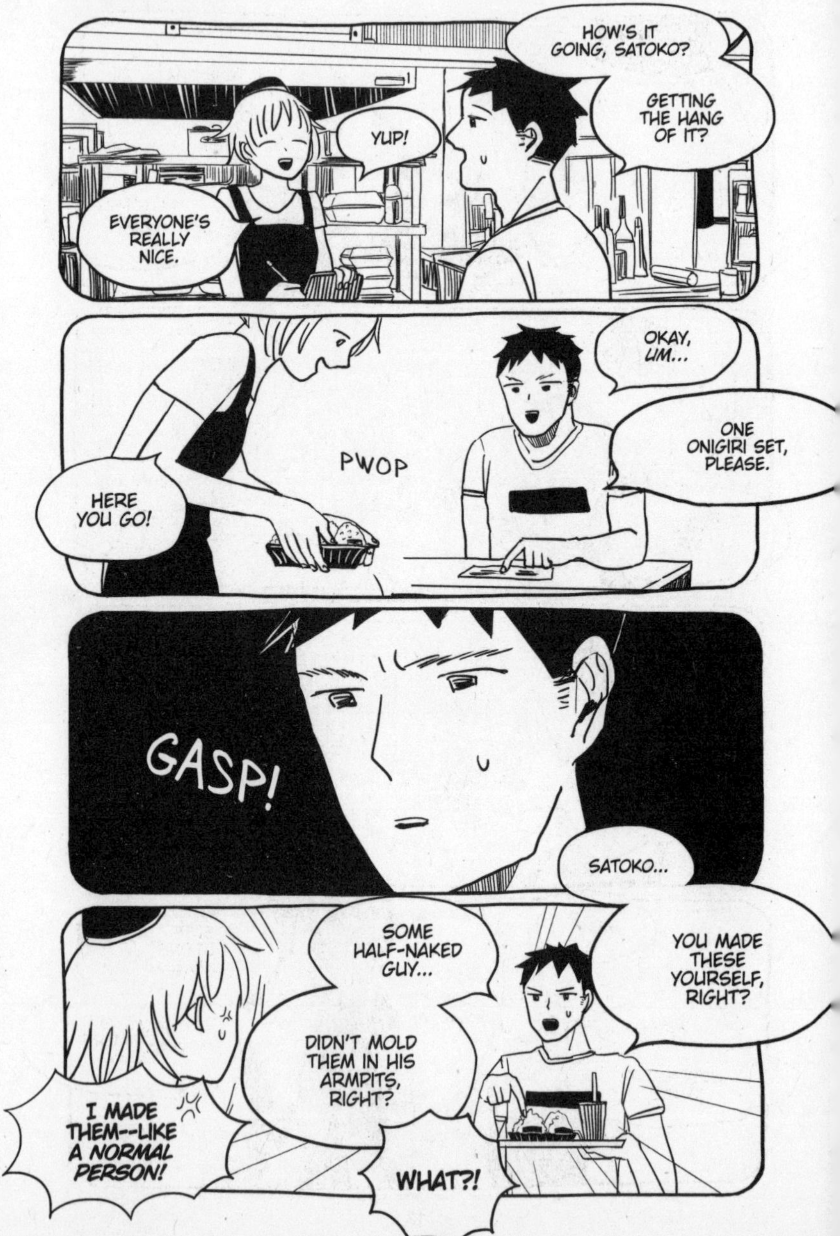
HOW'S IT GOING, SATOKO?
GETTING THE HANG OF IT?
YUP!
EVERYONE'S REALLY NICE.
OKAY, UM...
ONE ONIGIRI SET, PLEASE.
PWOP
HERE YOU GO!
GASP!
SATOKO...
YOU MADE THESE YOURSELF, RIGHT?
SOME HALF-NAKED GUY...
DIDN'T MOLD THEM IN HIS ARMPITS, RIGHT?
WHAT?!
I MADE THEM--LIKE A *NORMAL PERSON!*

TRANSACTION

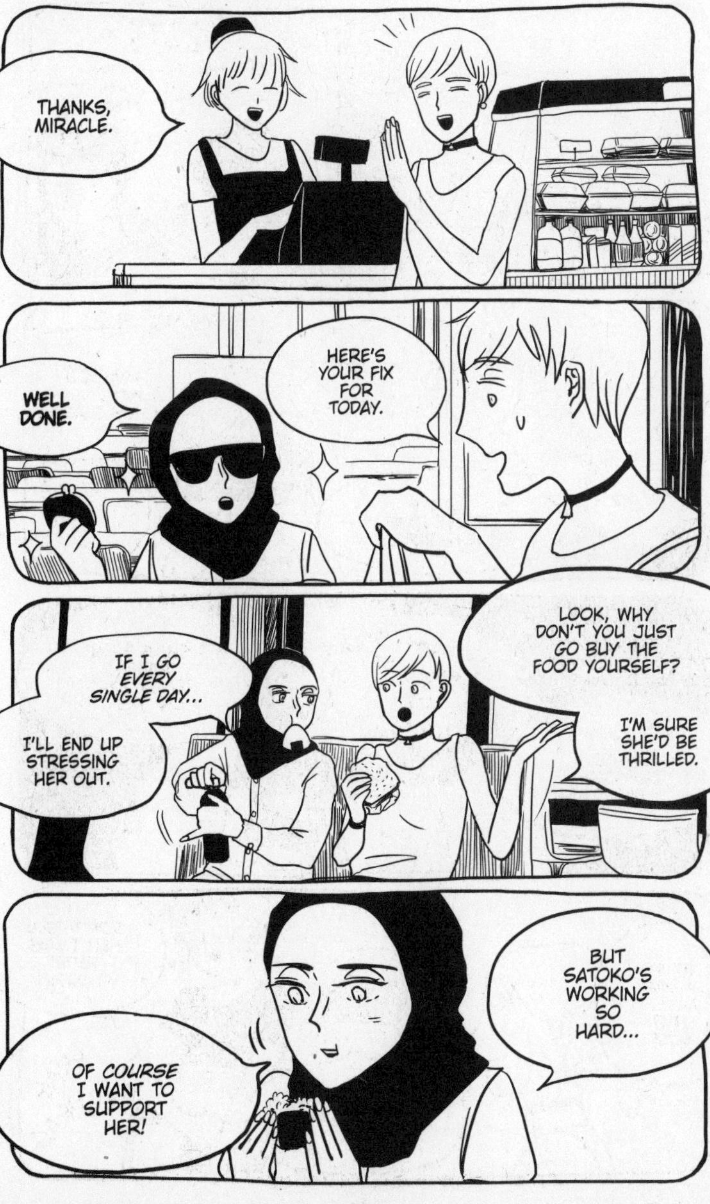
THANKS, MIRACLE.
HERE'S YOUR FIX FOR TODAY.
WELL DONE.
LOOK, WHY DON'T YOU JUST GO BUY THE FOOD YOURSELF?
I'M SURE SHE'D BE THRILLED.
IF I GO EVERY SINGLE DAY...
I'LL END UP STRESSING HER OUT.
BUT SATOKO'S WORKING SO HARD...
OF COURSE I WANT TO SUPPORT HER!

SNEAKY

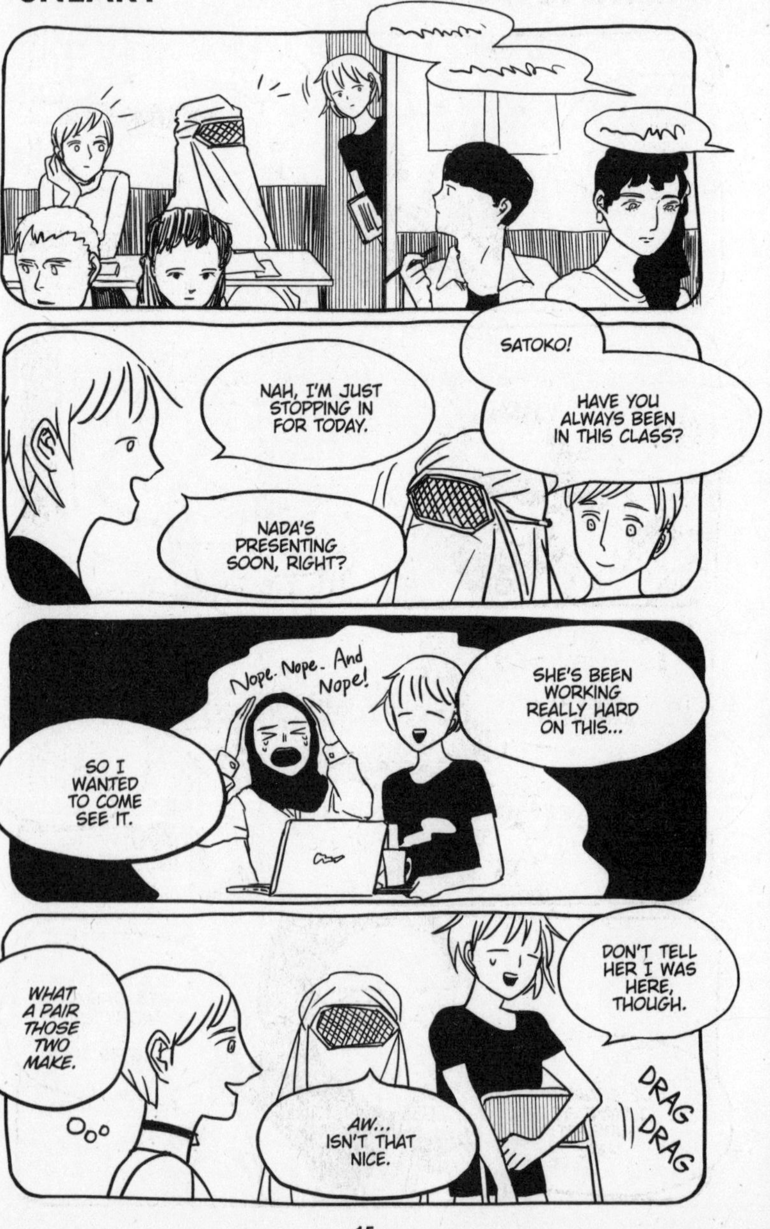
SATOKO!
HAVE YOU ALWAYS BEEN IN THIS CLASS?
NAH, I'M JUST STOPPING IN FOR TODAY.
NADA'S PRESENTING SOON, RIGHT?
SHE'S BEEN WORKING REALLY HARD ON THIS...
Nope. Nope. And Nope!
SO I WANTED TO COME SEE IT.
DON'T TELL HER I WAS HERE, THOUGH.
DRAG DRAG
AW... ISN'T THAT NICE.
WHAT A PAIR THOSE TWO MAKE.
Ooo

EARLOBE TEST

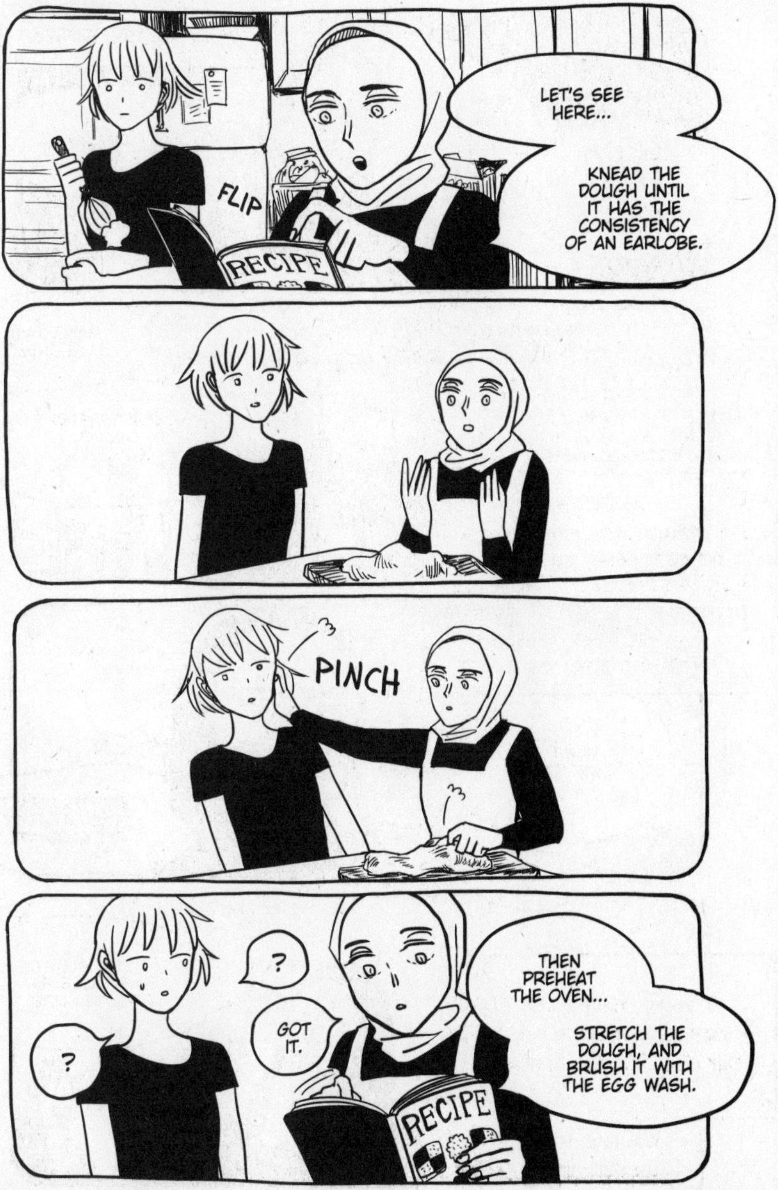
LET'S SEE HERE...
KNEAD THE DOUGH UNTIL IT HAS THE CONSISTENCY OF AN EARLOBE.
FLIP
RECIPE
PINCH
THEN PREHEAT THE OVEN...
STRETCH THE DOUGH, AND BRUSH IT WITH THE EGG WASH.
GOT IT.
?
?
RECIPE

NADA'S SOLO GOURMET DINING

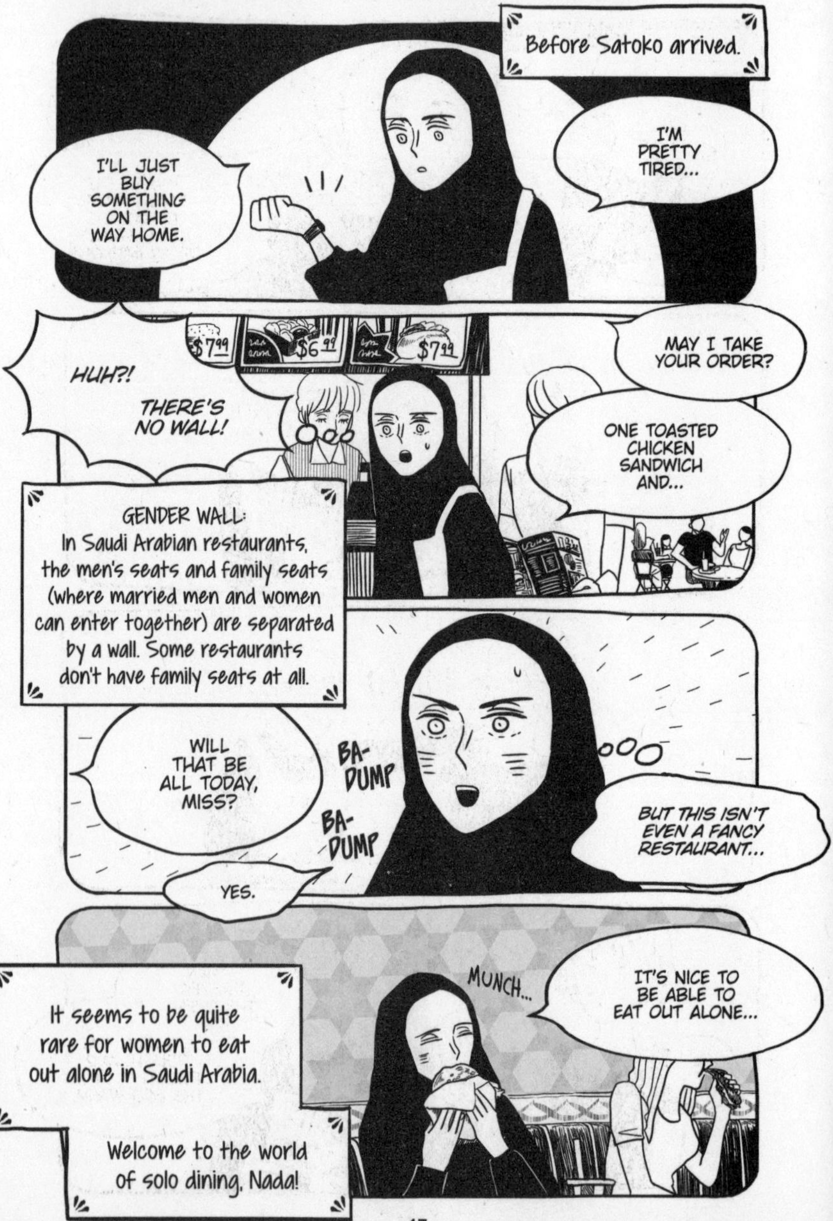
Before Satoko arrived.
I'M PRETTY TIRED...
I'LL JUST BUY SOMETHING ON THE WAY HOME.
MAY I TAKE YOUR ORDER?
ONE TOASTED CHICKEN SANDWICH AND...
HUH?!
THERE'S NO WALL!
GENDER WALL:
In Saudi Arabian restaurants, the men's seats and family seats (where married men and women can enter together) are separated by a wall. Some restaurants don't have family seats at all.
BA-DUMP
BA-DUMP
WILL THAT BE ALL TODAY, MISS?
YES.
BUT THIS ISN'T EVEN A FANCY RESTAURANT...
MUNCH...
IT'S NICE TO BE ABLE TO EAT OUT ALONE...
It seems to be quite rare for women to eat out alone in Saudi Arabia.
Welcome to the world of solo dining, Nada!

NADA'S SOLO GOURMET DINING: PART TWO

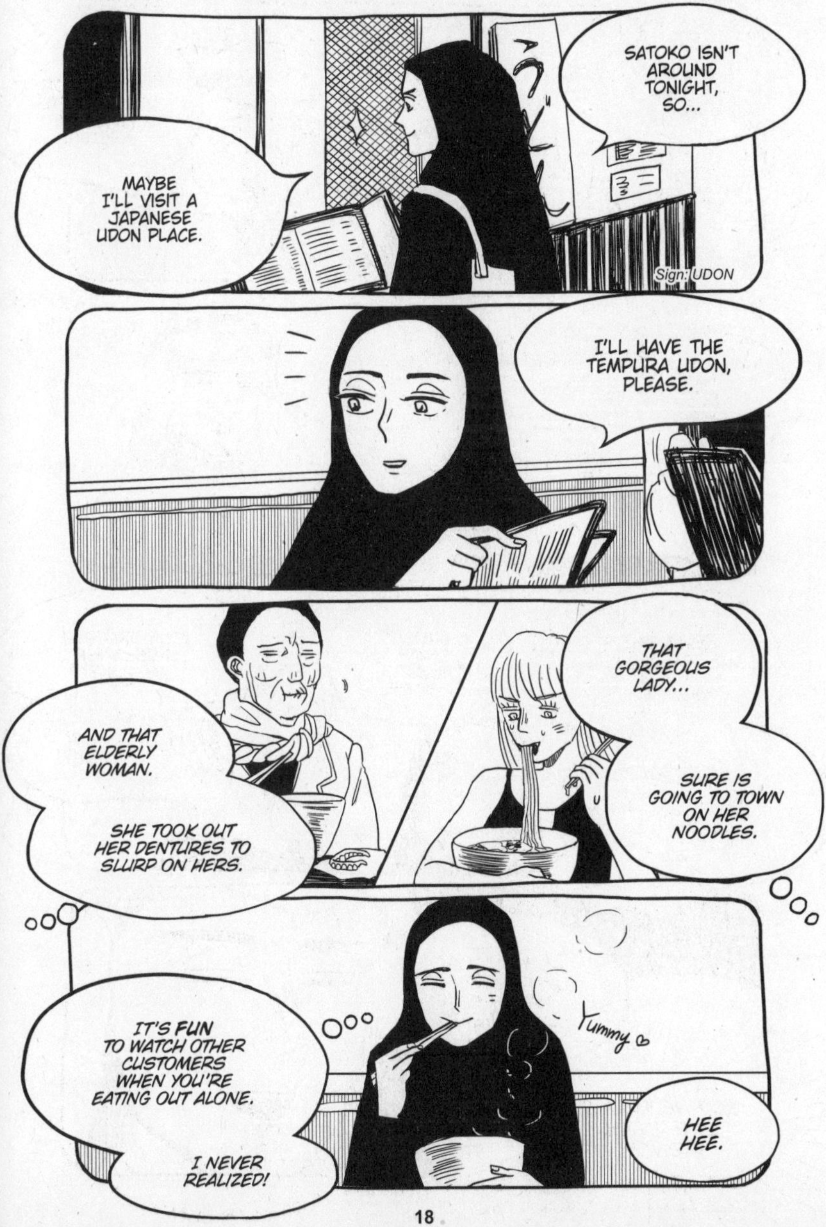

SATOKO ISN'T AROUND TONIGHT, SO...
MAYBE I'LL VISIT A JAPANESE UDON PLACE.
Sign: UDON
I'LL HAVE THE TEMPURA UDON, PLEASE.
THAT GORGEOUS LADY...
SURE IS GOING TO TOWN ON HER NOODLES.
AND THAT ELDERLY WOMAN.
SHE TOOK OUT HER DENTURES TO SLURP ON HERS.
Yummy
HEE HEE.
IT'S FUN TO WATCH OTHER CUSTOMERS WHEN YOU'RE EATING OUT ALONE.
I NEVER REALIZED!

RAHMAN

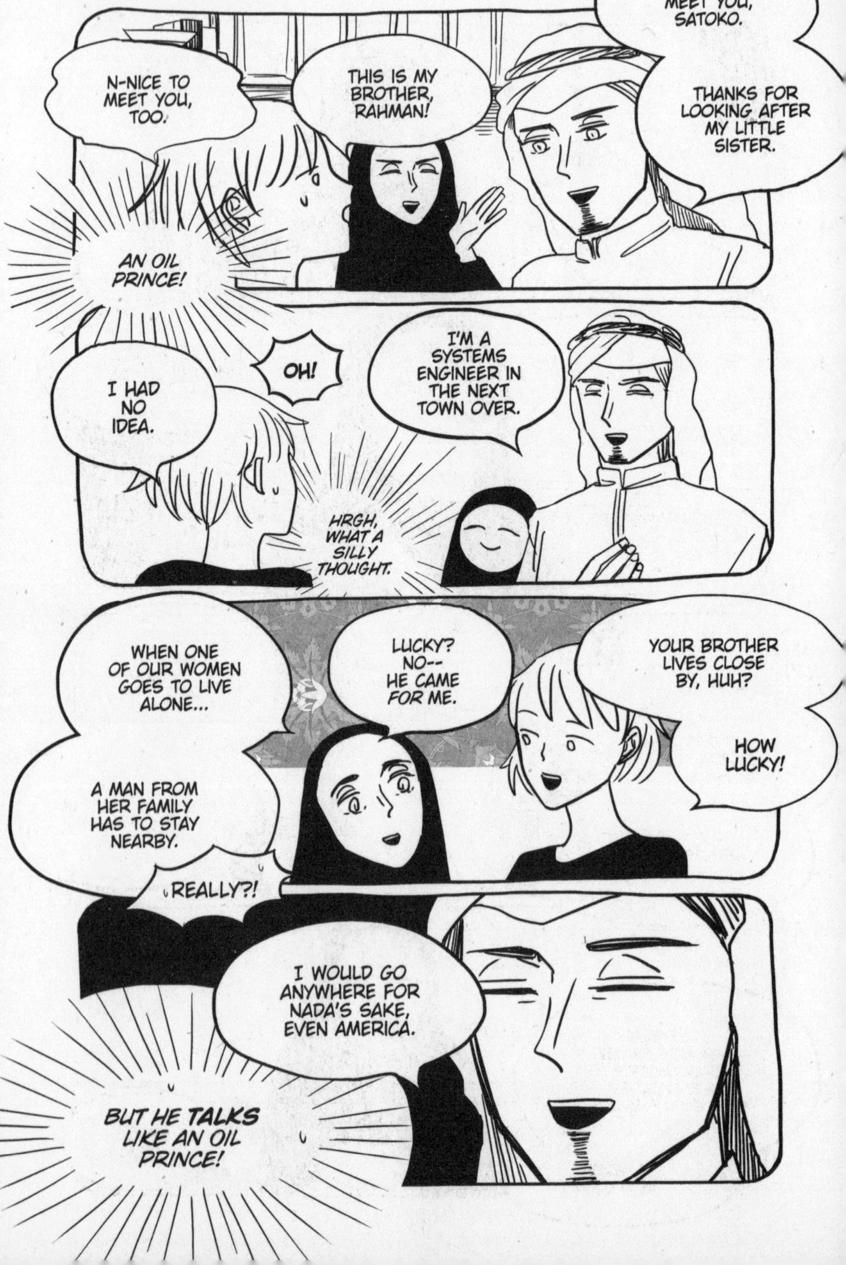
NICE TO MEET YOU, SATOKO.
THANKS FOR LOOKING AFTER MY LITTLE SISTER.
THIS IS MY BROTHER, RAHMAN!
N-NICE TO MEET YOU, TOO.
AN OIL PRINCE!
I'M A SYSTEMS ENGINEER IN THE NEXT TOWN OVER.
OH!
I HAD NO IDEA.
HRGH, WHAT A SILLY THOUGHT.
YOUR BROTHER LIVES CLOSE BY, HUH?
HOW LUCKY!
LUCKY? NO-- HE CAME FOR ME.
WHEN ONE OF OUR WOMEN GOES TO LIVE ALONE...
A MAN FROM HER FAMILY HAS TO STAY NEARBY.
REALLY?!
I WOULD GO ANYWHERE FOR NADA'S SAKE, EVEN AMERICA.
BUT HE TALKS LIKE AN OIL PRINCE!

SHOCK

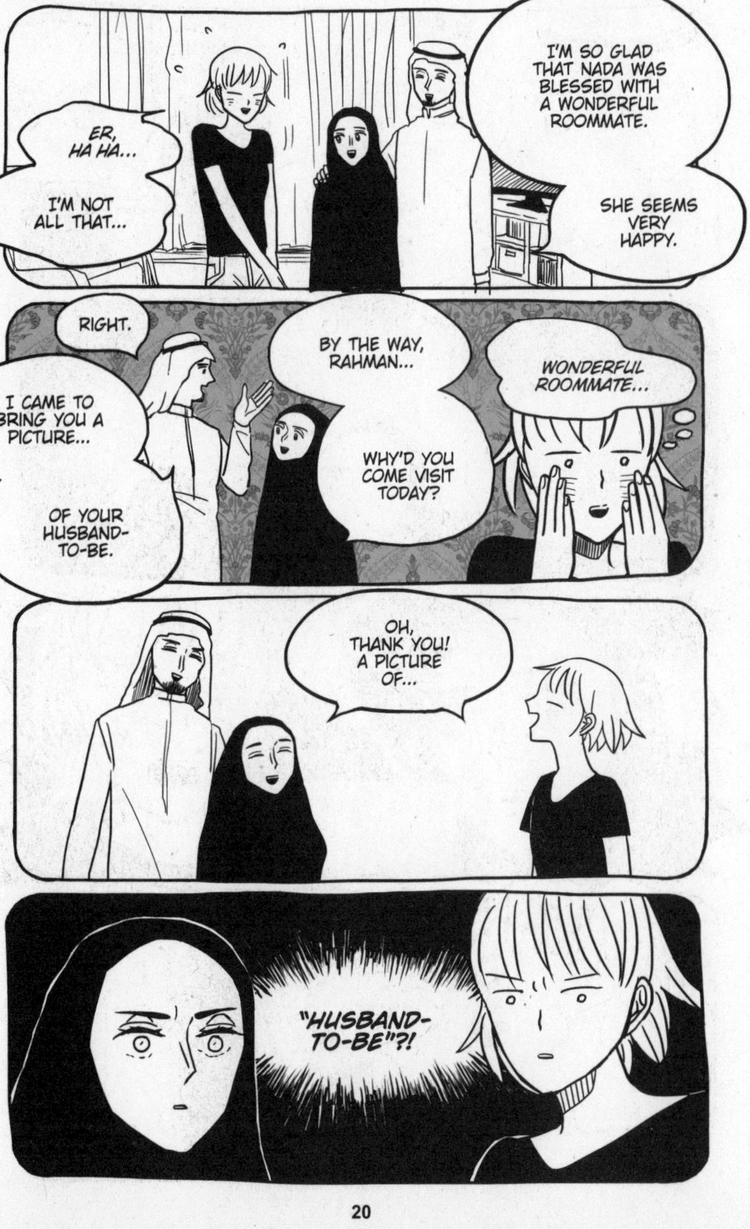
I'M SO GLAD THAT NADA WAS BLESSED WITH A WONDERFUL ROOMMATE.
SHE SEEMS VERY HAPPY.
ER, HA HA...
I'M NOT ALL THAT...
WONDERFUL ROOMMATE...
BY THE WAY, RAHMAN...
WHY'D YOU COME VISIT TODAY?
RIGHT.
I CAME TO BRING YOU A PICTURE...
OF YOUR HUSBAND-TO-BE.
OH, THANK YOU! A PICTURE OF...
"HUSBAND-TO-BE"?!

PHOTO

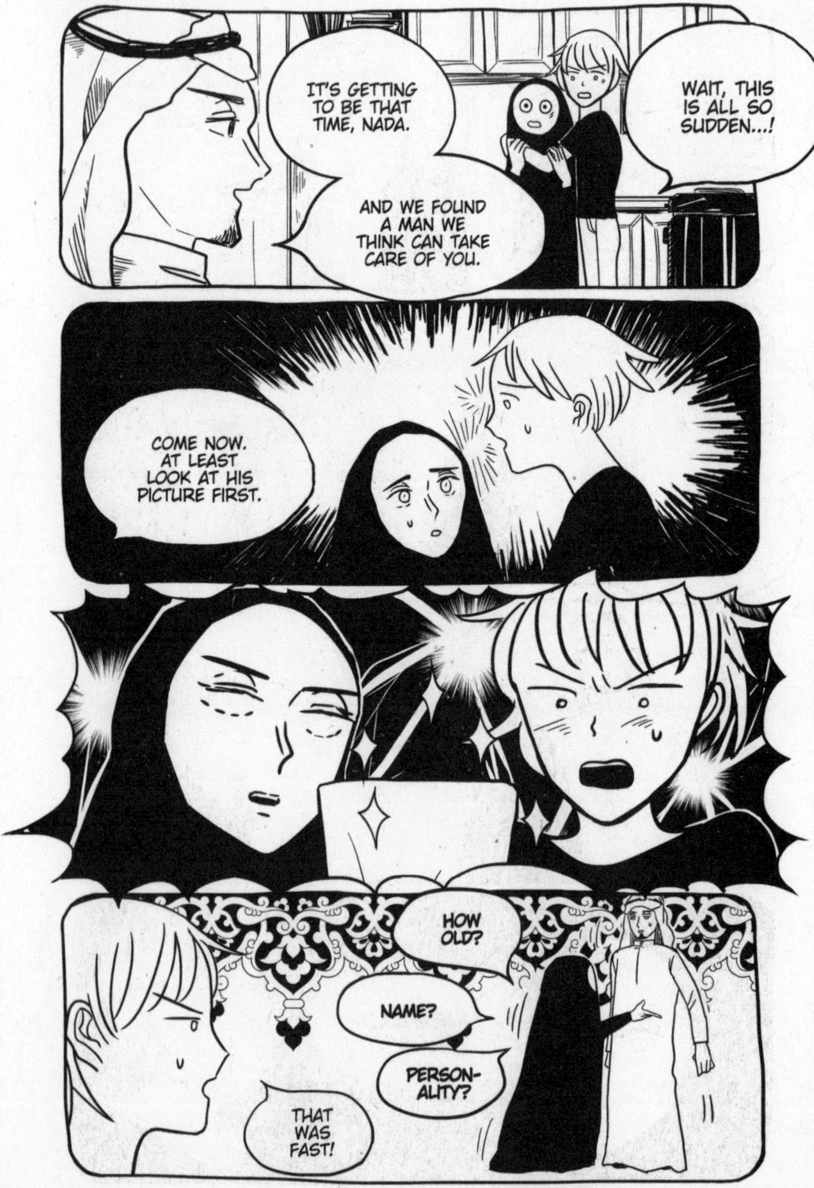
WAIT, THIS IS ALL SO SUDDEN...!
IT'S GETTING TO BE THAT TIME, NADA.
AND WE FOUND A MAN WE THINK CAN TAKE CARE OF YOU.
COME NOW. AT LEAST LOOK AT HIS PICTURE FIRST.
HOW OLD?
NAME?
PERSON-ALITY?
THAT WAS FAST!

SOMEDAY

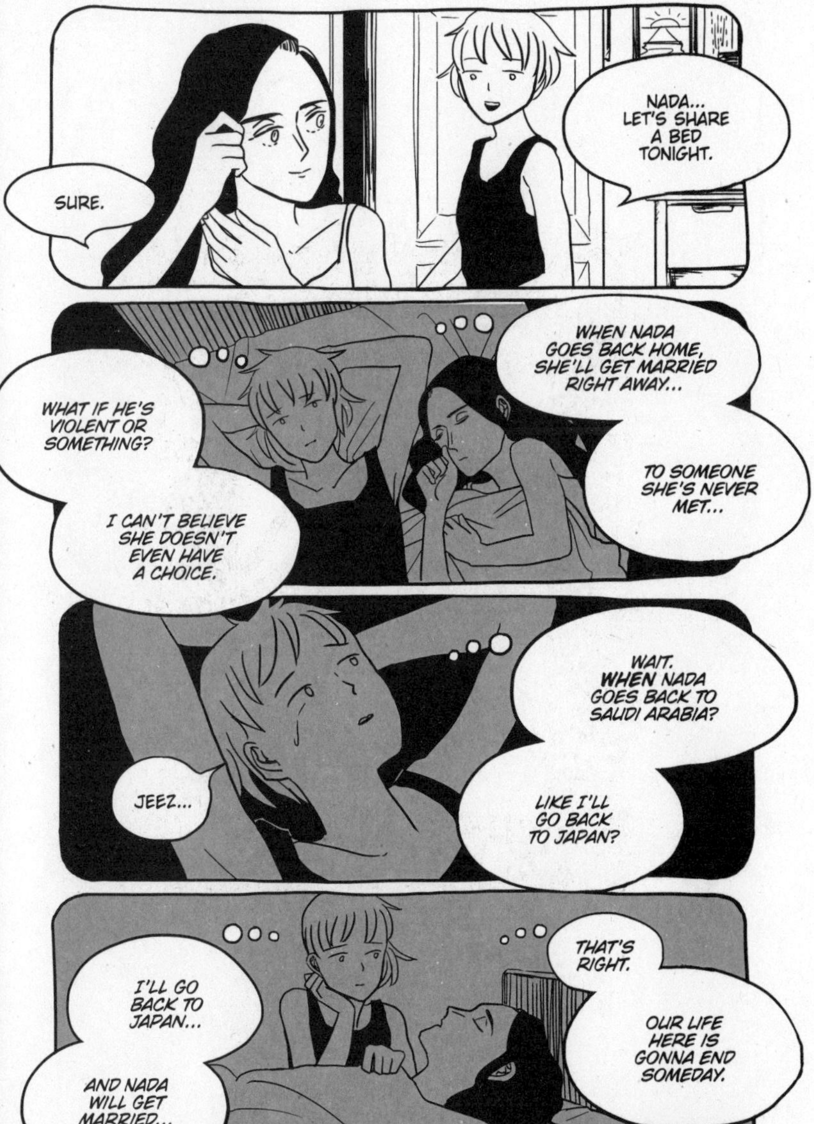
NADA... LET'S SHARE A BED TONIGHT.
SURE.
WHEN NADA GOES BACK HOME, SHE'LL GET MARRIED RIGHT AWAY...
TO SOMEONE SHE'S NEVER MET...
WHAT IF HE'S VIOLENT OR SOMETHING?
I CAN'T BELIEVE SHE DOESN'T EVEN HAVE A CHOICE.
WAIT. **WHEN** NADA GOES BACK TO SAUDI ARABIA?
LIKE I'LL GO BACK TO JAPAN?
JEEZ...
THAT'S RIGHT.
OUR LIFE HERE IS GONNA END SOMEDAY.
I'LL GO BACK TO JAPAN...
AND NADA WILL GET MARRIED...

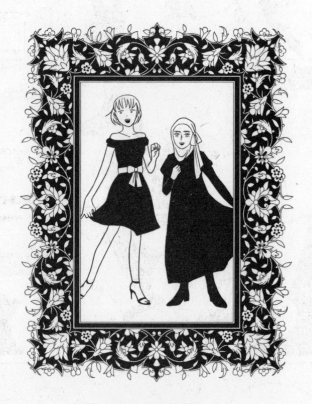

SATOKO AND NADA

Presented by Yupechika

SATOKO AND NADA

Presented by Yupechika

PAKEEZAH'S DARLING

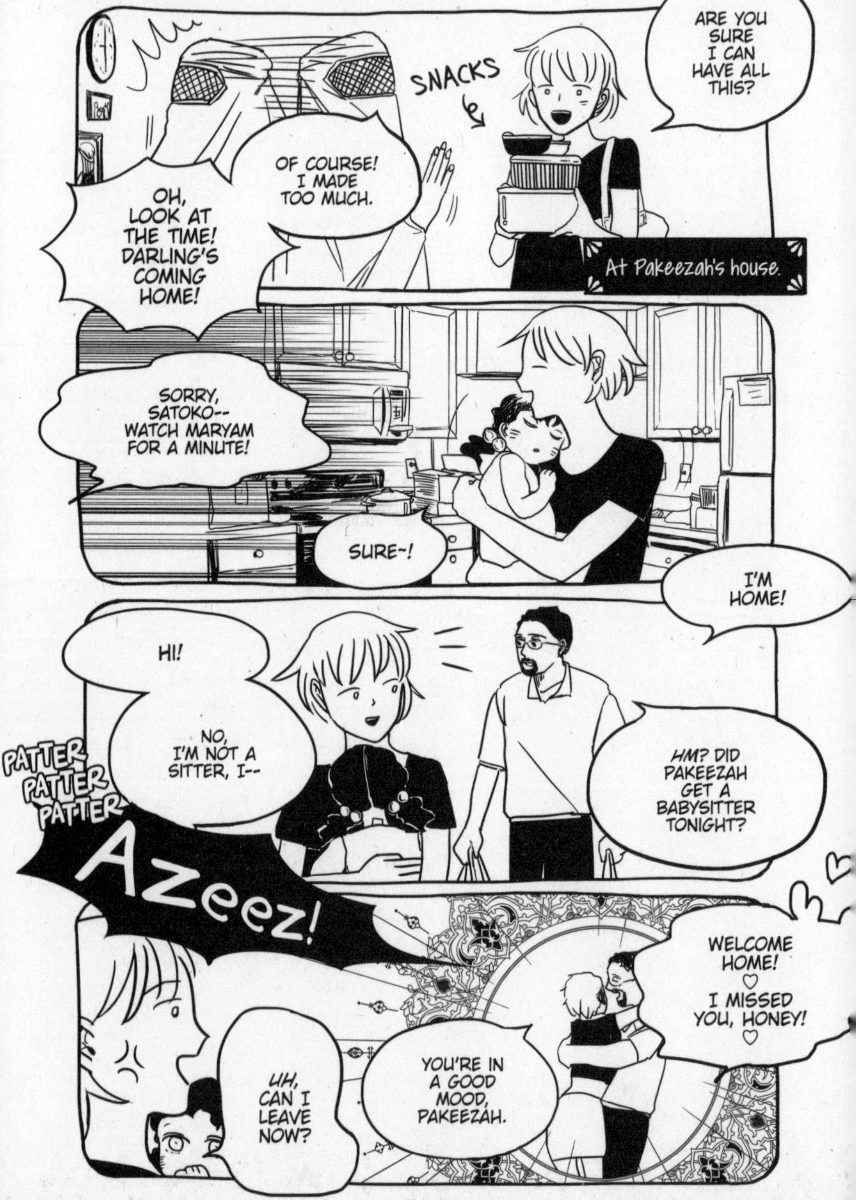

ARE YOU SURE I CAN HAVE ALL THIS?
SNACKS
OF COURSE! I MADE TOO MUCH.
At Pakeezah's house.
OH, LOOK AT THE TIME! DARLING'S COMING HOME!
SORRY, SATOKO-- WATCH MARYAM FOR A MINUTE!
SURE~!
I'M HOME!
HM? DID PAKEEZAH GET A BABYSITTER TONIGHT?
HI!
NO, I'M NOT A SITTER, I--
PATTER PATTER PATTER
Azeez!
WELCOME HOME! ♡ I MISSED YOU, HONEY! ♡
YOU'RE IN A GOOD MOOD, PAKEEZAH.
UH, CAN I LEAVE NOW?

VEGGIES

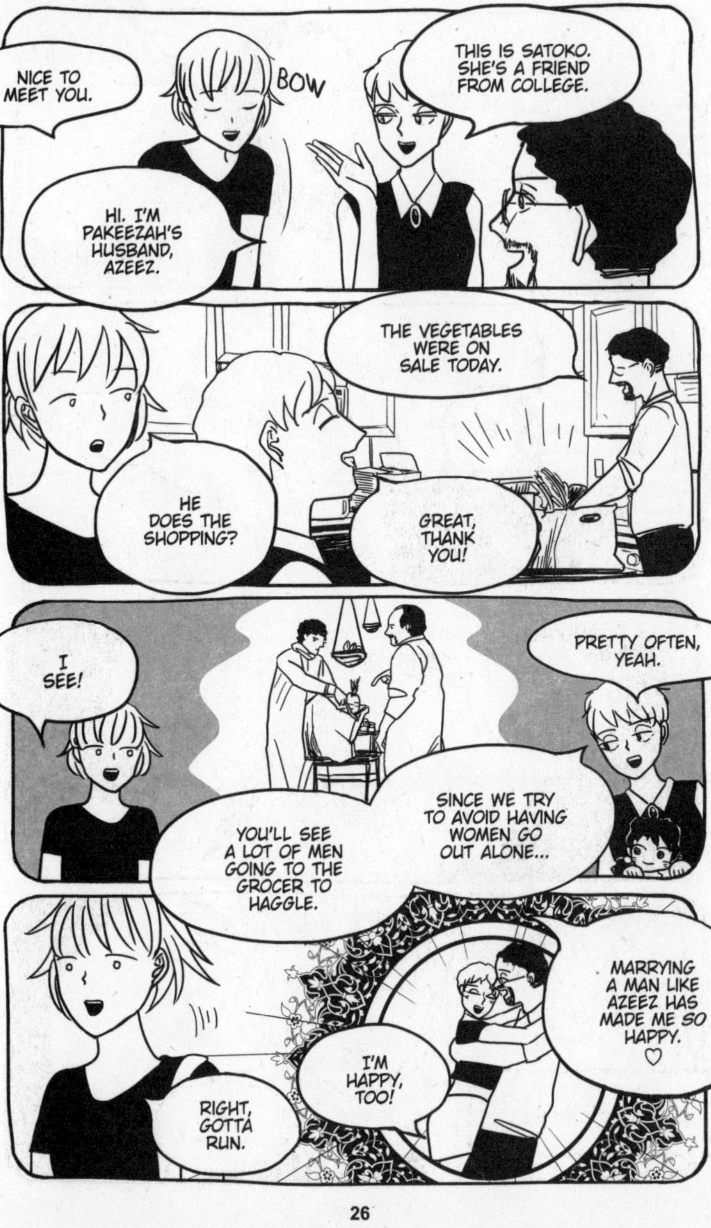

THIS IS SATOKO. SHE'S A FRIEND FROM COLLEGE.
BOW
NICE TO MEET YOU.
HI. I'M PAKEEZAH'S HUSBAND, AZEEZ.
THE VEGETABLES WERE ON SALE TODAY.
GREAT, THANK YOU!
HE DOES THE SHOPPING?
PRETTY OFTEN, YEAH.
I SEE!
SINCE WE TRY TO AVOID HAVING WOMEN GO OUT ALONE...
YOU'LL SEE A LOT OF MEN GOING TO THE GROCER TO HAGGLE.
MARRYING A MAN LIKE AZEEZ HAS MADE ME SO HAPPY. ♡
I'M HAPPY, TOO!
RIGHT, GOTTA RUN.

GESTURES

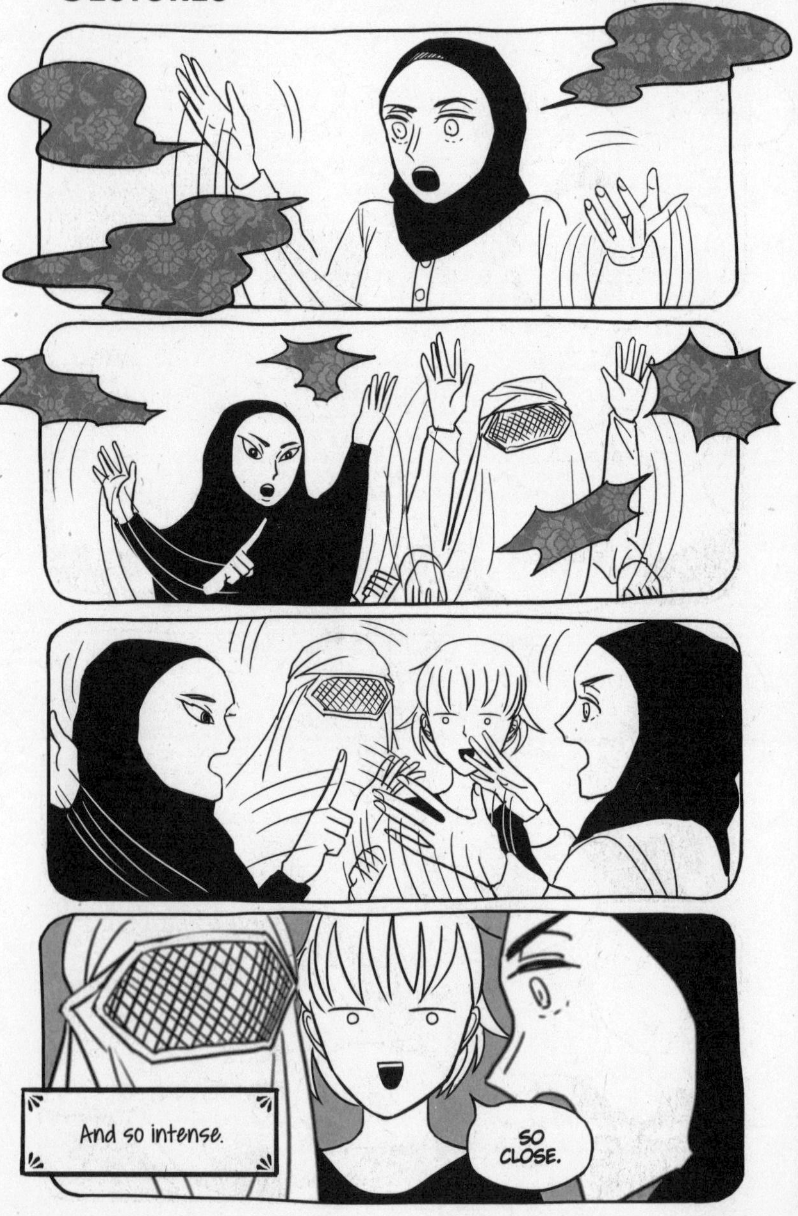
SO CLOSE.
And so intense.

MILK BREAD

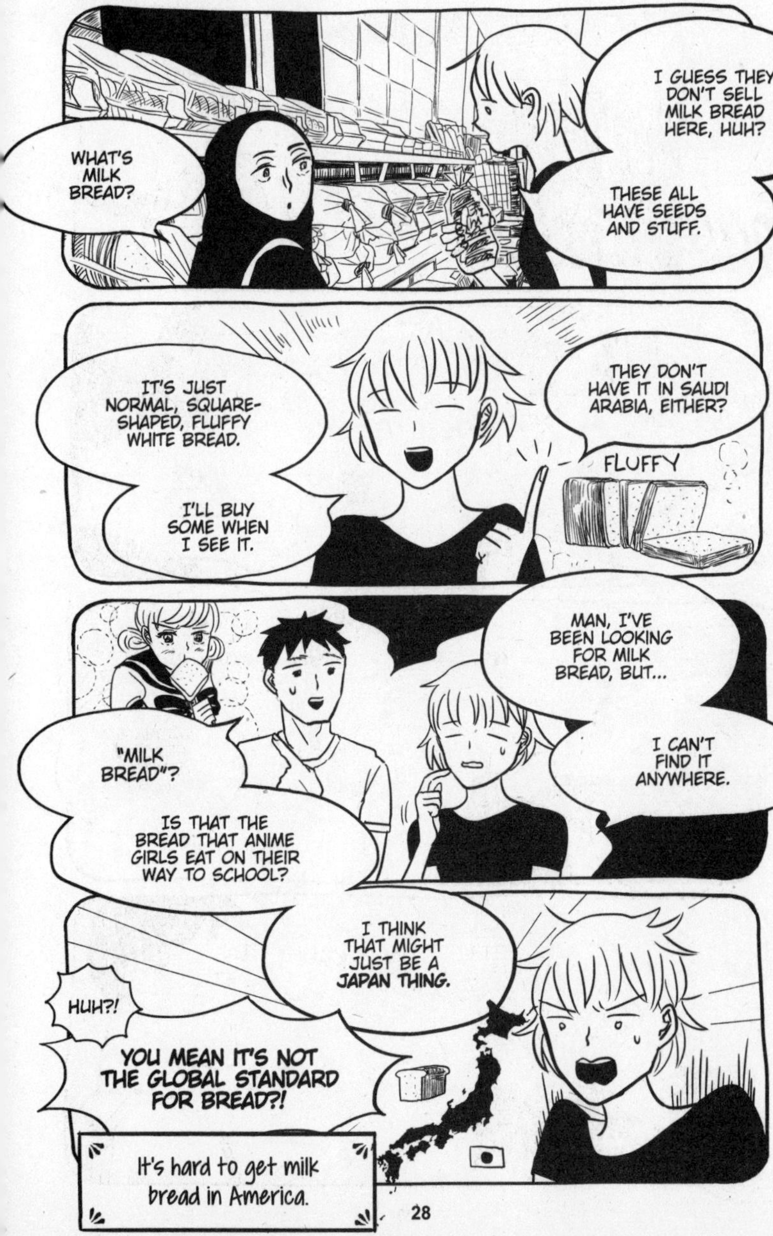
I GUESS THEY DON'T SELL MILK BREAD HERE, HUH?
THESE ALL HAVE SEEDS AND STUFF.
WHAT'S MILK BREAD?
IT'S JUST NORMAL, SQUARE-SHAPED, FLUFFY WHITE BREAD.
I'LL BUY SOME WHEN I SEE IT.
THEY DON'T HAVE IT IN SAUDI ARABIA, EITHER?
FLUFFY
MAN, I'VE BEEN LOOKING FOR MILK BREAD, BUT...
I CAN'T FIND IT ANYWHERE.
"MILK BREAD"?
IS THAT THE BREAD THAT ANIME GIRLS EAT ON THEIR WAY TO SCHOOL?
I THINK THAT MIGHT JUST BE A JAPAN THING.
HUH?!
YOU MEAN IT'S NOT THE GLOBAL STANDARD FOR BREAD?!
It's hard to get milk bread in America.

SWEET RELIEF

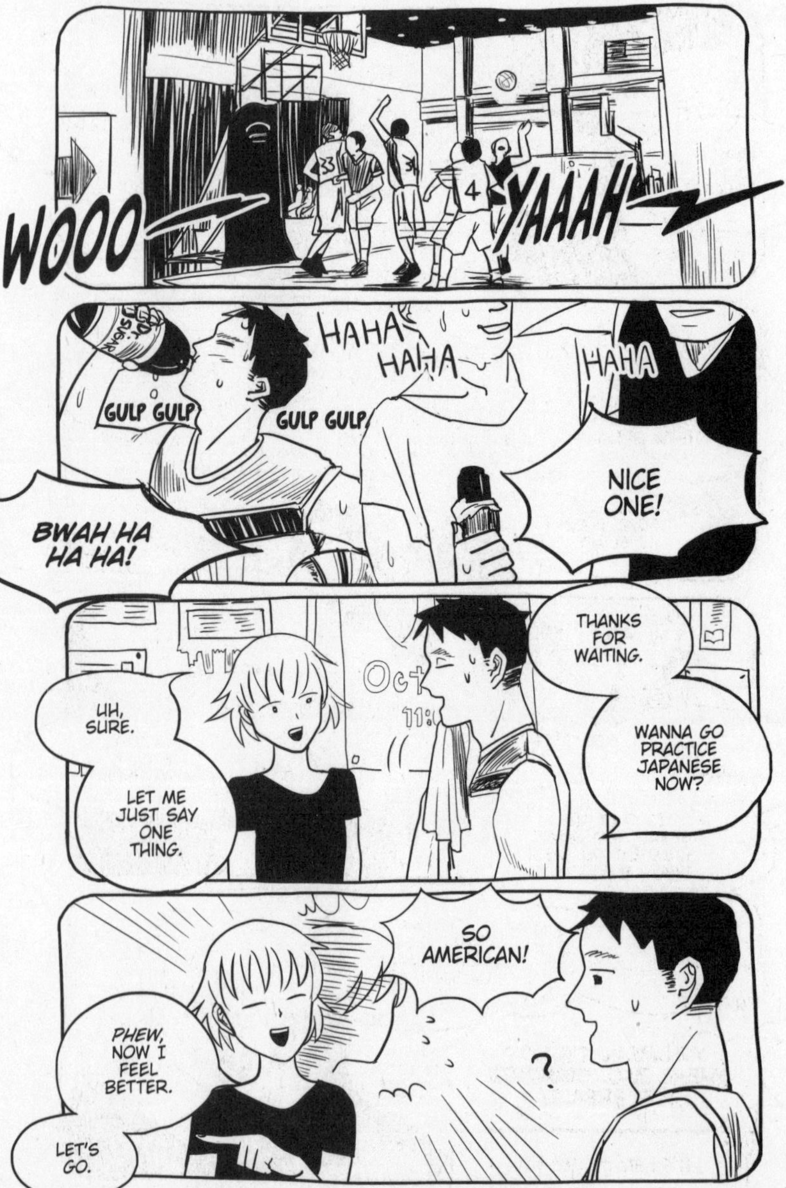
YAAAH
WOOO
HAHA
NICE ONE!
HAHA HAHA
GULP GULP
GULP GULP
BWAH HA HA HA!
THANKS FOR WAITING.
WANNA GO PRACTICE JAPANESE NOW?
Oct
UH, SURE.
LET ME JUST SAY ONE THING.
SO AMERICAN!
?
PHEW, NOW I FEEL BETTER.
LET'S GO.

FOOD MODELS

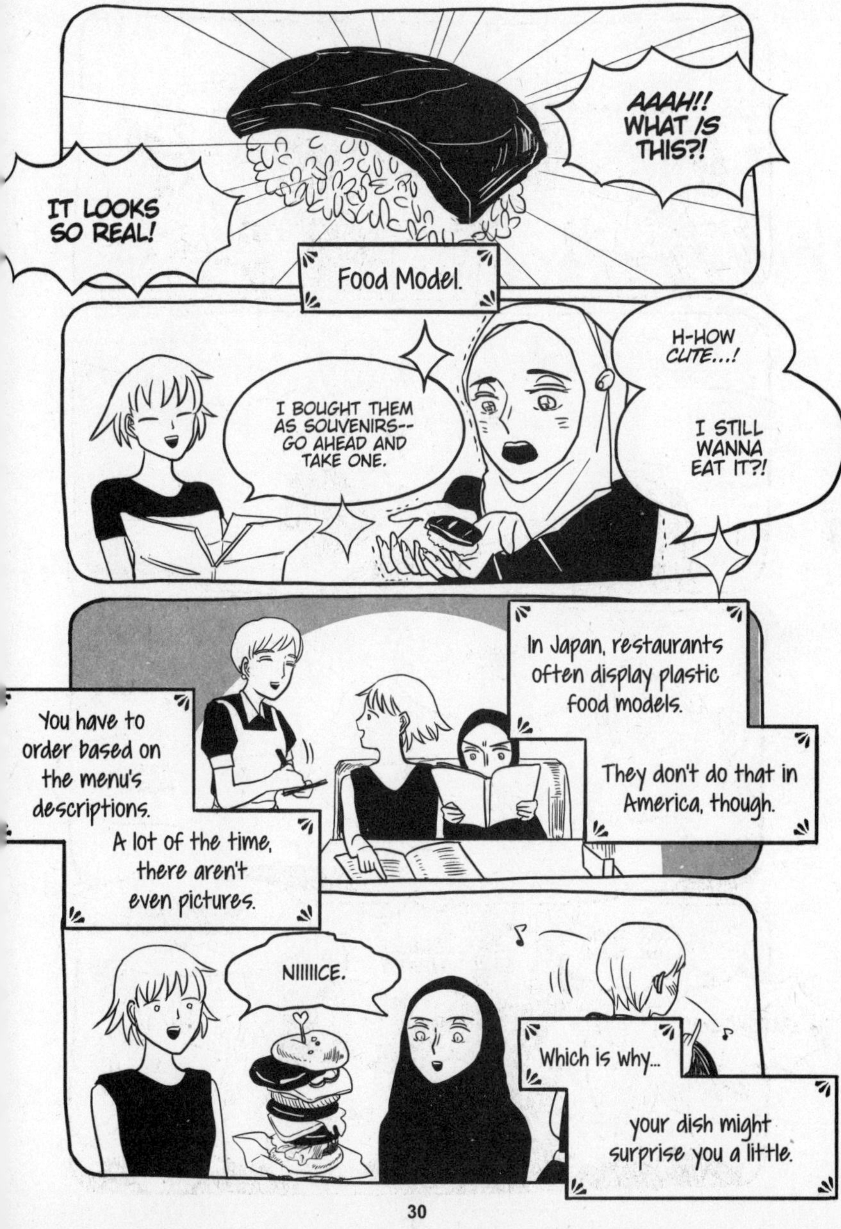
AAAH!! WHAT IS THIS?!
IT LOOKS SO REAL!
Food Model.
H-HOW CUTE...!
I STILL WANNA EAT IT?!
I BOUGHT THEM AS SOUVENIRS-- GO AHEAD AND TAKE ONE.
In Japan, restaurants often display plastic food models.
They don't do that in America, though.
You have to order based on the menu's descriptions.
A lot of the time, there aren't even pictures.
Which is why...
your dish might surprise you a little.
NIIIIICE.

POWERFUL PRESENCE

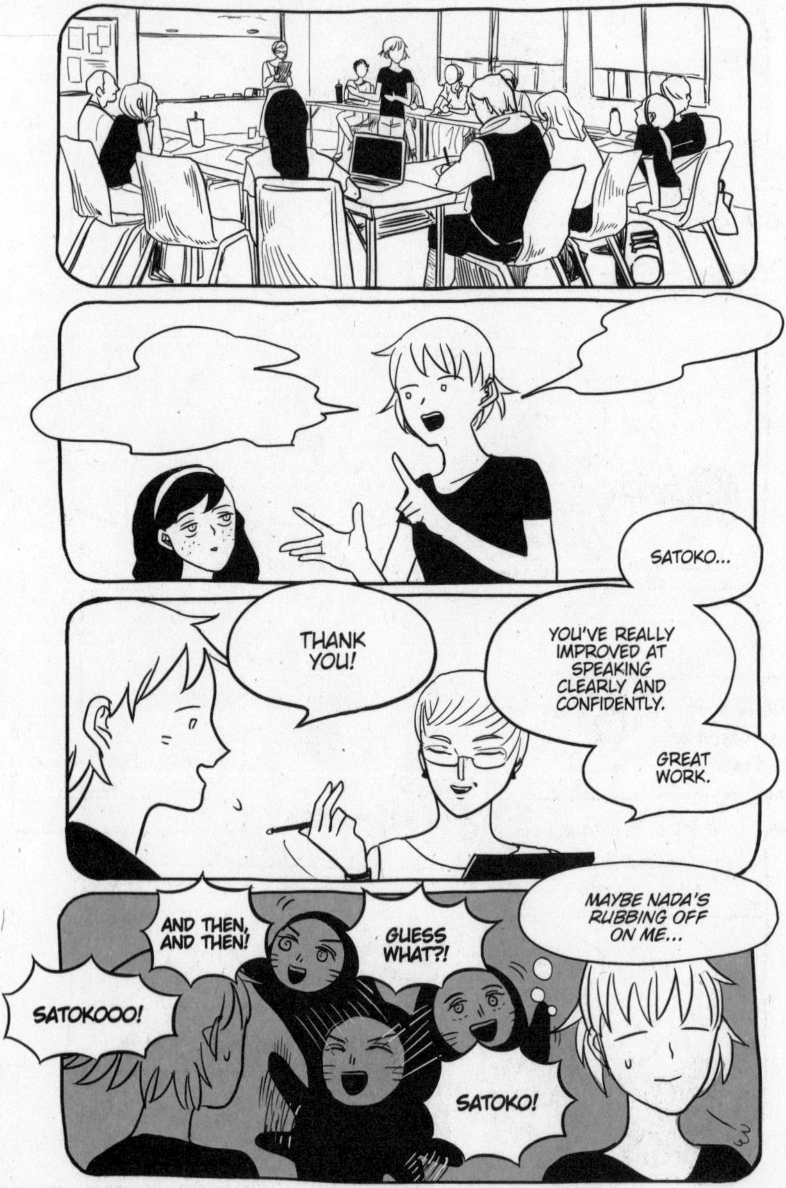
SATOKO...
YOU'VE REALLY IMPROVED AT SPEAKING CLEARLY AND CONFIDENTLY.
GREAT WORK.
THANK YOU!
MAYBE NADA'S RUBBING OFF ON ME...
GUESS WHAT?!
AND THEN, AND THEN!
SATOKOOO!
SATOKO!

GOODY TWO-SHOES

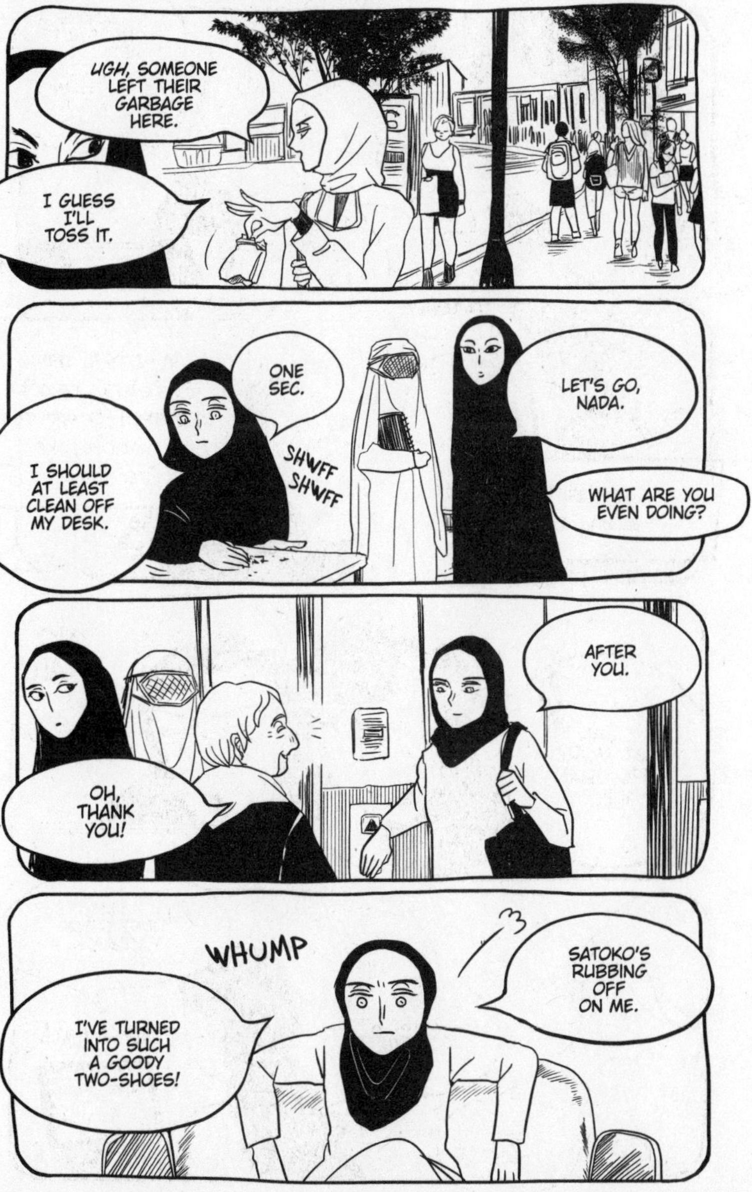
UGH, SOMEONE LEFT THEIR GARBAGE HERE.
I GUESS I'LL TOSS IT.
LET'S GO, NADA.
ONE SEC.
WHAT ARE YOU EVEN DOING?
SHWFF SHWFF
I SHOULD AT LEAST CLEAN OFF MY DESK.
AFTER YOU.
OH, THANK YOU!
SATOKO'S RUBBING OFF ON ME.
WHUMP
I'VE TURNED INTO SUCH A GOODY TWO-SHOES!

INVESTIGATION

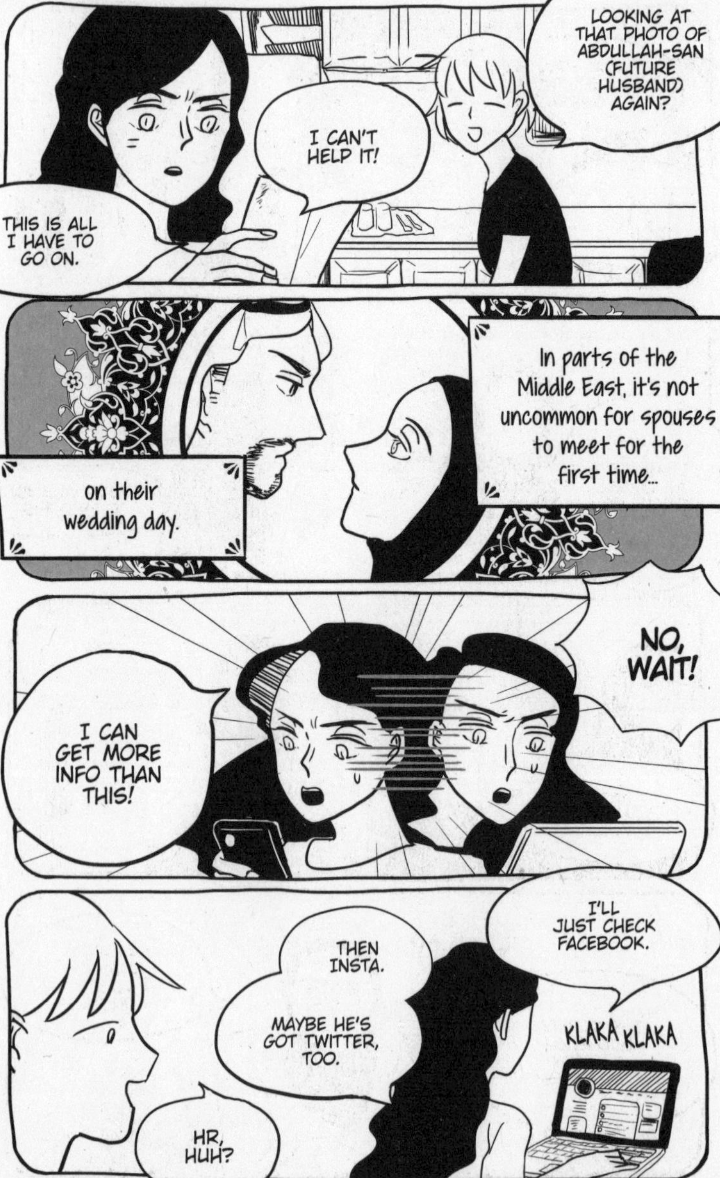
LOOKING AT THAT PHOTO OF ABDULLAH-SAN (FUTURE HUSBAND) AGAIN?
I CAN'T HELP IT!
THIS IS ALL I HAVE TO GO ON.
In parts of the Middle East, it's not uncommon for spouses to meet for the first time...
on their wedding day.
NO, WAIT!
I CAN GET MORE INFO THAN THIS!
I'LL JUST CHECK FACEBOOK.
KLAKA KLAKA
THEN INSTA.
MAYBE HE'S GOT TWITTER, TOO.
HR, HUH?

CHANCE

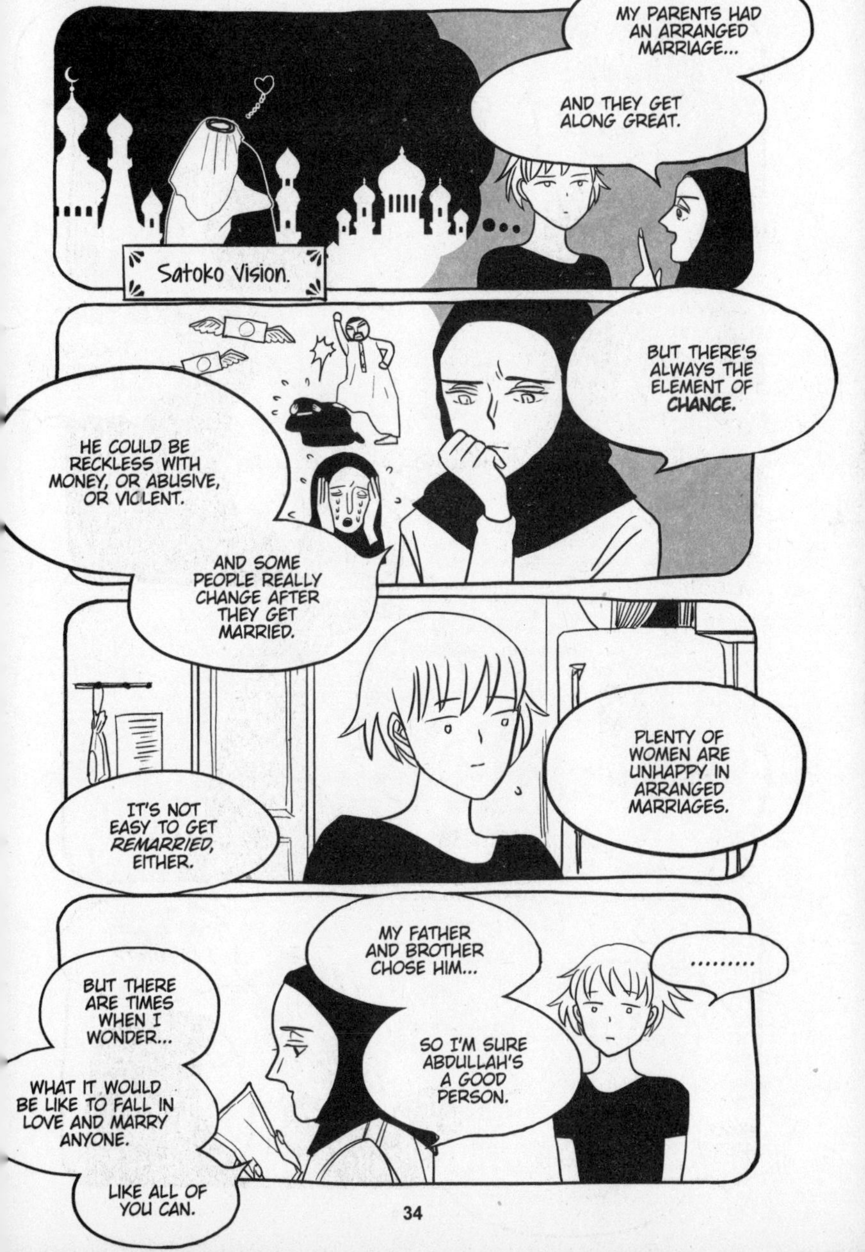
MY PARENTS HAD AN ARRANGED MARRIAGE...
AND THEY GET ALONG GREAT.
...
Satoko Vision.
BUT THERE'S ALWAYS THE ELEMENT OF **CHANCE.**
HE COULD BE RECKLESS WITH MONEY, OR ABUSIVE, OR VIOLENT.
AND SOME PEOPLE REALLY CHANGE AFTER THEY GET MARRIED.
PLENTY OF WOMEN ARE UNHAPPY IN ARRANGED MARRIAGES.
IT'S NOT EASY TO GET *REMARRIED*, EITHER.
....
MY FATHER AND BROTHER CHOSE HIM...
SO I'M SURE ABDULLAH'S A GOOD PERSON.
BUT THERE ARE TIMES WHEN I WONDER...
WHAT IT WOULD BE LIKE TO FALL IN LOVE AND MARRY ANYONE.
LIKE ALL OF YOU CAN.

WAIT, WHAT

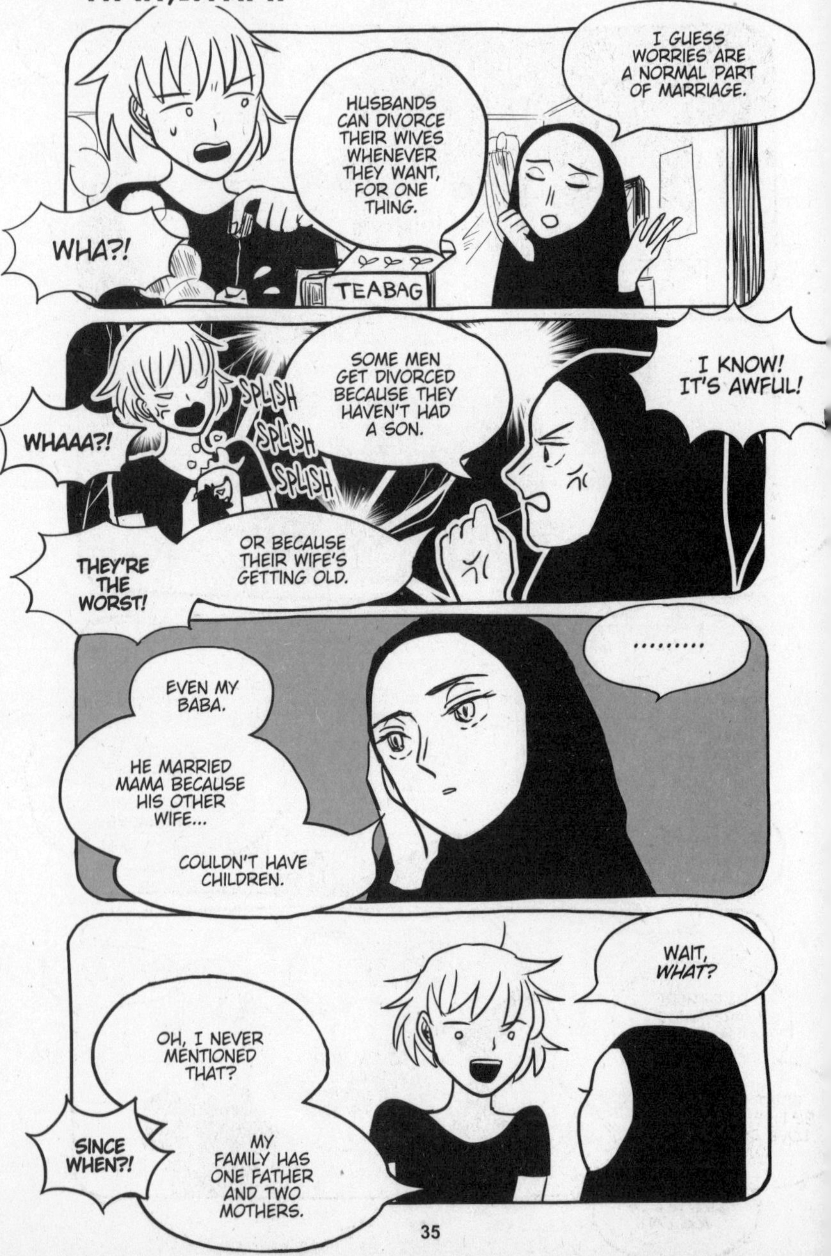
I GUESS WORRIES ARE A NORMAL PART OF MARRIAGE.
HUSBANDS CAN DIVORCE THEIR WIVES WHENEVER THEY WANT, FOR ONE THING.
WHA?!
TEABAG
I KNOW! IT'S AWFUL!
SOME MEN GET DIVORCED BECAUSE THEY HAVEN'T HAD A SON.
SPLISH
SPLISH
SPLISH
WHAAA?!
OR BECAUSE THEIR WIFE'S GETTING OLD.
THEY'RE THE WORST!
....
EVEN MY BABA.
HE MARRIED MAMA BECAUSE HIS OTHER WIFE...
COULDN'T HAVE CHILDREN.
WAIT, *WHAT?*
OH, I NEVER MENTIONED THAT?
MY FAMILY HAS ONE FATHER AND TWO MOTHERS.
SINCE WHEN?!

NOT JUST A FANTASY

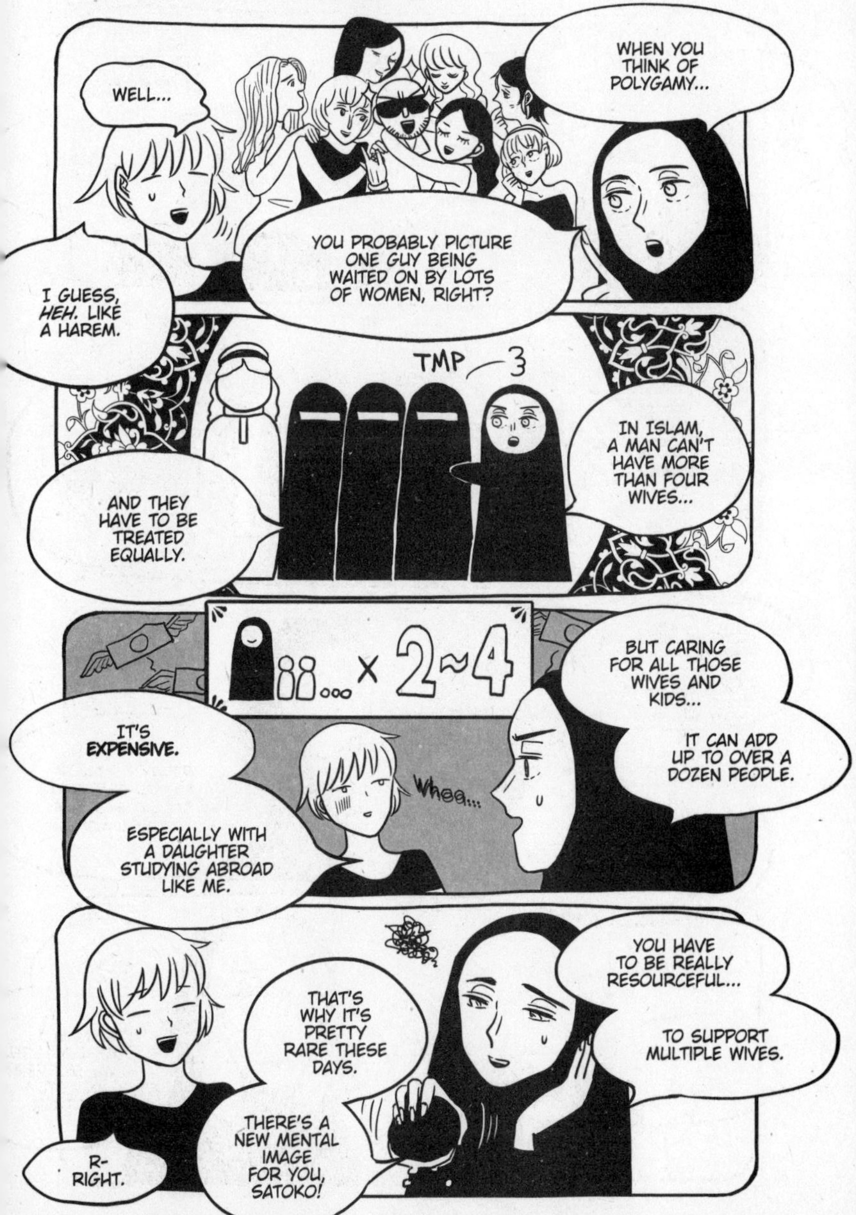
WHEN YOU THINK OF POLYGAMY...
YOU PROBABLY PICTURE ONE GUY BEING WAITED ON BY LOTS OF WOMEN, RIGHT?
WELL...
I GUESS, *HEH.* LIKE A HAREM.
TMP
IN ISLAM, A MAN CAN'T HAVE MORE THAN FOUR WIVES...
AND THEY HAVE TO BE TREATED EQUALLY.
× 2~4
BUT CARING FOR ALL THOSE WIVES AND KIDS...
IT CAN ADD UP TO OVER A DOZEN PEOPLE.
Whoa...
IT'S **EXPENSIVE.**
ESPECIALLY WITH A DAUGHTER STUDYING ABROAD LIKE ME.
YOU HAVE TO BE REALLY RESOURCEFUL...
TO SUPPORT MULTIPLE WIVES.
THAT'S WHY IT'S PRETTY RARE THESE DAYS.
THERE'S A NEW MENTAL IMAGE FOR YOU, SATOKO!
R-RIGHT.

NADA'S STEPMOTHER

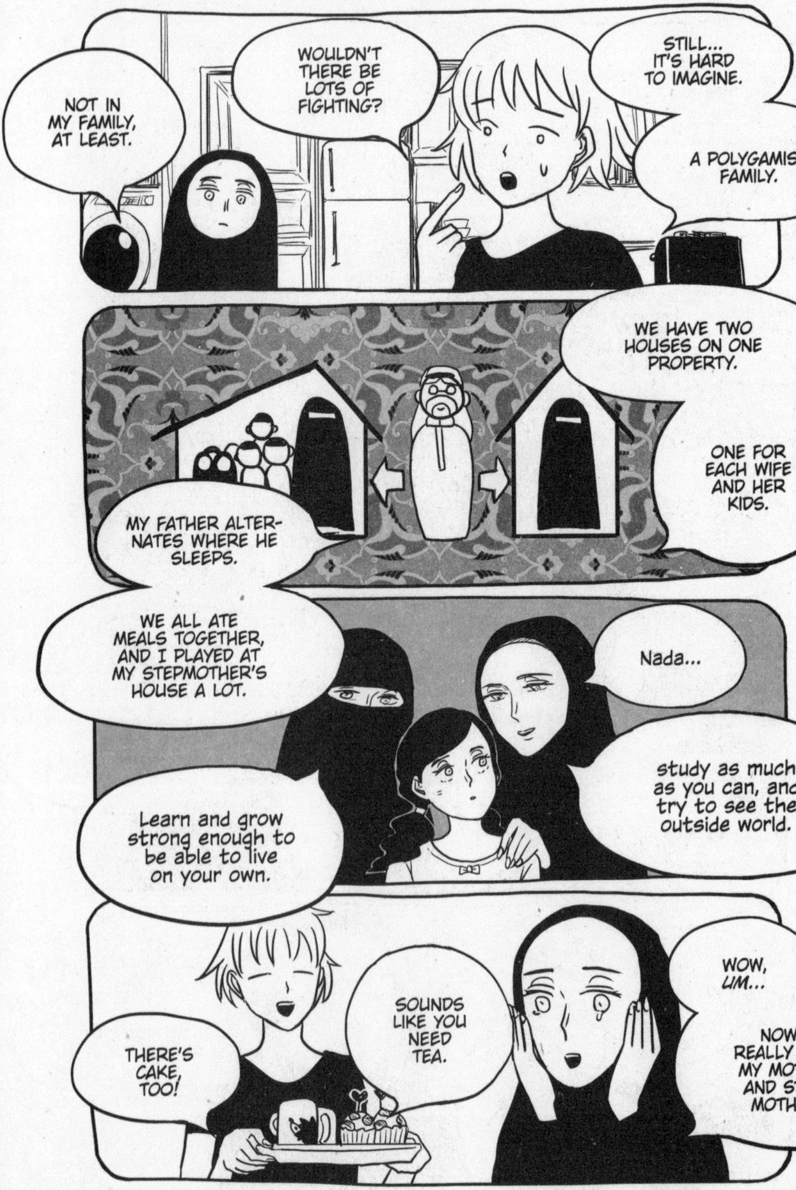

STILL... IT'S HARD TO IMAGINE.
A POLYGAMIST FAMILY.
WOULDN'T THERE BE LOTS OF FIGHTING?
NOT IN MY FAMILY, AT LEAST.
WE HAVE TWO HOUSES ON ONE PROPERTY.
ONE FOR EACH WIFE AND HER KIDS.
MY FATHER ALTERNATES WHERE HE SLEEPS.
Nada...
WE ALL ATE MEALS TOGETHER, AND I PLAYED AT MY STEPMOTHER'S HOUSE A LOT.
study as much as you can, and try to see the outside world.
Learn and grow strong enough to be able to live on your own.
WOW, UM...
NOW I REALLY MISS MY MOTHER AND STEPMOTHER.
SOUNDS LIKE YOU NEED TEA.
THERE'S CAKE, TOO!

FAIRNESS

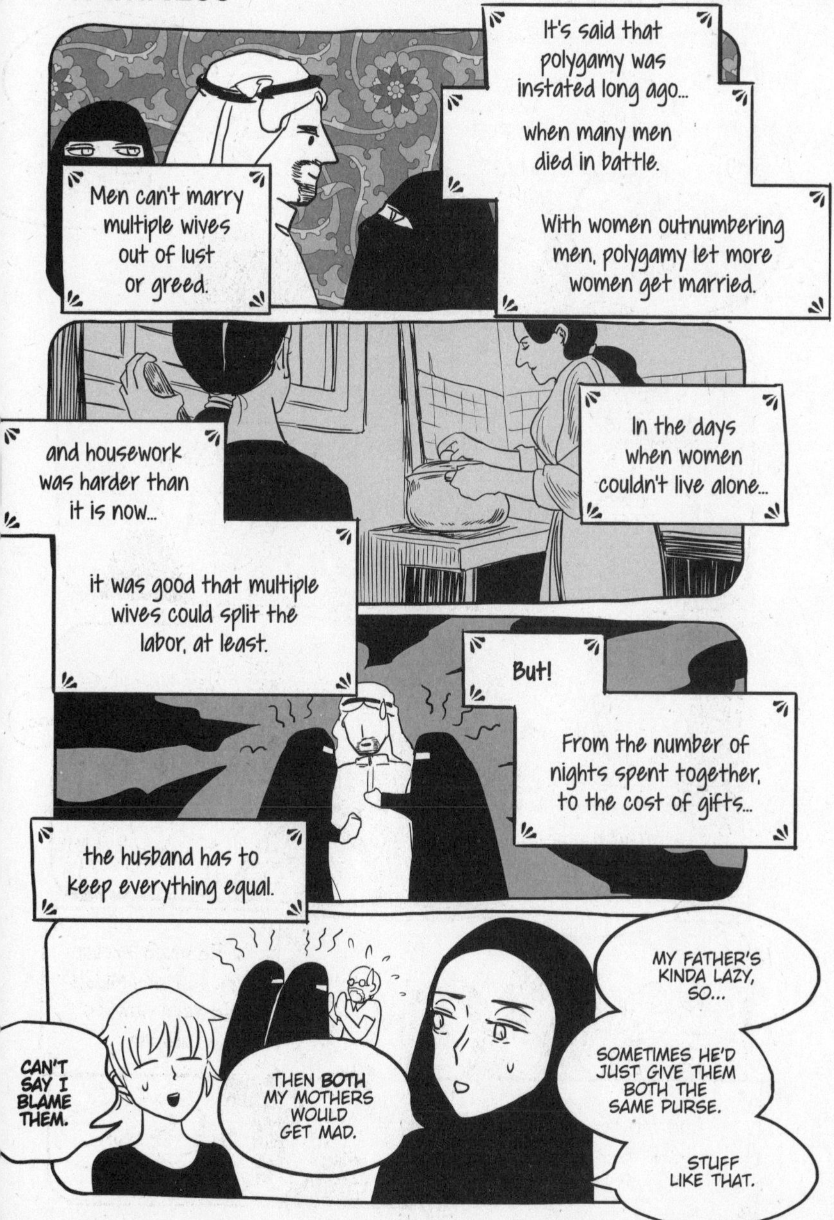
It's said that polygamy was instated long ago...
when many men died in battle.
With women outnumbering men, polygamy let more women get married.
Men can't marry multiple wives out of lust or greed.
In the days when women couldn't live alone...
and housework was harder than it is now...
it was good that multiple wives could split the labor, at least.
But!
From the number of nights spent together, to the cost of gifts...
the husband has to keep everything equal.
MY FATHER'S KINDA LAZY, SO...
SOMETIMES HE'D JUST GIVE THEM BOTH THE SAME PURSE.
STUFF LIKE THAT.
THEN **BOTH** MY MOTHERS WOULD GET MAD.
CAN'T SAY I BLAME THEM.

MANY SIBLINGS

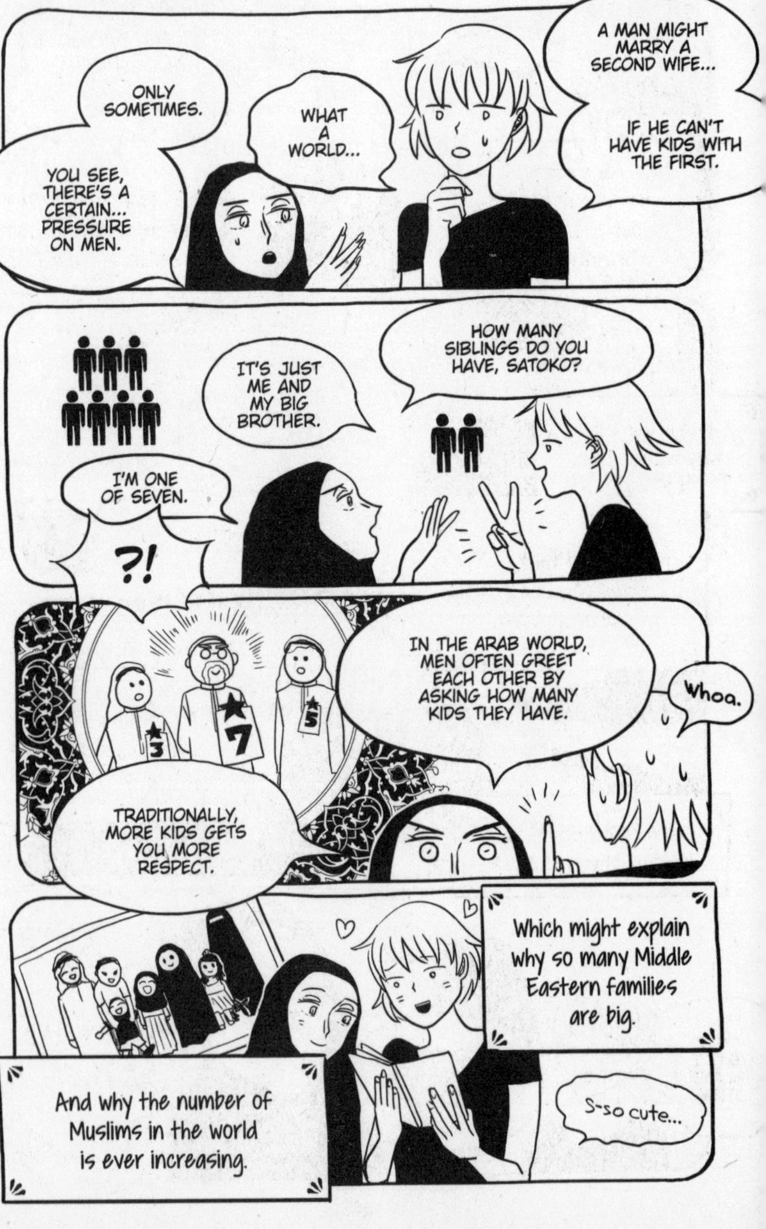
A MAN MIGHT MARRY A SECOND WIFE...
IF HE CAN'T HAVE KIDS WITH THE FIRST.
WHAT A WORLD...
ONLY SOMETIMES.
YOU SEE, THERE'S A CERTAIN... PRESSURE ON MEN.
HOW MANY SIBLINGS DO YOU HAVE, SATOKO?
IT'S JUST ME AND MY BIG BROTHER.
I'M ONE OF SEVEN.
?!
Whoa.
IN THE ARAB WORLD, MEN OFTEN GREET EACH OTHER BY ASKING HOW MANY KIDS THEY HAVE.
3
7
5
TRADITIONALLY, MORE KIDS GETS YOU MORE RESPECT.
Which might explain why so many Middle Eastern families are big.
S-so cute...
And why the number of Muslims in the world is ever increasing.

DOUBLE EYELIDS

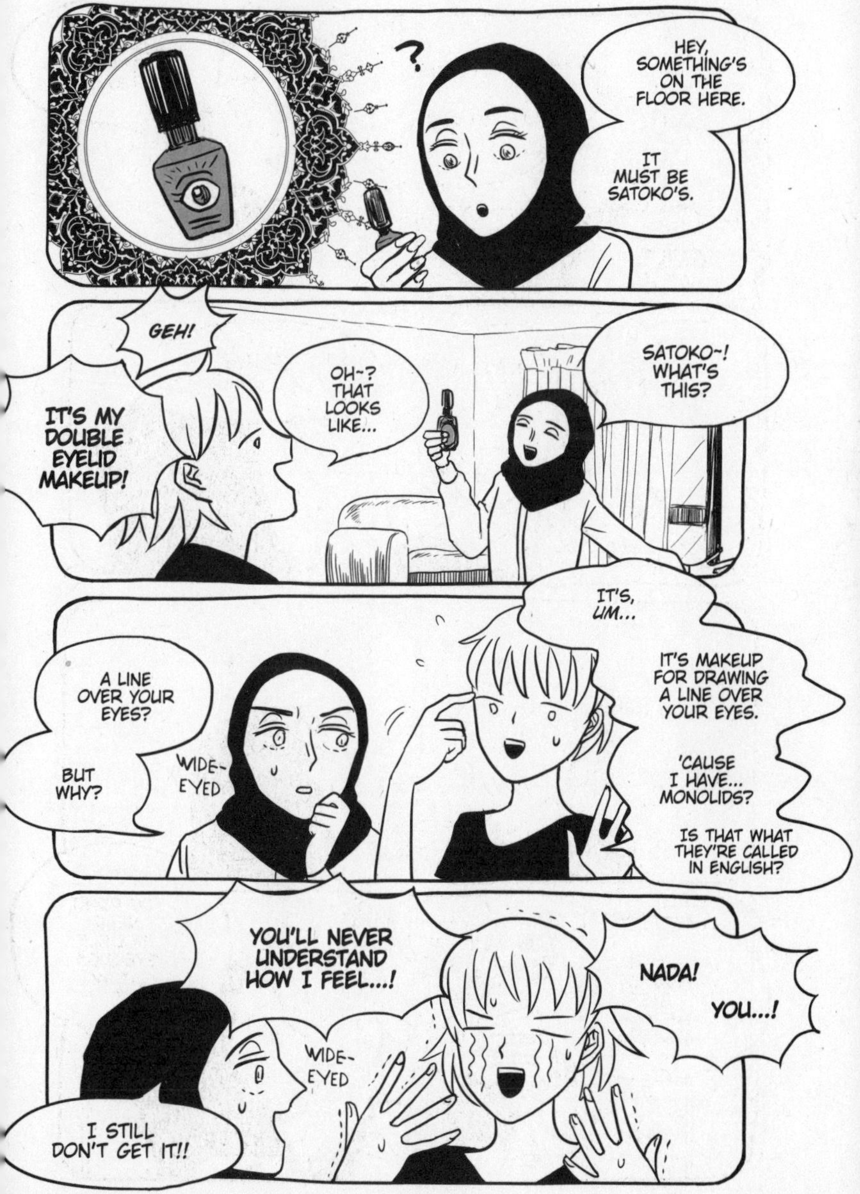
HEY, SOMETHING'S ON THE FLOOR HERE.
IT MUST BE SATOKO'S.
SATOKO~! WHAT'S THIS?
OH~? THAT LOOKS LIKE...
GEH!
IT'S MY DOUBLE EYELID MAKEUP!
IT'S, UM...
IT'S MAKEUP FOR DRAWING A LINE OVER YOUR EYES.
'CAUSE I HAVE... MONOLIDS?
IS THAT WHAT THEY'RE CALLED IN ENGLISH?
A LINE OVER YOUR EYES?
WIDE-EYED
BUT WHY?
NADA!
YOU...!
YOU'LL NEVER UNDERSTAND HOW I FEEL...!
WIDE-EYED
I STILL DON'T GET IT!!

THE WAY YOU ARE

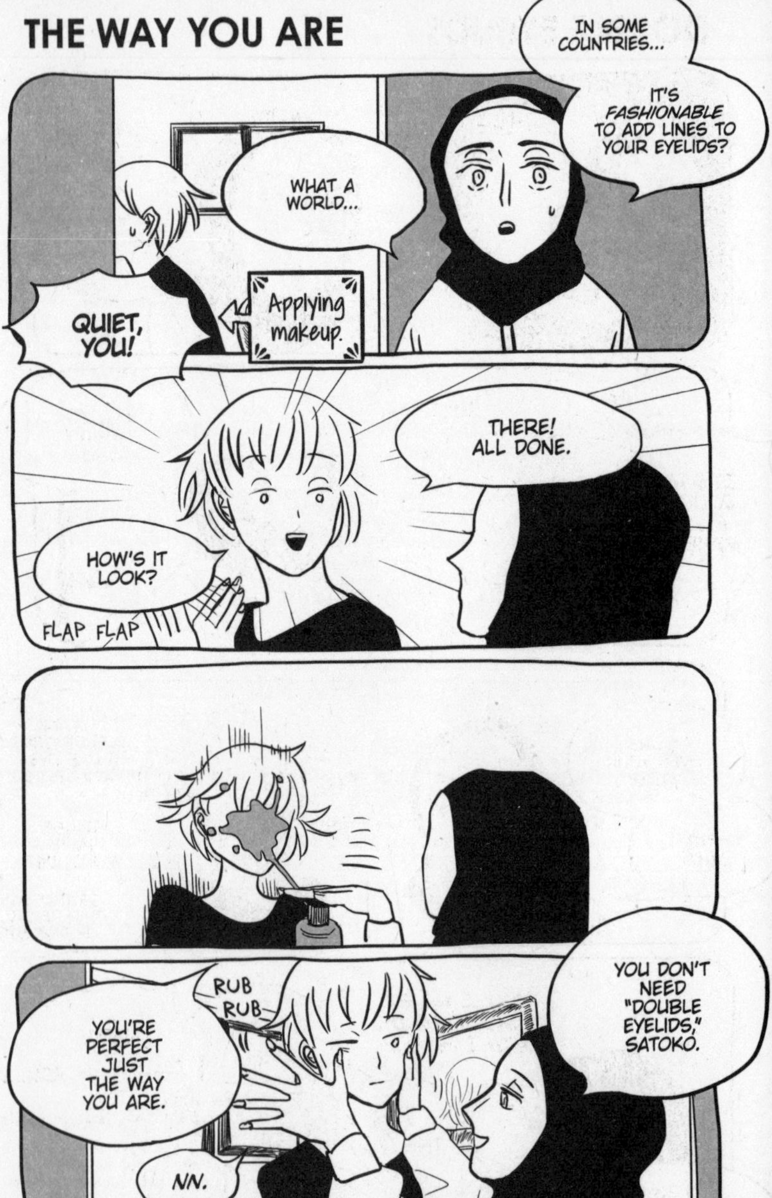
IN SOME COUNTRIES...
IT'S *FASHIONABLE* TO ADD LINES TO YOUR EYELIDS?
WHAT A WORLD...
Applying makeup.
QUIET, YOU!
THERE! ALL DONE.
HOW'S IT LOOK?
FLAP FLAP
YOU DON'T NEED "DOUBLE EYELIDS," SATOKO.
RUB RUB
YOU'RE PERFECT JUST THE WAY YOU ARE.
NN.

BIKE

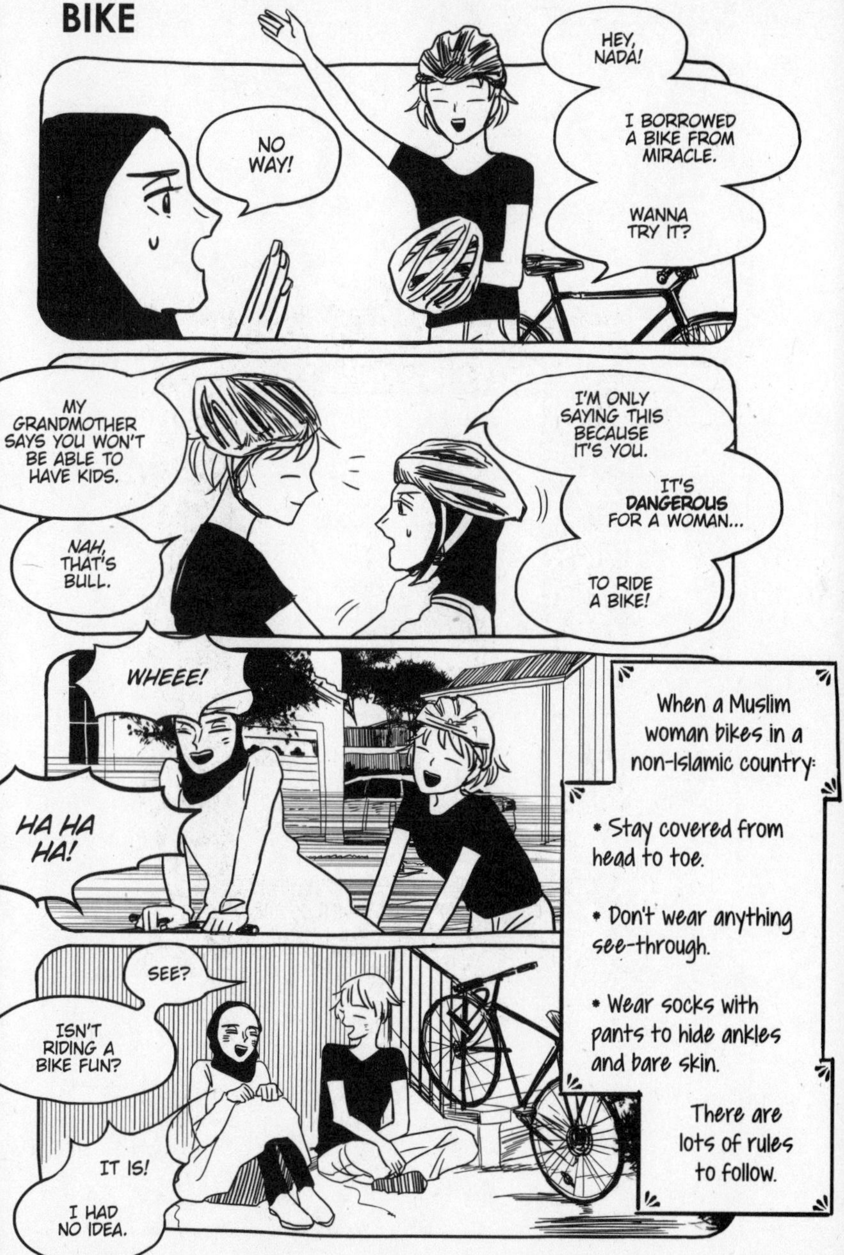
HEY, NADA!
I BORROWED A BIKE FROM MIRACLE.
WANNA TRY IT?
NO WAY!
I'M ONLY SAYING THIS BECAUSE IT'S YOU.
IT'S **DANGEROUS** FOR A WOMAN...
TO RIDE A BIKE!
MY GRANDMOTHER SAYS YOU WON'T BE ABLE TO HAVE KIDS.
NAH, THAT'S BULL.
When a Muslim woman bikes in a non-Islamic country:
• Stay covered from head to toe.
• Don't wear anything see-through.
• Wear socks with pants to hide ankles and bare skin.
There are lots of rules to follow.
WHEEE!
HA HA HA!
SEE?
ISN'T RIDING A BIKE FUN?
IT IS!
I HAD NO IDEA.

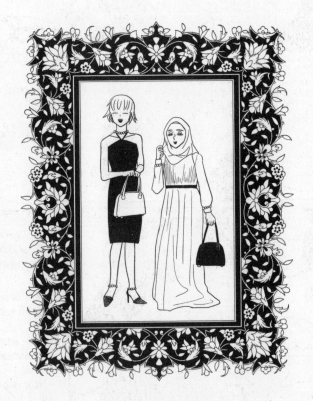

SATOKO AND NADA

Presented by Yupechika

SATOKO AND NADA

Presented by Yupechika

ALMSGIVING

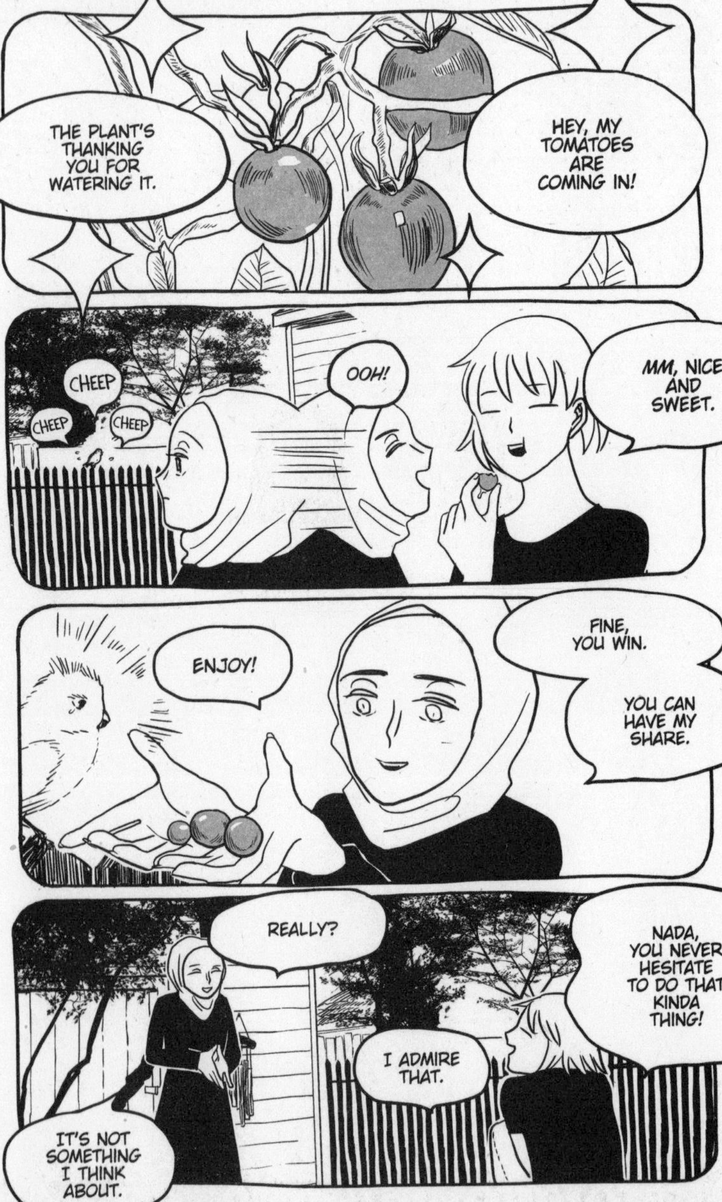
HEY, MY TOMATOES ARE COMING IN!
THE PLANT'S THANKING YOU FOR WATERING IT.
MM, NICE AND SWEET.
OOH!
CHEEP
CHEEP
CHEEP
FINE, YOU WIN.
YOU CAN HAVE MY SHARE.
ENJOY!
NADA, YOU NEVER HESITATE TO DO THAT KINDA THING!
I ADMIRE THAT.
REALLY?
IT'S NOT SOMETHING I THINK ABOUT.

SINGING VOICE

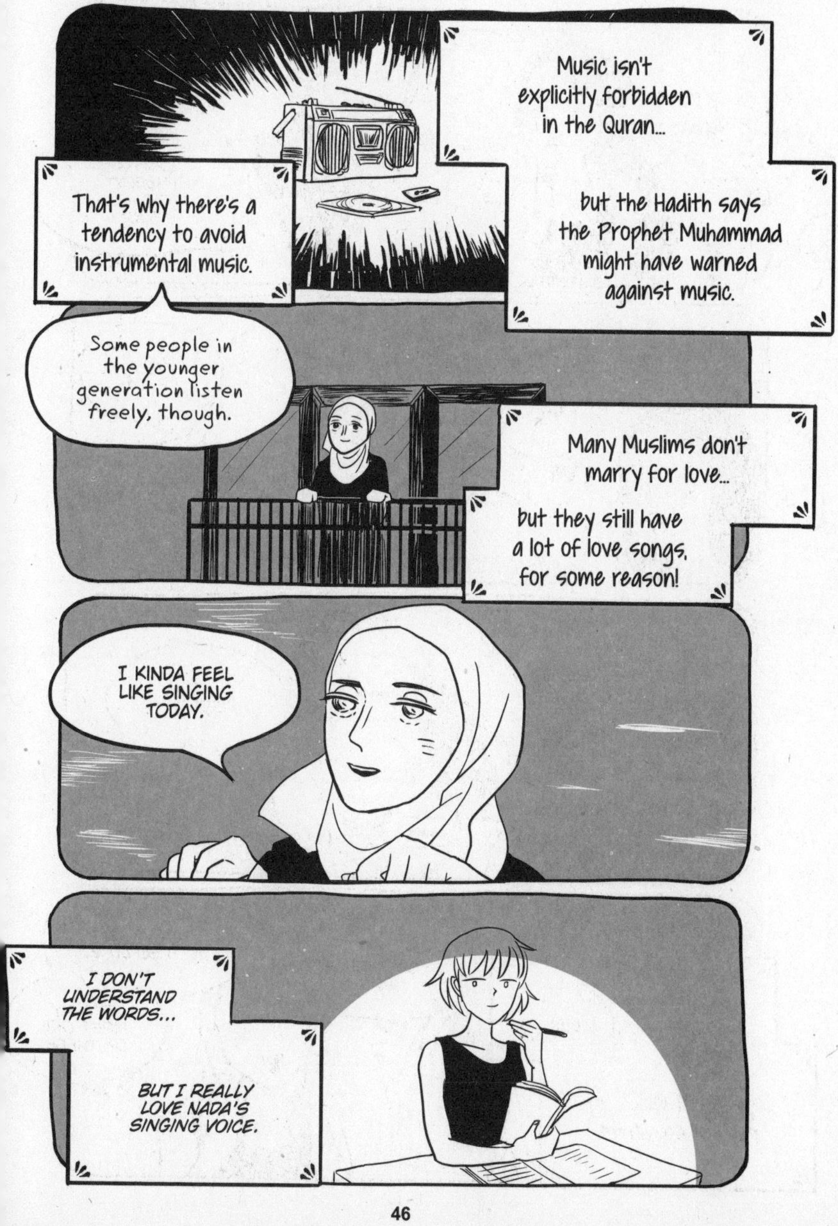

Music isn't explicitly forbidden in the Quran...
but the Hadith says the Prophet Muhammad might have warned against music.
That's why there's a tendency to avoid instrumental music.
Some people in the younger generation listen freely, though.
Many Muslims don't marry for love...
but they still have a lot of love songs, for some reason!
I KINDA FEEL LIKE SINGING TODAY.
I DON'T UNDERSTAND THE WORDS...
BUT I REALLY LOVE NADA'S SINGING VOICE.

FROM SATOKO'S MOM

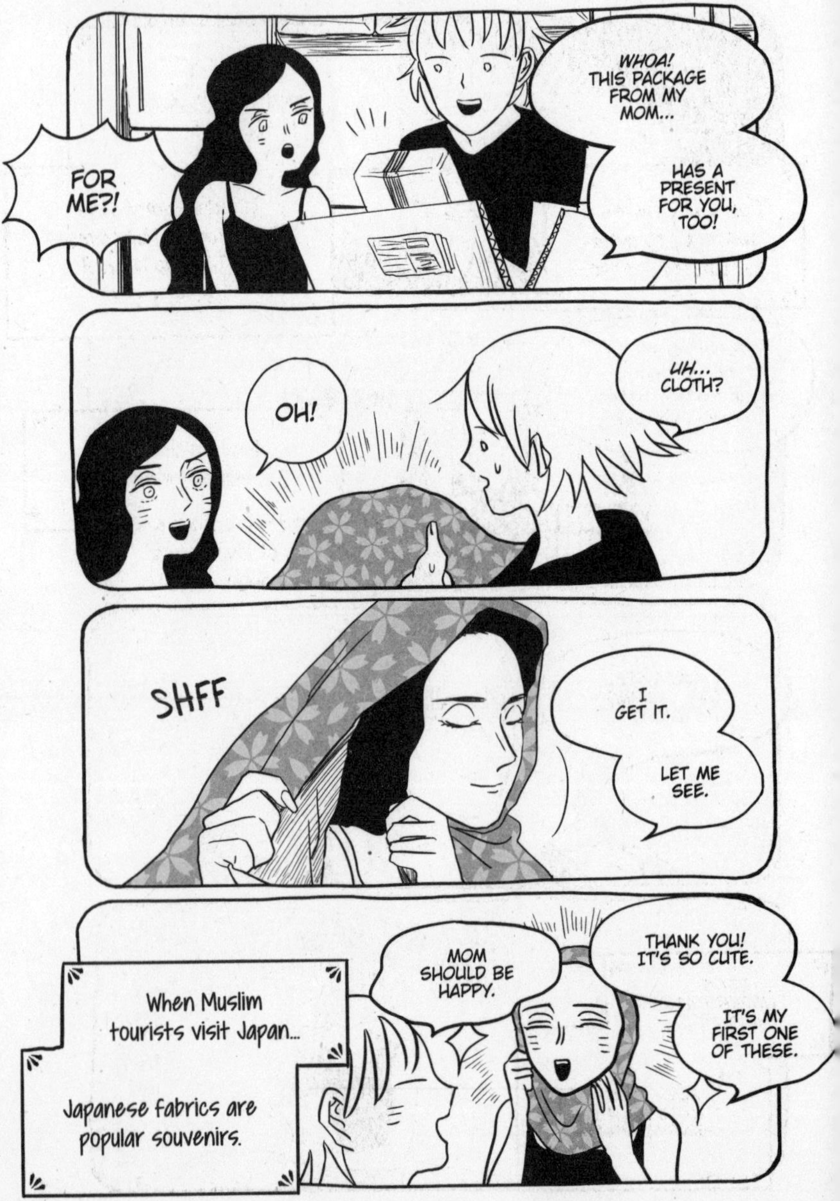
WHOA! THIS PACKAGE FROM MY MOM...
HAS A PRESENT FOR YOU, TOO!
FOR ME?!
UH... CLOTH?
OH!
I GET IT.
LET ME SEE.
SHFF
THANK YOU! IT'S SO CUTE.
IT'S MY FIRST ONE OF THESE.
MOM SHOULD BE HAPPY.
When Muslim tourists visit Japan...
Japanese fabrics are popular souvenirs.

NOT QUITE

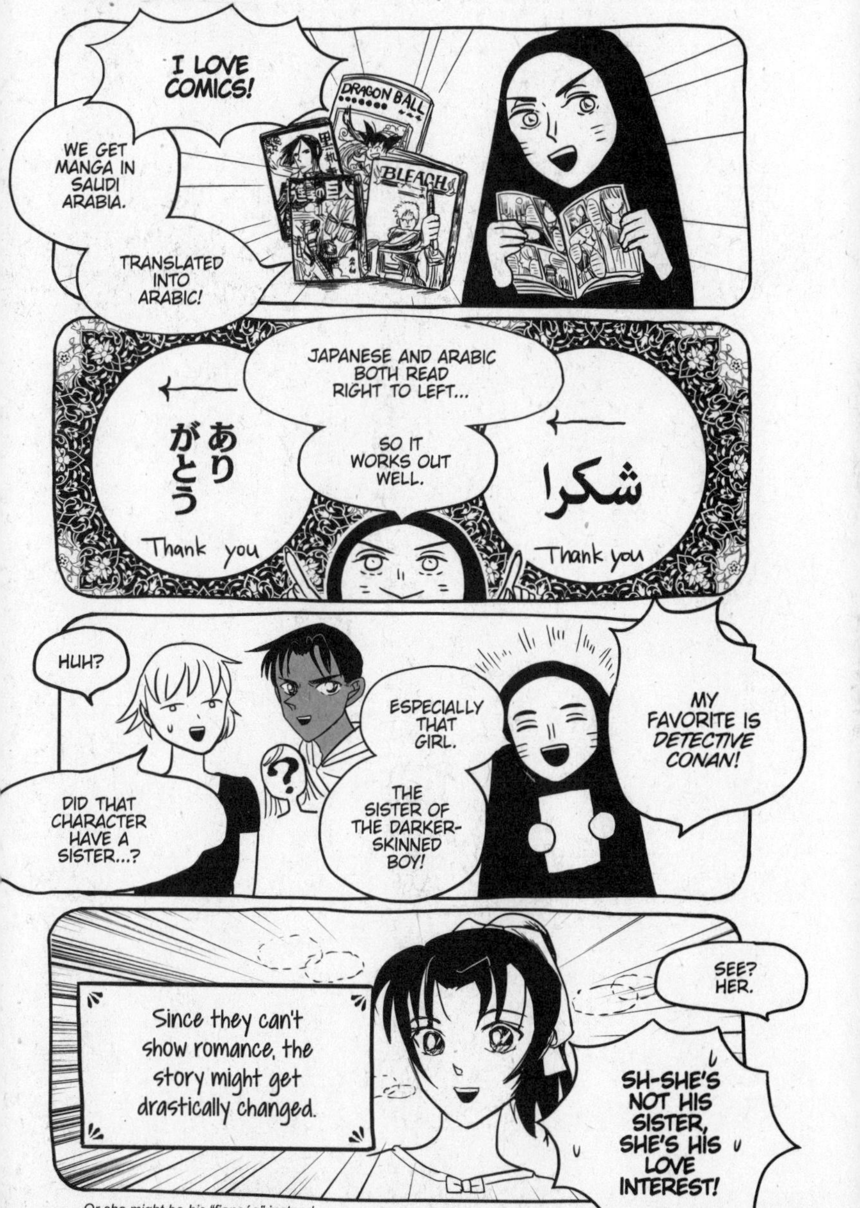
I LOVE COMICS!
WE GET MANGA IN SAUDI ARABIA.
TRANSLATED INTO ARABIC!
DRAGON BALL
BLEACH
JAPANESE AND ARABIC BOTH READ RIGHT TO LEFT...
SO IT WORKS OUT WELL.
شكرا
Thank you
ありがとう
Thank you
MY FAVORITE IS DETECTIVE CONAN!
ESPECIALLY THAT GIRL.
THE SISTER OF THE DARKER-SKINNED BOY!
HUH?
DID THAT CHARACTER HAVE A SISTER...?
SEE? HER.
SH-SHE'S NOT HIS SISTER, SHE'S HIS LOVE INTEREST!
Since they can't show romance, the story might get drastically changed.

Or she might be his "fiancée" instead.

GORE IS OKAY

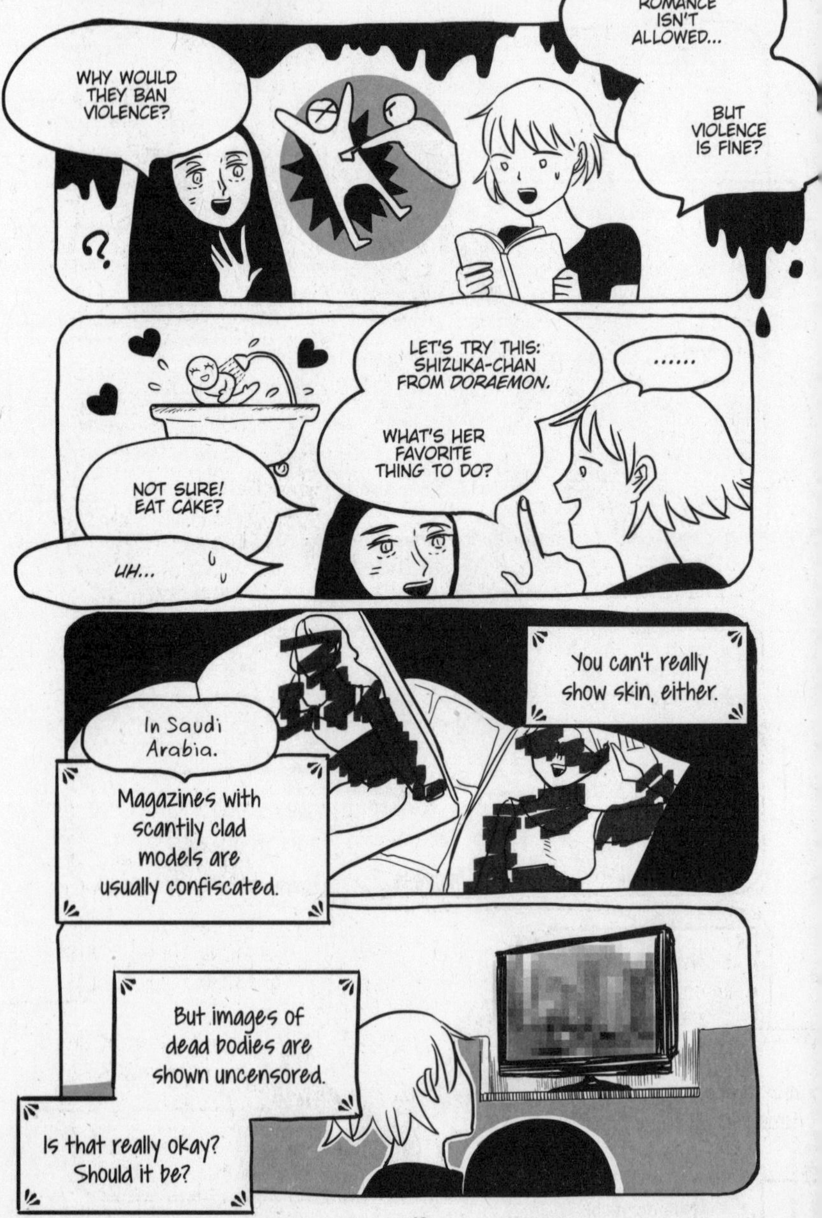
SO ROMANCE ISN'T ALLOWED...
BUT VIOLENCE IS FINE?
WHY WOULD THEY BAN VIOLENCE?
......
LET'S TRY THIS: SHIZUKA-CHAN FROM *DORAEMON*.
WHAT'S HER FAVORITE THING TO DO?
NOT SURE! EAT CAKE?
UH...
You can't really show skin, either.
In Saudi Arabia.
Magazines with scantily clad models are usually confiscated.
But images of dead bodies are shown uncensored.
Is that really okay? Should it be?

NO SKIN

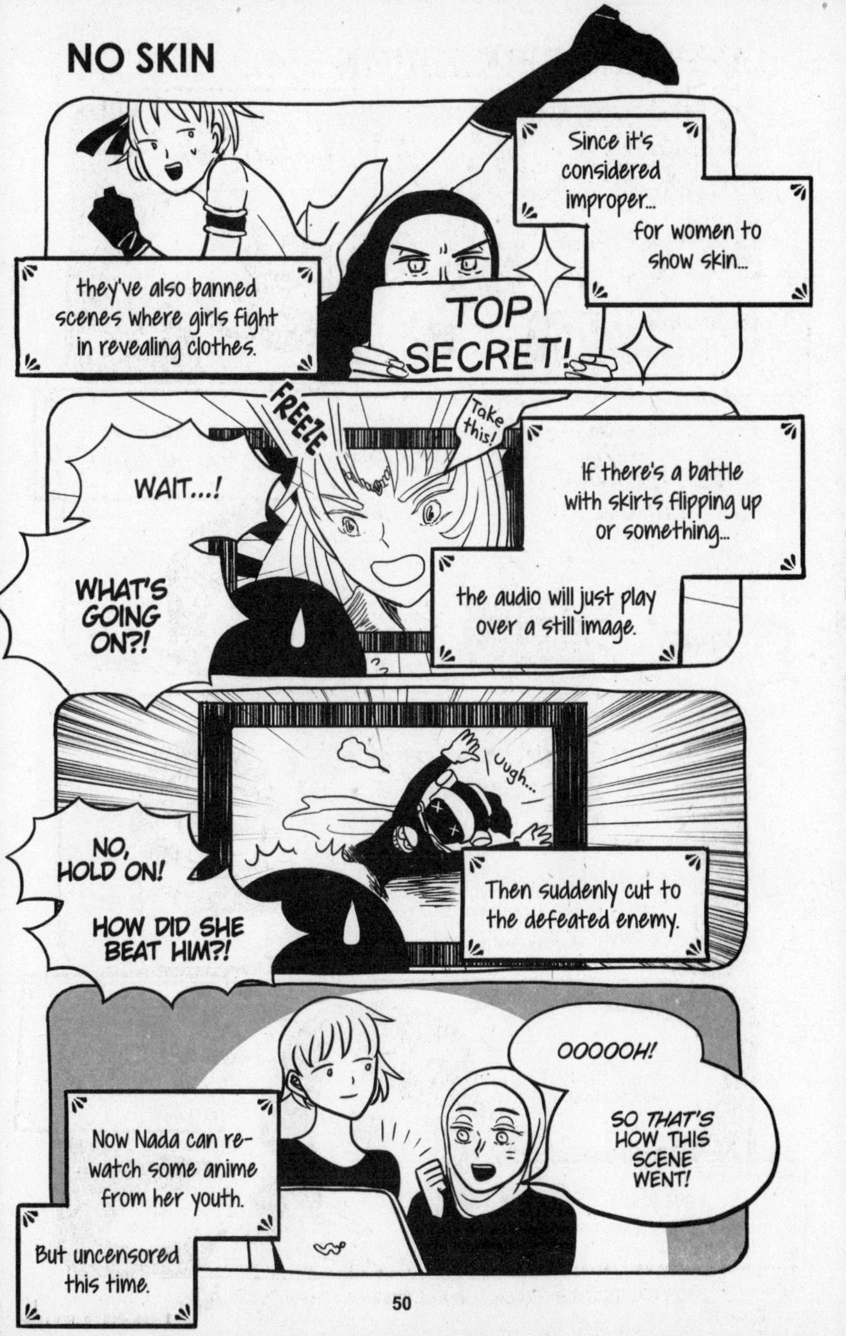

Since it's considered improper...
for women to show skin...
TOP SECRET!
they've also banned scenes where girls fight in revealing clothes.
Take this!
FREEZE
If there's a battle with skirts flipping up or something...
the audio will just play over a still image.
WAIT...!
WHAT'S GOING ON?!
Uugh...
Then suddenly cut to the defeated enemy.
NO, HOLD ON!
HOW DID SHE BEAT HIM?!
OOOOOH!
SO *THAT'S* HOW THIS SCENE WENT!
Now Nada can re-watch some anime from her youth.
But uncensored this time.

THEORY OF EVOLUTION

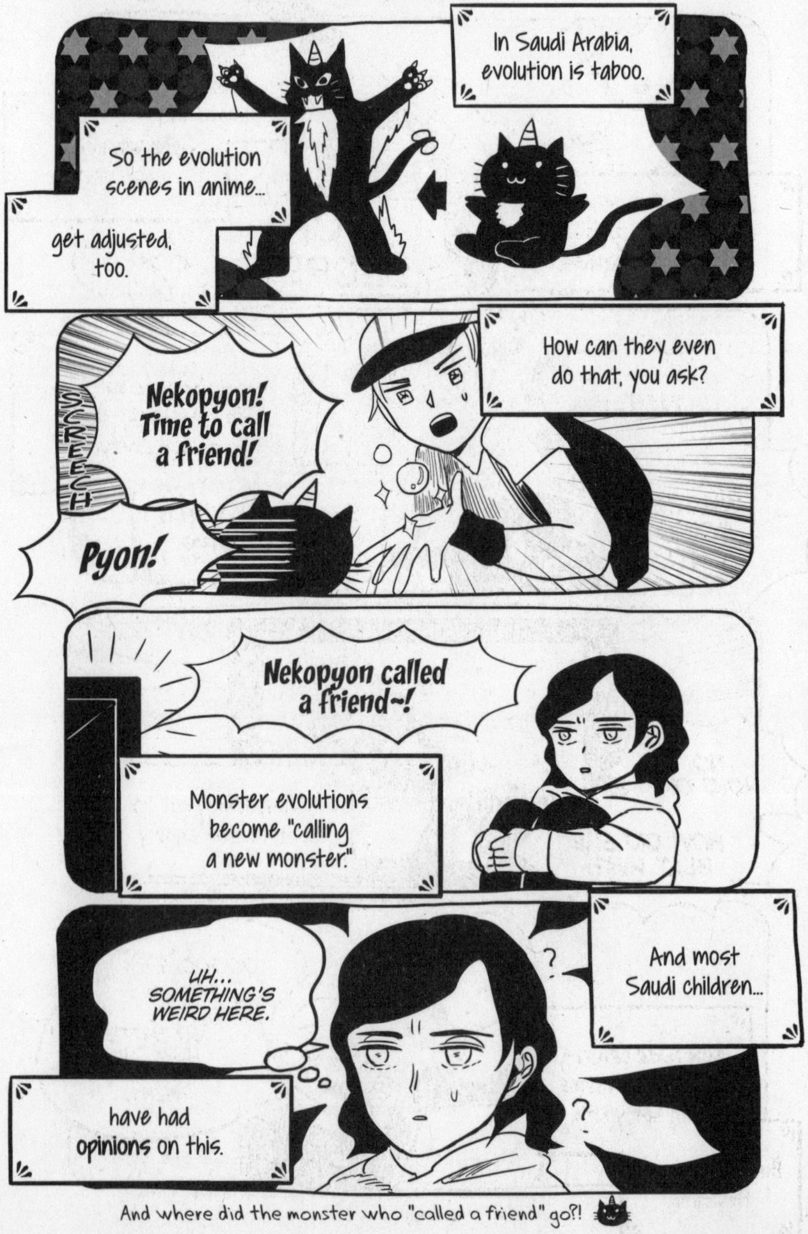
In Saudi Arabia, evolution is taboo.
So the evolution scenes in anime...
get adjusted, too.
How can they even do that, you ask?
Nekopyon! Time to call a friend!
SCREECH
Pyon!
Nekopyon called a friend~!
Monster evolutions become "calling a new monster."
And most Saudi children...
UH... SOMETHING'S WEIRD HERE.
?
?
have had opinions on this.

And where did the monster who "called a friend" go?!

UNIFORM

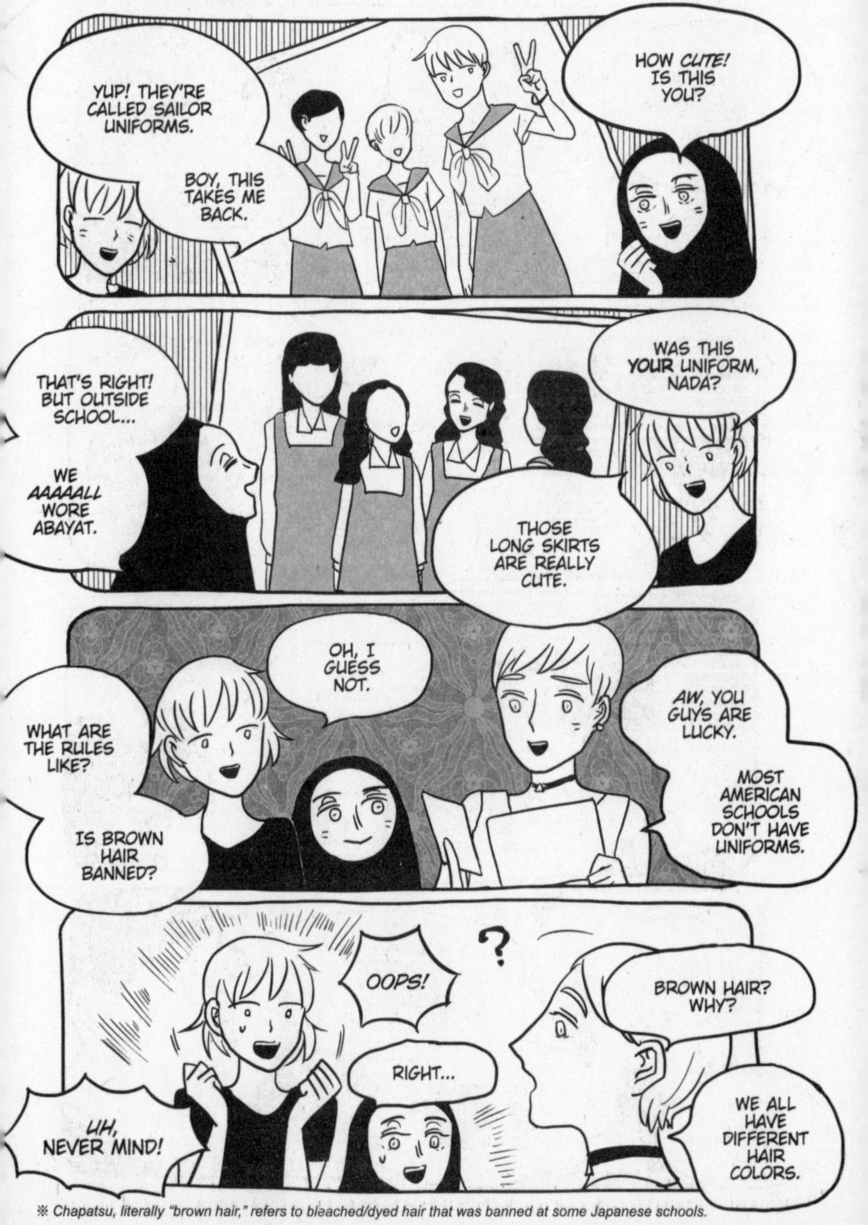
HOW *CUTE!* IS THIS YOU?
YUP! THEY'RE CALLED SAILOR UNIFORMS.
BOY, THIS TAKES ME BACK.
WAS THIS **YOUR** UNIFORM, NADA?
THOSE LONG SKIRTS ARE REALLY CUTE.
THAT'S RIGHT! BUT OUTSIDE SCHOOL...
WE *AAAAALL* WORE ABAYAT.
AW, YOU GUYS ARE LUCKY.
MOST AMERICAN SCHOOLS DON'T HAVE UNIFORMS.
OH, I GUESS NOT.
WHAT ARE THE RULES LIKE?
IS BROWN HAIR BANNED?
?
BROWN HAIR? WHY?
WE ALL HAVE DIFFERENT HAIR COLORS.
OOPS!
RIGHT...
UH, NEVER MIND!

※ *Chapatsu, literally "brown hair," refers to bleached/dyed hair that was banned at some Japanese schools.*

SCHOOL LIFE

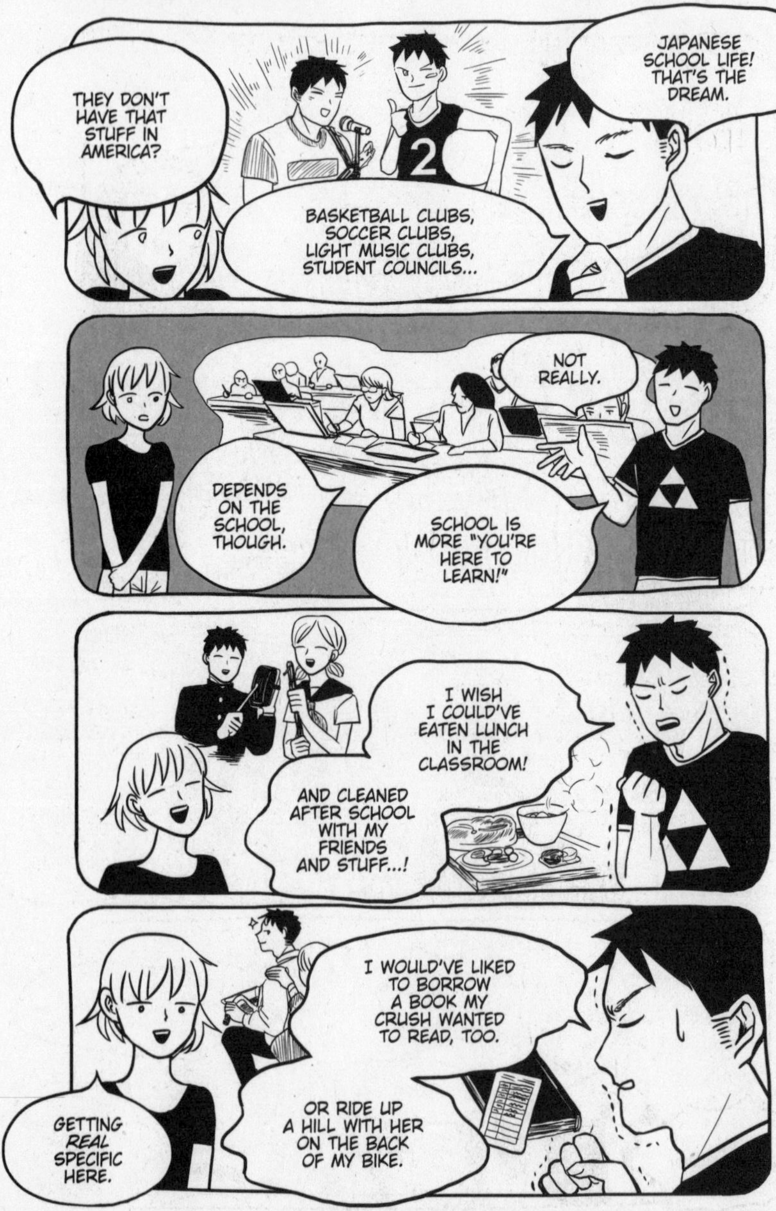
JAPANESE SCHOOL LIFE! THAT'S THE DREAM.
BASKETBALL CLUBS, SOCCER CLUBS, LIGHT MUSIC CLUBS, STUDENT COUNCILS...
THEY DON'T HAVE THAT STUFF IN AMERICA?
NOT REALLY.
SCHOOL IS MORE "YOU'RE HERE TO LEARN!"
DEPENDS ON THE SCHOOL, THOUGH.
I WISH I COULD'VE EATEN LUNCH IN THE CLASSROOM!
AND CLEANED AFTER SCHOOL WITH MY FRIENDS AND STUFF...!
I WOULD'VE LIKED TO BORROW A BOOK MY CRUSH WANTED TO READ, TOO.
OR RIDE UP A HILL WITH HER ON THE BACK OF MY BIKE.
GETTING *REAL* SPECIFIC HERE.

SCHOOL MEALS

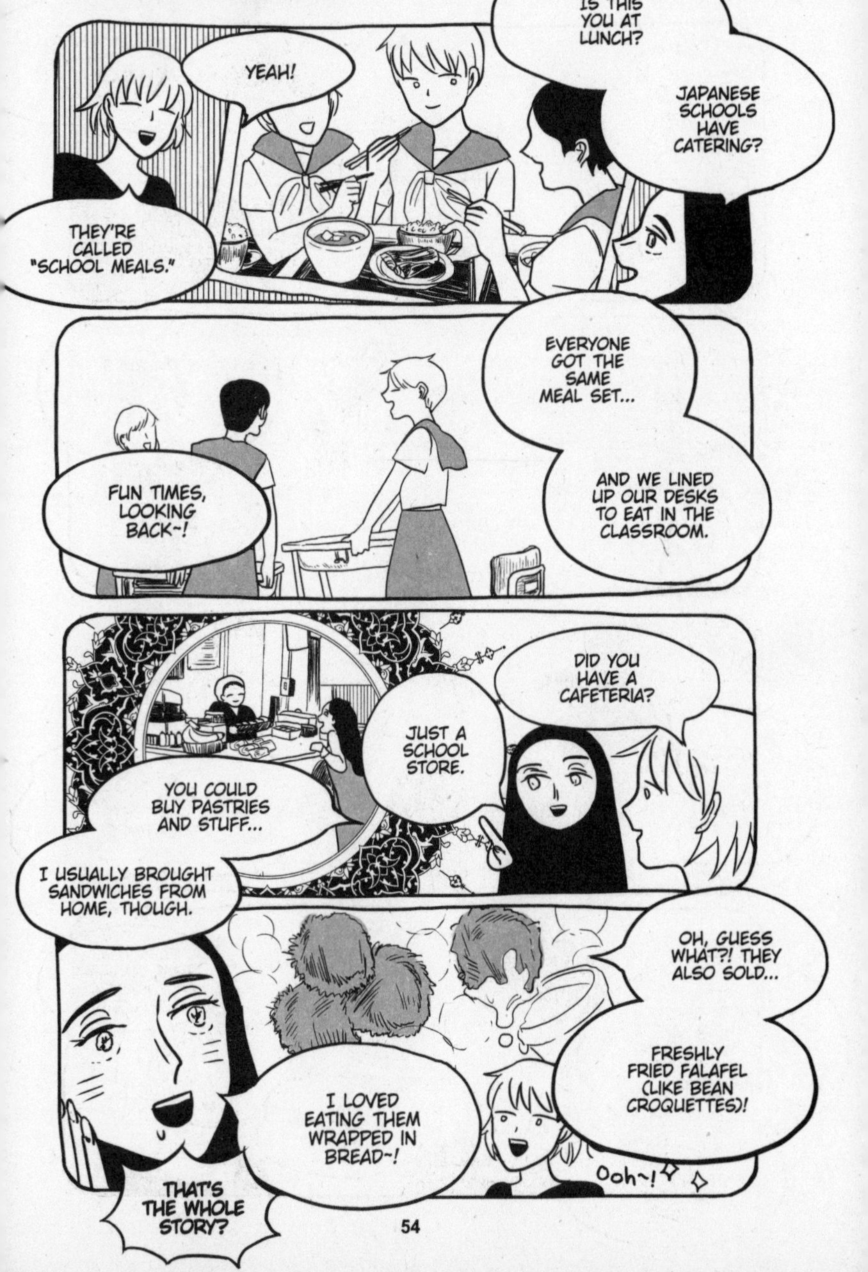
IS THIS YOU AT LUNCH?
JAPANESE SCHOOLS HAVE CATERING?
YEAH!
THEY'RE CALLED "SCHOOL MEALS."
EVERYONE GOT THE SAME MEAL SET...
AND WE LINED UP OUR DESKS TO EAT IN THE CLASSROOM.
FUN TIMES, LOOKING BACK~!
DID YOU HAVE A CAFETERIA?
JUST A SCHOOL STORE.
YOU COULD BUY PASTRIES AND STUFF...
I USUALLY BROUGHT SANDWICHES FROM HOME, THOUGH.
OH, GUESS WHAT?! THEY ALSO SOLD...
FRESHLY FRIED FALAFEL (LIKE BEAN CROQUETTES)!
Ooh~!
I LOVED EATING THEM WRAPPED IN BREAD~!
THAT'S THE WHOLE STORY?

HOMESCHOOLING

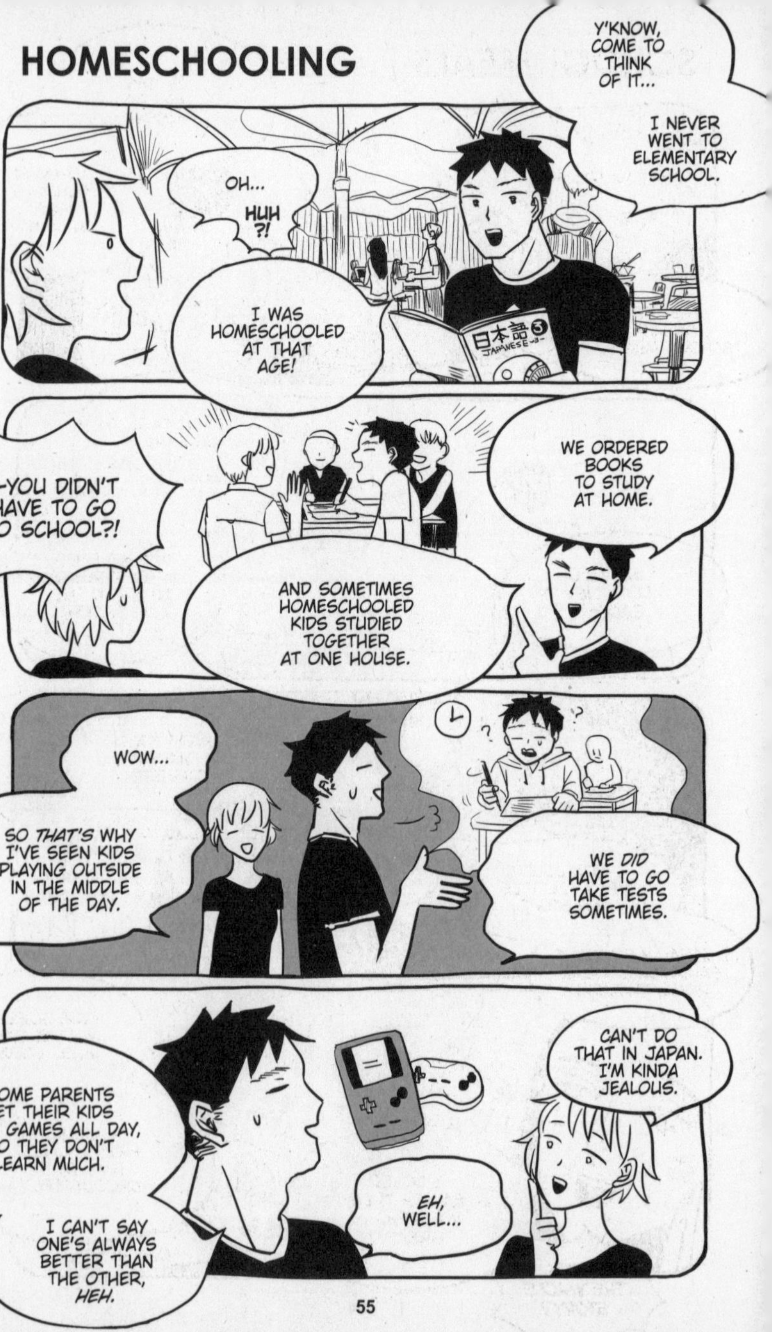
Y'KNOW, COME TO THINK OF IT...
I NEVER WENT TO ELEMENTARY SCHOOL.
OH...
HUH?!
I WAS HOMESCHOOLED AT THAT AGE!
日本語 3 JAPANESE -3-
WE ORDERED BOOKS TO STUDY AT HOME.
Y-YOU DIDN'T HAVE TO GO TO SCHOOL?!
AND SOMETIMES HOMESCHOOLED KIDS STUDIED TOGETHER AT ONE HOUSE.
WOW...
SO *THAT'S* WHY I'VE SEEN KIDS PLAYING OUTSIDE IN THE MIDDLE OF THE DAY.
WE *DID* HAVE TO GO TAKE TESTS SOMETIMES.
CAN'T DO THAT IN JAPAN. I'M KINDA JEALOUS.
SOME PARENTS LET THEIR KIDS PLAY GAMES ALL DAY, SO THEY DON'T LEARN MUCH.
EH, WELL...
I CAN'T SAY ONE'S ALWAYS BETTER THAN THE OTHER, *HEH.*

ADHAN

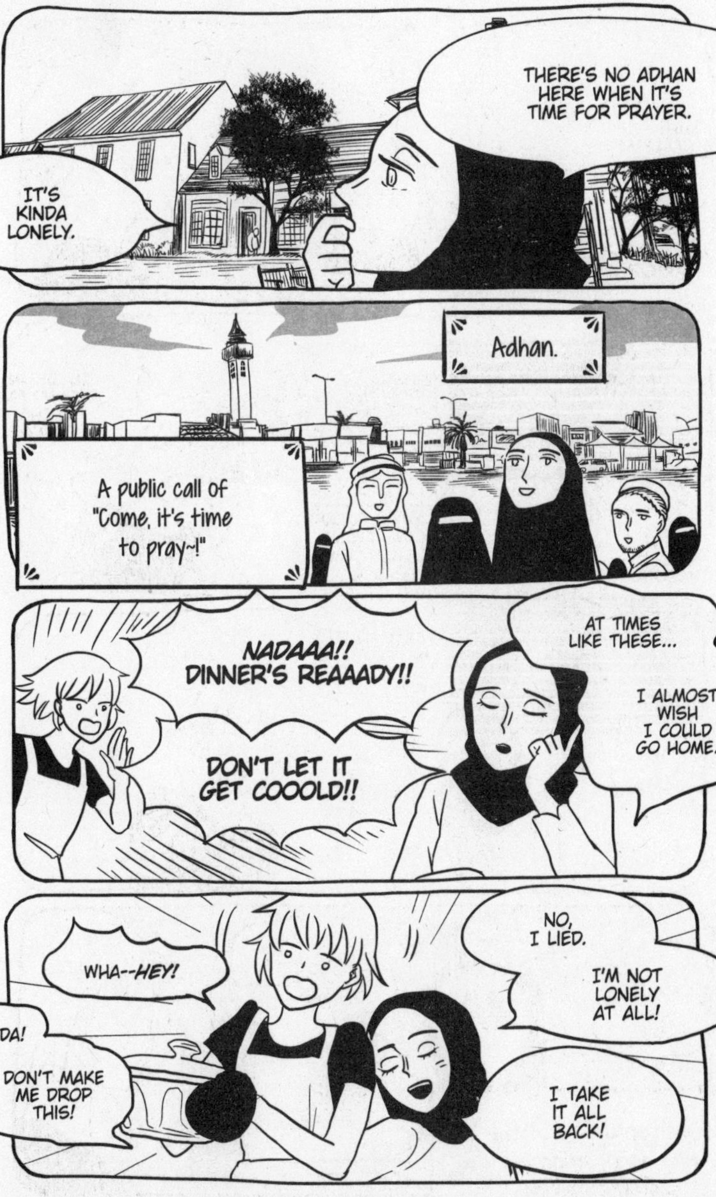
THERE'S NO ADHAN HERE WHEN IT'S TIME FOR PRAYER.
IT'S KINDA LONELY.
Adhan.
A public call of "Come, it's time to pray~!"
AT TIMES LIKE THESE...
I ALMOST WISH I COULD GO HOME.
NADAAA!! DINNER'S REAAADY!!
DON'T LET IT GET COOOLD!!
NO, I LIED.
I'M NOT LONELY AT ALL!
WHA--*HEY!*
I TAKE IT ALL BACK!
NADA!
DON'T MAKE ME DROP THIS!

SUNSET

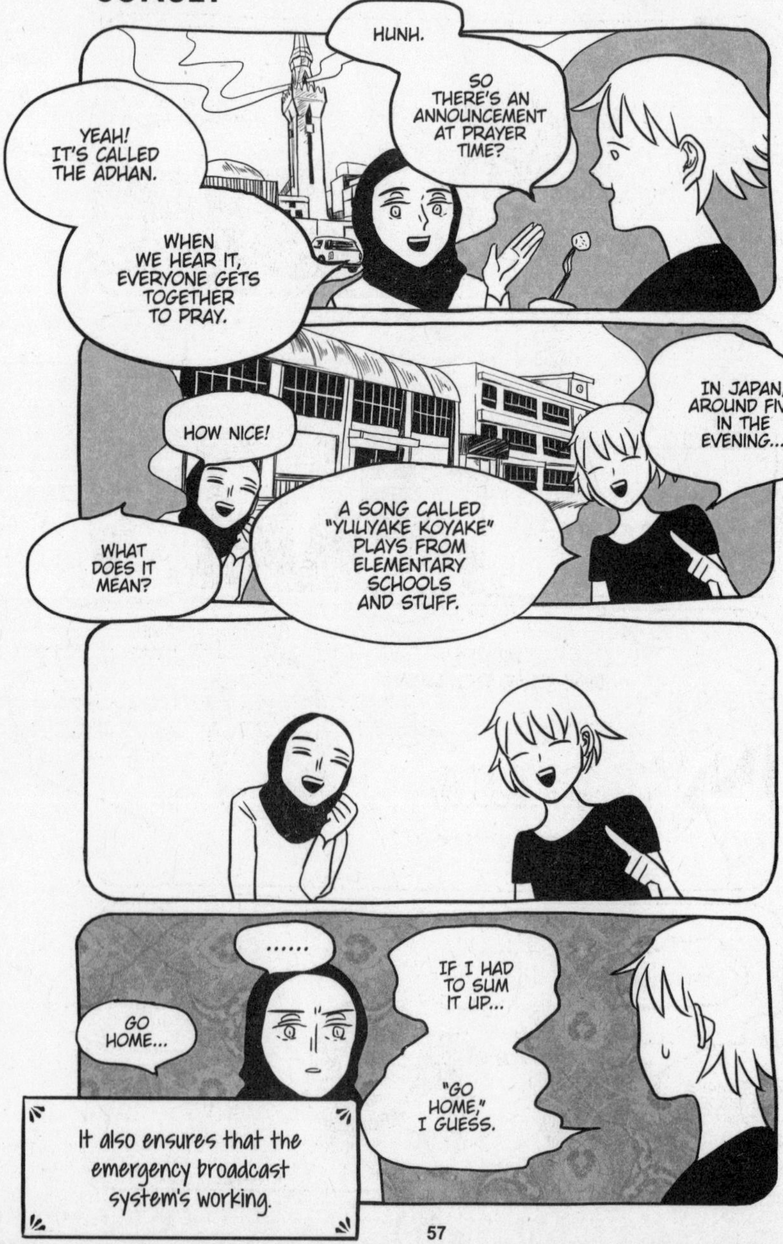
HUNH.
SO THERE'S AN ANNOUNCEMENT AT PRAYER TIME?
YEAH! IT'S CALLED THE ADHAN.
WHEN WE HEAR IT, EVERYONE GETS TOGETHER TO PRAY.
IN JAPAN, AROUND FIVE IN THE EVENING...
A SONG CALLED "YUUYAKE KOYAKE" PLAYS FROM ELEMENTARY SCHOOLS AND STUFF.
HOW NICE!
WHAT DOES IT MEAN?
IF I HAD TO SUM IT UP...
"GO HOME," I GUESS.
......
GO HOME...
It also ensures that the emergency broadcast system's working.

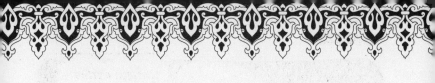

SATOKO AND NADA

Presented by Yupechika

LINDA

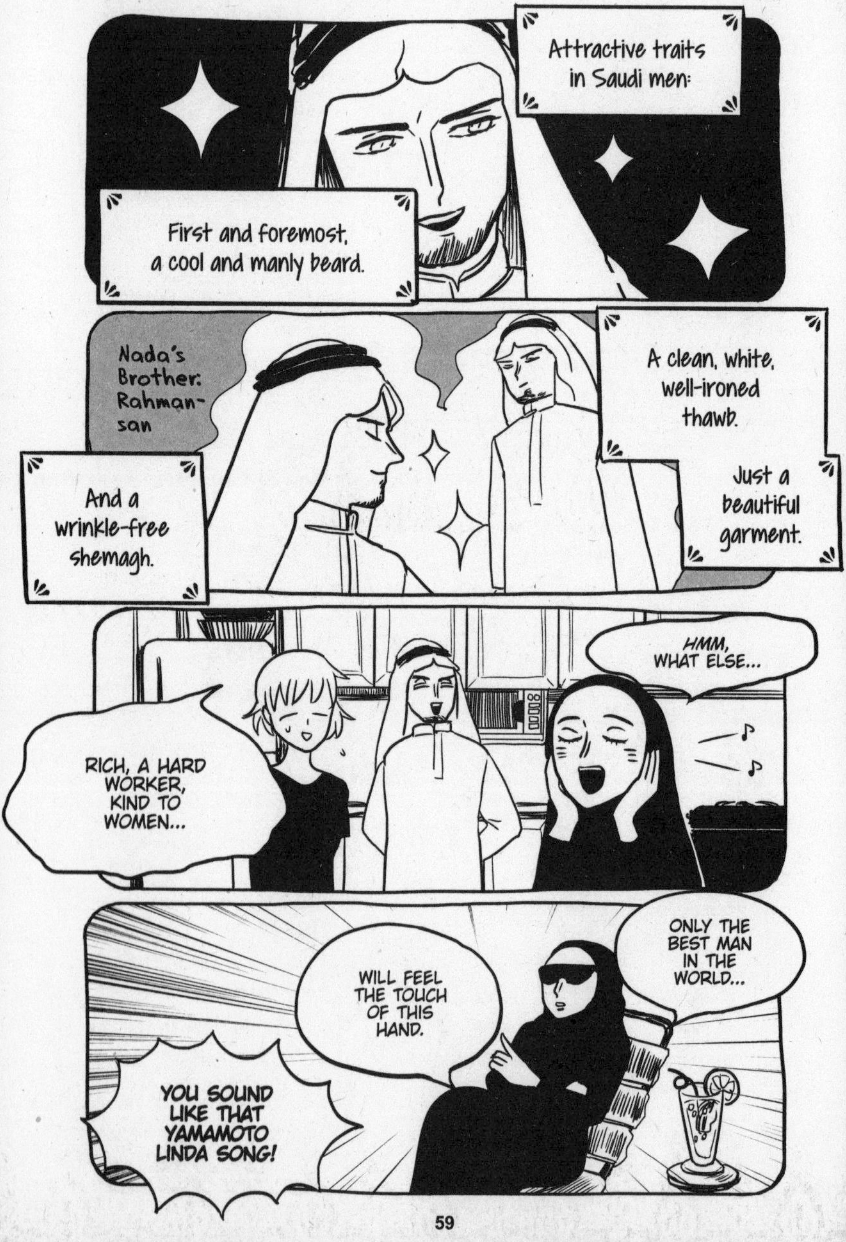
Attractive traits in Saudi men:
First and foremost, a cool and manly beard.
A clean, white, well-ironed thawb.
Just a beautiful garment.
Nada's Brother: Rahman-san
And a wrinkle-free shemagh.
HMM, WHAT ELSE...
RICH, A HARD WORKER, KIND TO WOMEN...
ONLY THE BEST MAN IN THE WORLD...
WILL FEEL THE TOUCH OF THIS HAND.
YOU SOUND LIKE THAT YAMAMOTO LINDA SONG!

IDENTITY

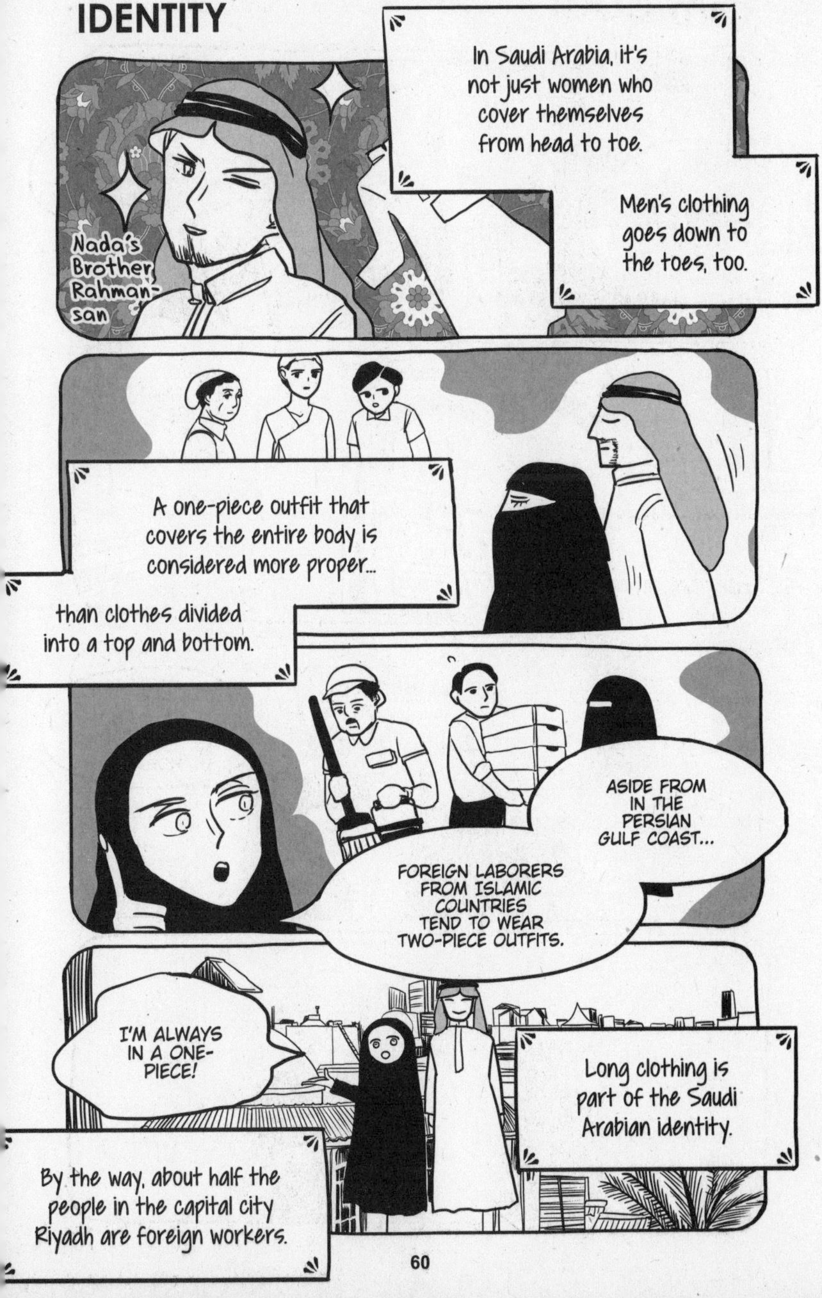

In Saudi Arabia, it's not just women who cover themselves from head to toe.
Men's clothing goes down to the toes, too.
Nada's Brother Rahman-san
A one-piece outfit that covers the entire body is considered more proper...
than clothes divided into a top and bottom.
ASIDE FROM IN THE PERSIAN GULF COAST...
FOREIGN LABORERS FROM ISLAMIC COUNTRIES TEND TO WEAR TWO-PIECE OUTFITS.
Long clothing is part of the Saudi Arabian identity.
I'M ALWAYS IN A ONE-PIECE!
By the way, about half the people in the capital city Riyadh are foreign workers.

HOW COOL

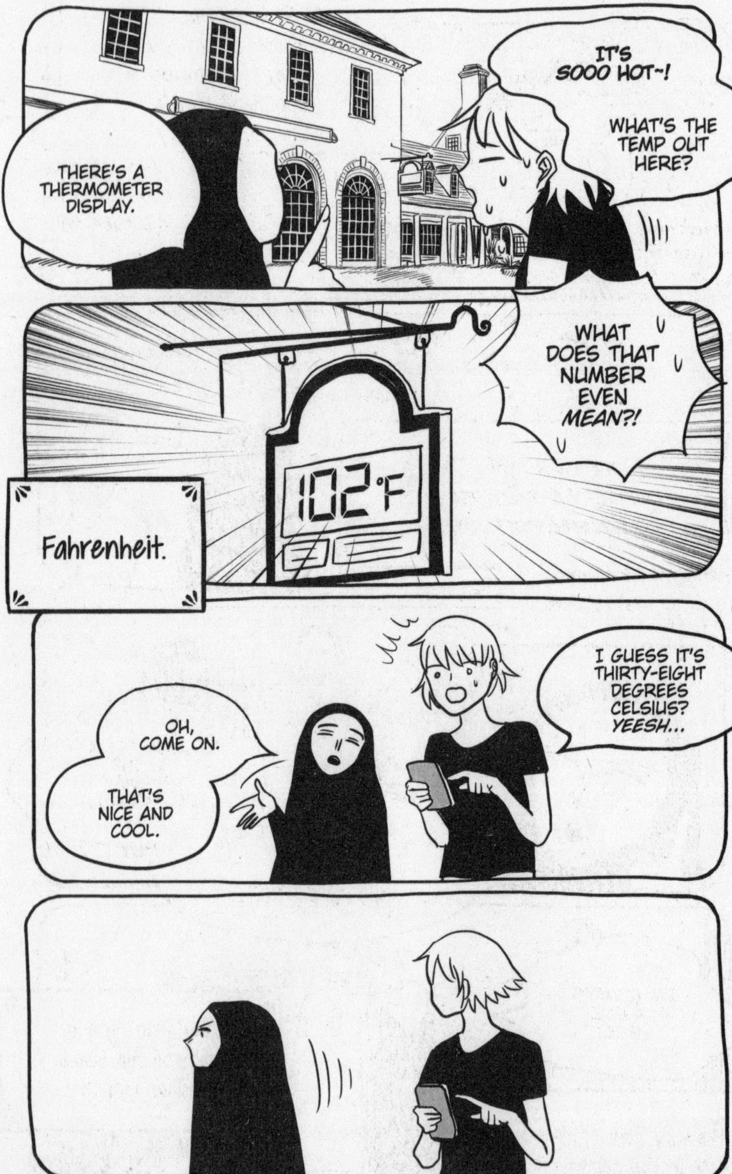
IT'S *SOOO* HOT~!
WHAT'S THE TEMP OUT HERE?
THERE'S A THERMOMETER DISPLAY.
WHAT DOES THAT NUMBER EVEN *MEAN?!*
102°F
Fahrenheit.
I GUESS IT'S THIRTY-EIGHT DEGREES CELSIUS? *YEESH...*
OH, COME ON.
THAT'S NICE AND COOL.

SHRIMP

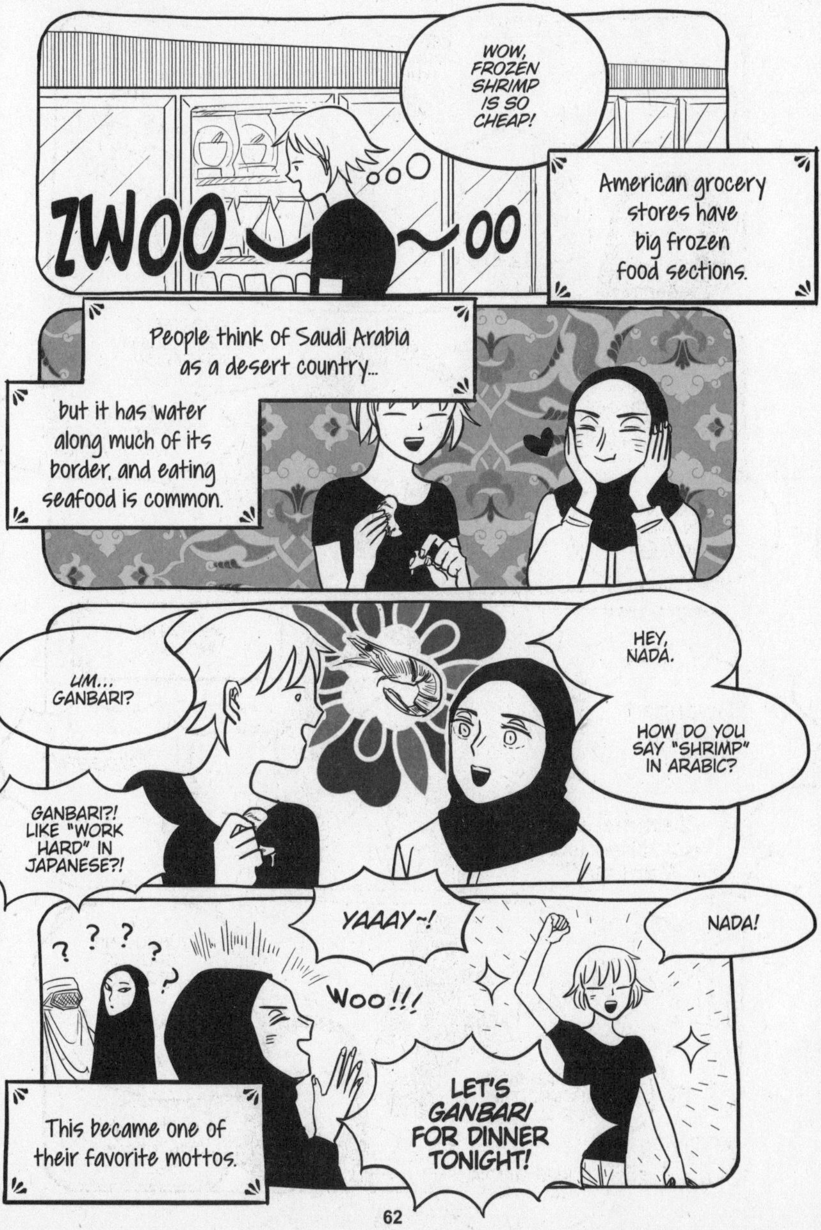
WOW, FROZEN SHRIMP IS SO CHEAP!
American grocery stores have big frozen food sections.
ZWOO~~OO
People think of Saudi Arabia as a desert country...
but it has water along much of its border, and eating seafood is common.
HEY, NADA.
HOW DO YOU SAY "SHRIMP" IN ARABIC?
UM... GANBARI?
GANBARI?! LIKE "WORK HARD" IN JAPANESE?!
NADA!
YAAAY~!
Woo!!!
LET'S GANBARI FOR DINNER TONIGHT!
? ? ? ? ?
This became one of their favorite mottos.

HOW LONG

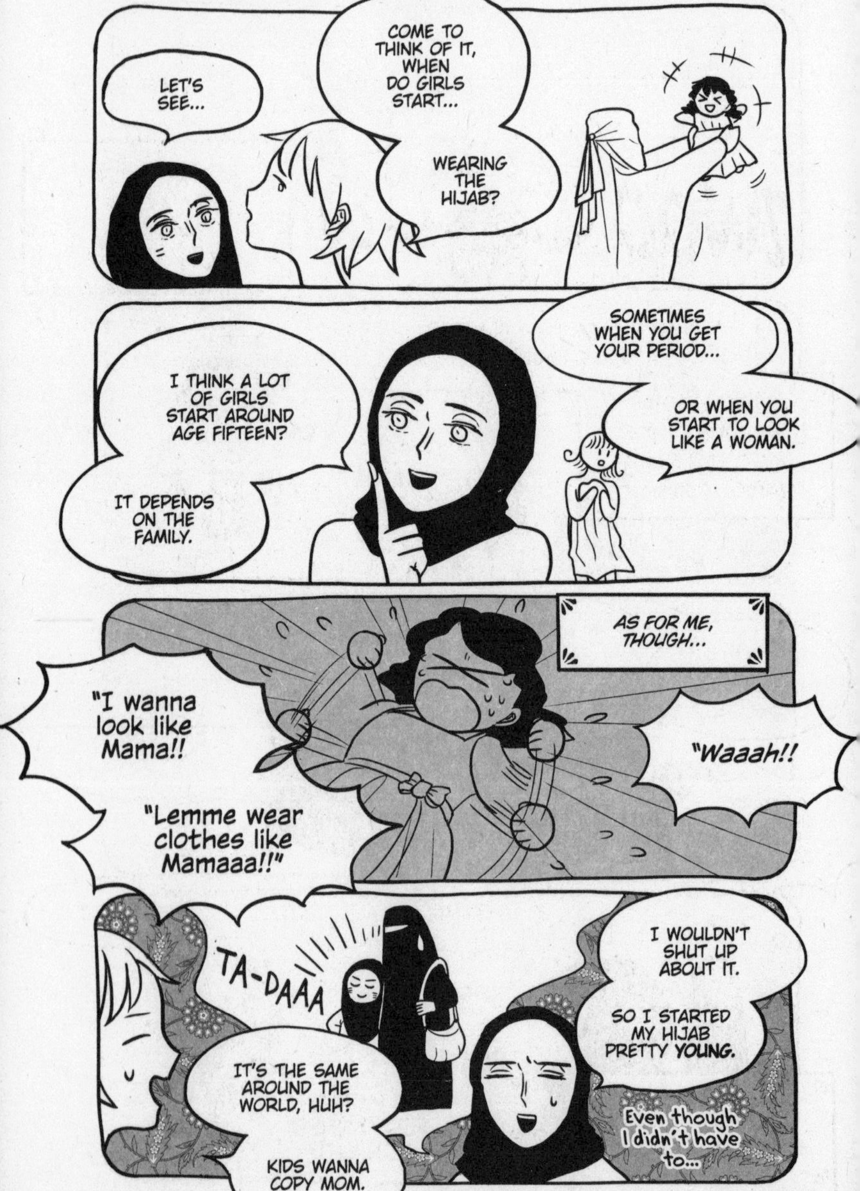

COME TO THINK OF IT, WHEN DO GIRLS START...
WEARING THE HIJAB?
LET'S SEE...
SOMETIMES WHEN YOU GET YOUR PERIOD...
OR WHEN YOU START TO LOOK LIKE A WOMAN.
I THINK A LOT OF GIRLS START AROUND AGE FIFTEEN?
IT DEPENDS ON THE FAMILY.
AS FOR ME, THOUGH...
"Waaah!!
"I wanna look like Mama!!
"Lemme wear clothes like Mamaaa!!"
I WOULDN'T SHUT UP ABOUT IT.
SO I STARTED MY HIJAB PRETTY **YOUNG.**
Even though I didn't have to...
TA-DAAA
IT'S THE SAME AROUND THE WORLD, HUH?
KIDS WANNA COPY MOM.

FINGER FOOD

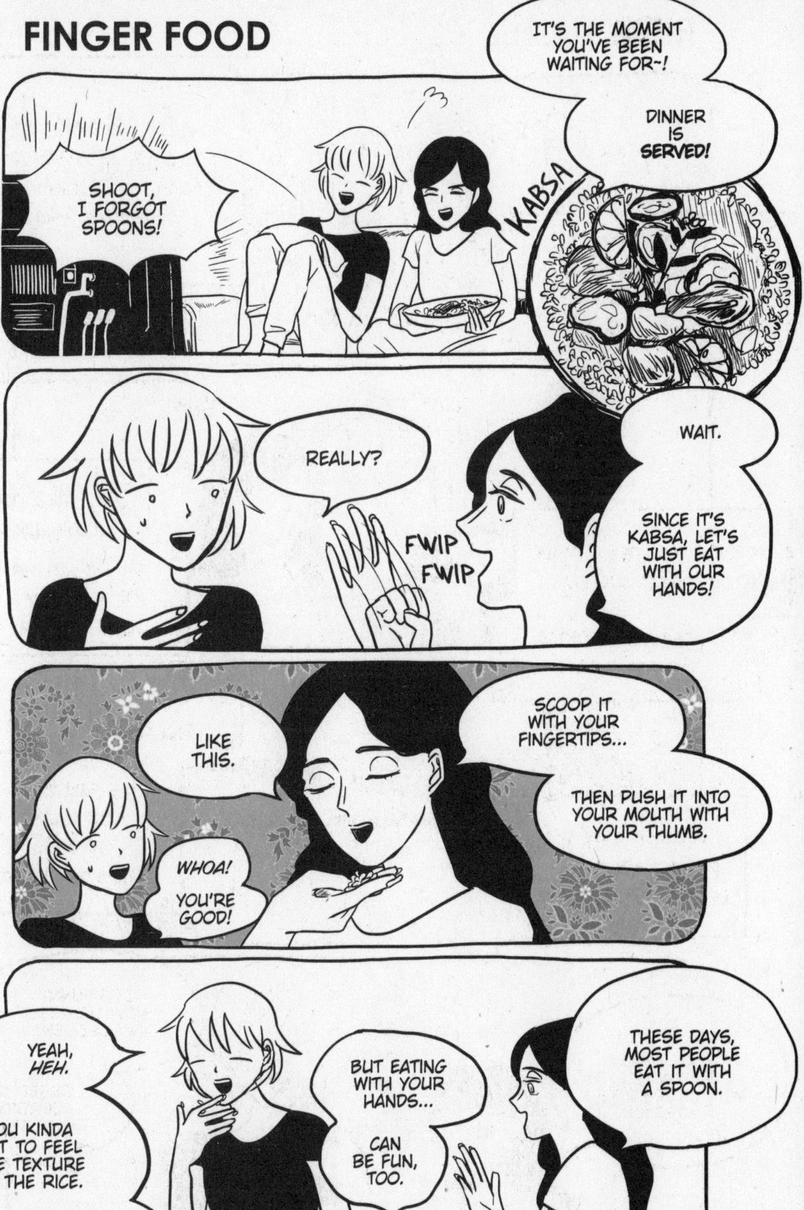

IT'S THE MOMENT YOU'VE BEEN WAITING FOR~!
DINNER IS SERVED!
KABSA
SHOOT, I FORGOT SPOONS!
WAIT.
SINCE IT'S KABSA, LET'S JUST EAT WITH OUR HANDS!
FWIP FWIP
REALLY?
SCOOP IT WITH YOUR FINGERTIPS...
LIKE THIS.
THEN PUSH IT INTO YOUR MOUTH WITH YOUR THUMB.
WHOA! YOU'RE GOOD!
THESE DAYS, MOST PEOPLE EAT IT WITH A SPOON.
BUT EATING WITH YOUR HANDS...
CAN BE FUN, TOO.
YEAH, HEH.
YOU KINDA GET TO FEEL THE TEXTURE OF THE RICE.
YUM!

RICE

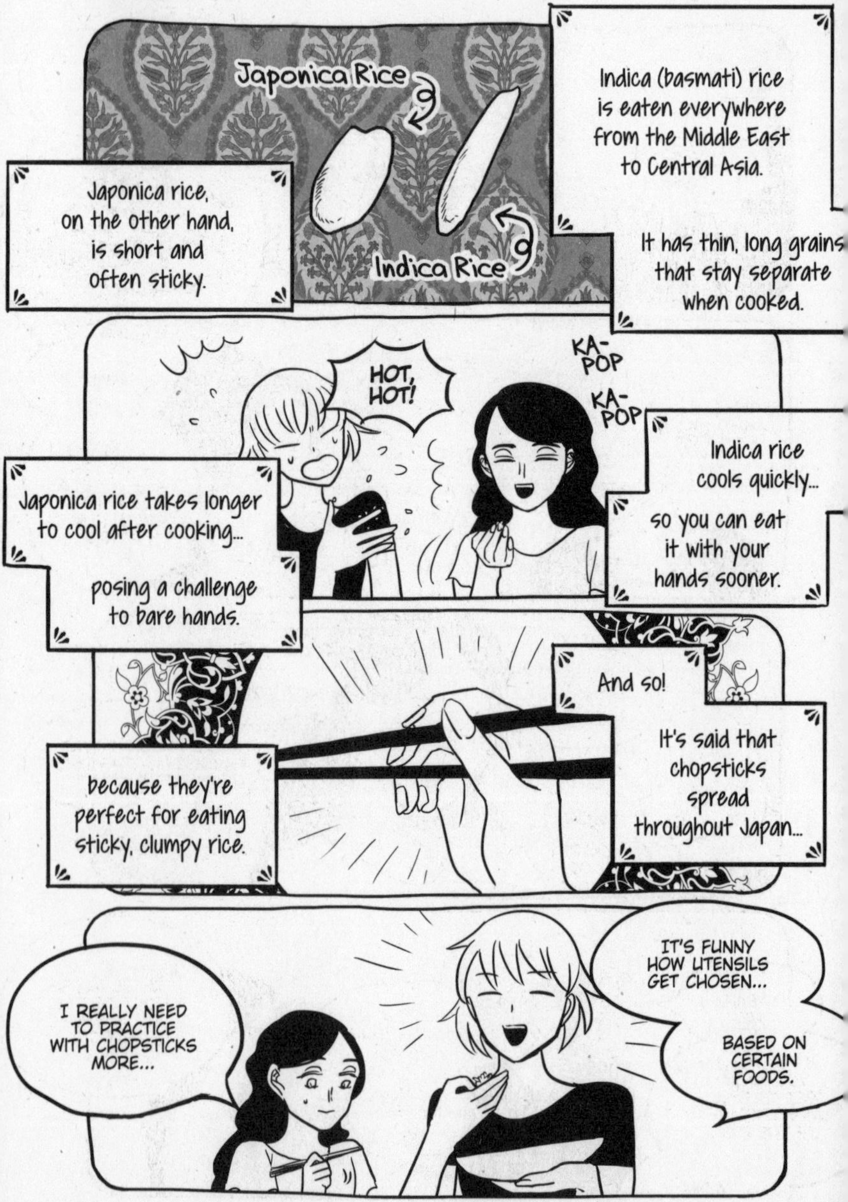

Indica (basmati) rice is eaten everywhere from the Middle East to Central Asia.
It has thin, long grains that stay separate when cooked.
Japonica Rice
Indica Rice
Japonica rice, on the other hand, is short and often sticky.
KA-POP
KA-POP
Indica rice cools quickly...
so you can eat it with your hands sooner.
HOT, HOT!
Japonica rice takes longer to cool after cooking...
posing a challenge to bare hands.
And so!
It's said that chopsticks spread throughout Japan...
because they're perfect for eating sticky, clumpy rice.
IT'S FUNNY HOW UTENSILS GET CHOSEN...
BASED ON CERTAIN FOODS.
I REALLY NEED TO PRACTICE WITH CHOPSTICKS MORE...

KABSA

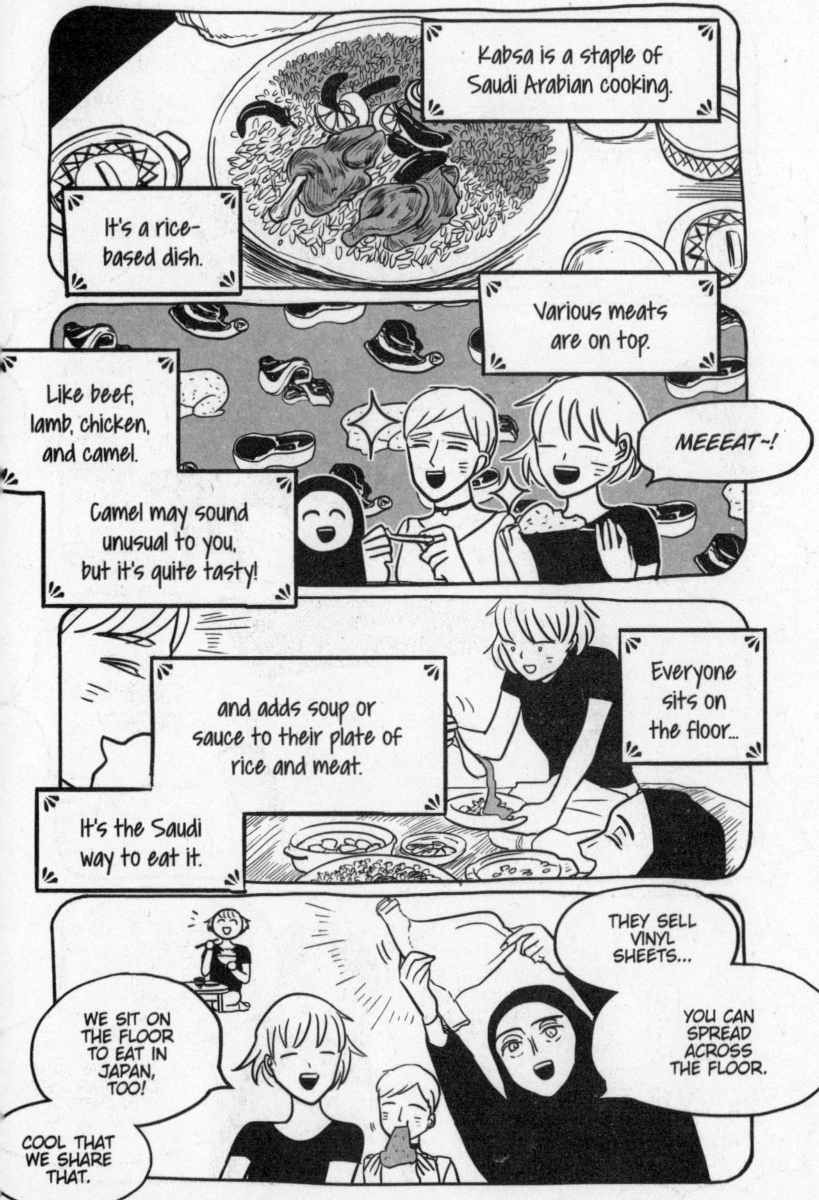

Kabsa is a staple of Saudi Arabian cooking.
It's a rice-based dish.
Various meats are on top.
MEEEAT~!
Like beef, lamb, chicken, and camel.
Camel may sound unusual to you, but it's quite tasty!
Everyone sits on the floor...
and adds soup or sauce to their plate of rice and meat.
It's the Saudi way to eat it.
THEY SELL VINYL SHEETS...
YOU CAN SPREAD ACROSS THE FLOOR.
WE SIT ON THE FLOOR TO EAT IN JAPAN, TOO!
COOL THAT WE SHARE THAT.

NUMERALS

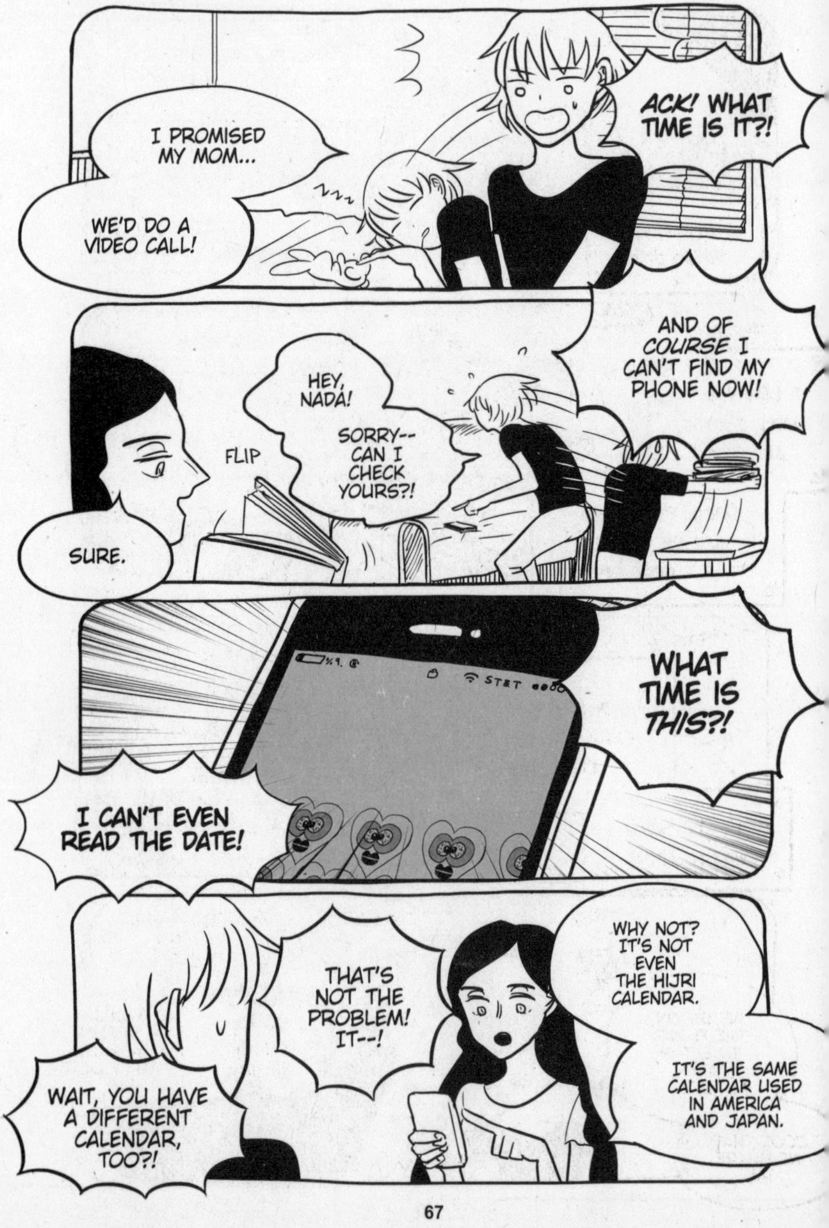
ACK! WHAT TIME IS IT?!
I PROMISED MY MOM...
WE'D DO A VIDEO CALL!
AND OF COURSE I CAN'T FIND MY PHONE NOW!
HEY, NADA!
SORRY-- CAN I CHECK YOURS?!
FLIP
SURE.
WHAT TIME IS THIS?!
I CAN'T EVEN READ THE DATE!
WHY NOT? IT'S NOT EVEN THE HIJRI CALENDAR.
IT'S THE SAME CALENDAR USED IN AMERICA AND JAPAN.
THAT'S NOT THE PROBLEM! IT--!
WAIT, YOU HAVE A DIFFERENT CALENDAR, TOO?!

NADA'S EASTERN ARABIC NUMERAL COURSE:
PART 1

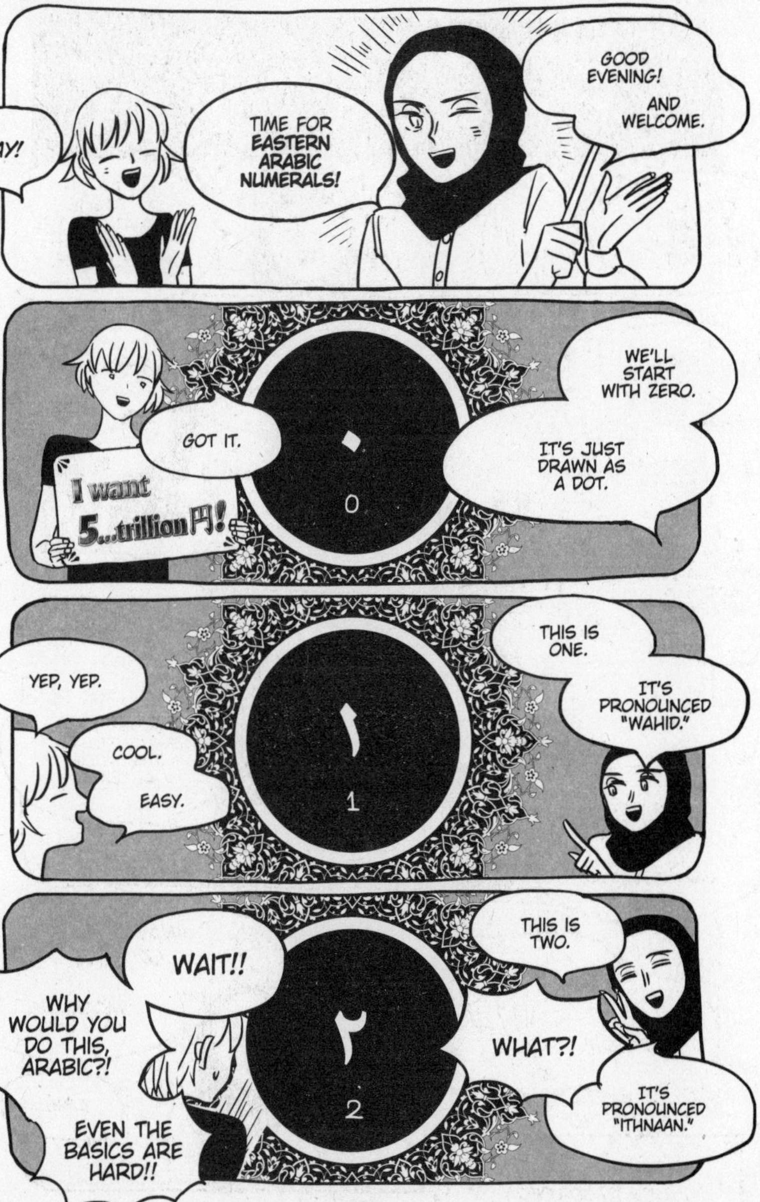

GOOD EVENING!
AND WELCOME.
TIME FOR EASTERN ARABIC NUMERALS!
YAY!
WE'LL START WITH ZERO.
IT'S JUST DRAWN AS A DOT.
٠
0
GOT IT.
I want 5...trillion円!
THIS IS ONE.
IT'S PRONOUNCED "WAHID."
١
1
YEP, YEP.
COOL.
EASY.
THIS IS TWO.
WAIT!!
WHAT?!
IT'S PRONOUNCED "ITHNAAN."
٢
2
WHY WOULD YOU DO THIS, ARABIC?!
EVEN THE BASICS ARE HARD!!

NADA'S EASTERN ARABIC NUMERAL COURSE: PART 2

| wahid | 2 thalaatha | 4 | Khamsa | 6 | sab'a | 8 | tis'a | 10 |
| 1 | ithnaan 3 | arba'a | 5 | sitta | 7 | thamanya | 9 | ashra |

١ ٢ ٣ ٤ ٥ ٦ ٧ ٨ ٩ ١٠

I DUNNO IF I CAN REMEMBER ALL THAT.

THIS IS WHAT ALL THE NUMERALS LOOK LIKE.

KHAM...

S-SABA...?

TESSA... ASURA...?

THEY SOUND LIKE CHARACTER NAMES IN A FANTASY STORY.

IN ORDER, THEY'RE PRONOUNCED:

WAHID, ITHNAAN...

SINCE YOU LIVE WITH ME, SATOKO-SAN...

MAYBE YOU *SHOULD* LEARN THIS MUCH, AT LEAST.

YEAH?

THEN *YOU* SHOULD LEARN TO COUNT TO TEN IN JAPANESE, TOO!

WAY AHEAD OF YOU!

WHOA, NOT BAD!

KEEP AT IT.

WICCHI, NII, SAN, SHII, GYOH...

WICCHI, NII, SAN, SHII...

ERM...

"WICCHI" WAS TOO CUTE TO CORRECT.

69

REVENGE

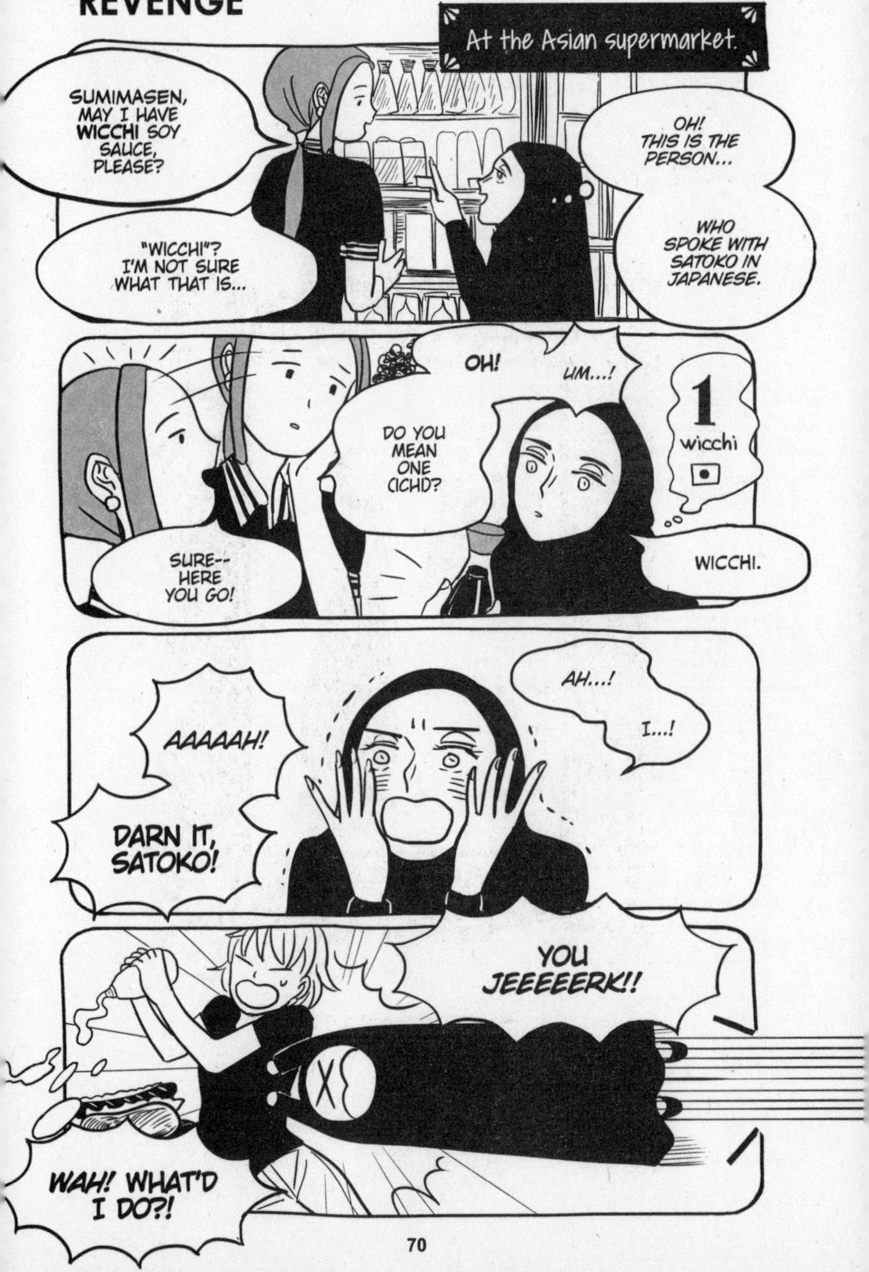
At the Asian supermarket.
OH! THIS IS THE PERSON...
WHO SPOKE WITH SATOKO IN JAPANESE.
SUMIMASEN, MAY I HAVE **WICCHI** SOY SAUCE, PLEASE?
"WICCHI"? I'M NOT SURE WHAT THAT IS...
1 wicchi
UM...!
OH!
DO YOU MEAN ONE CICHD?
WICCHI.
SURE-- HERE YOU GO!
AH...! I...!
AAAAAH!
DARN IT, SATOKO!
YOU JEEEEERK!!
WAH! WHAT'D I DO?!

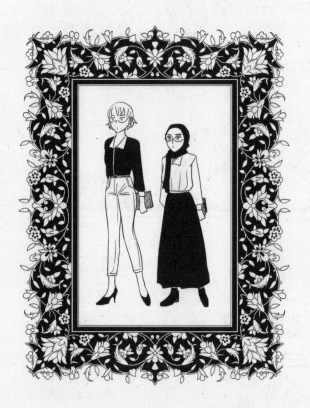

SATOKO AND NADA

Presented by Yupechika

INVITATION

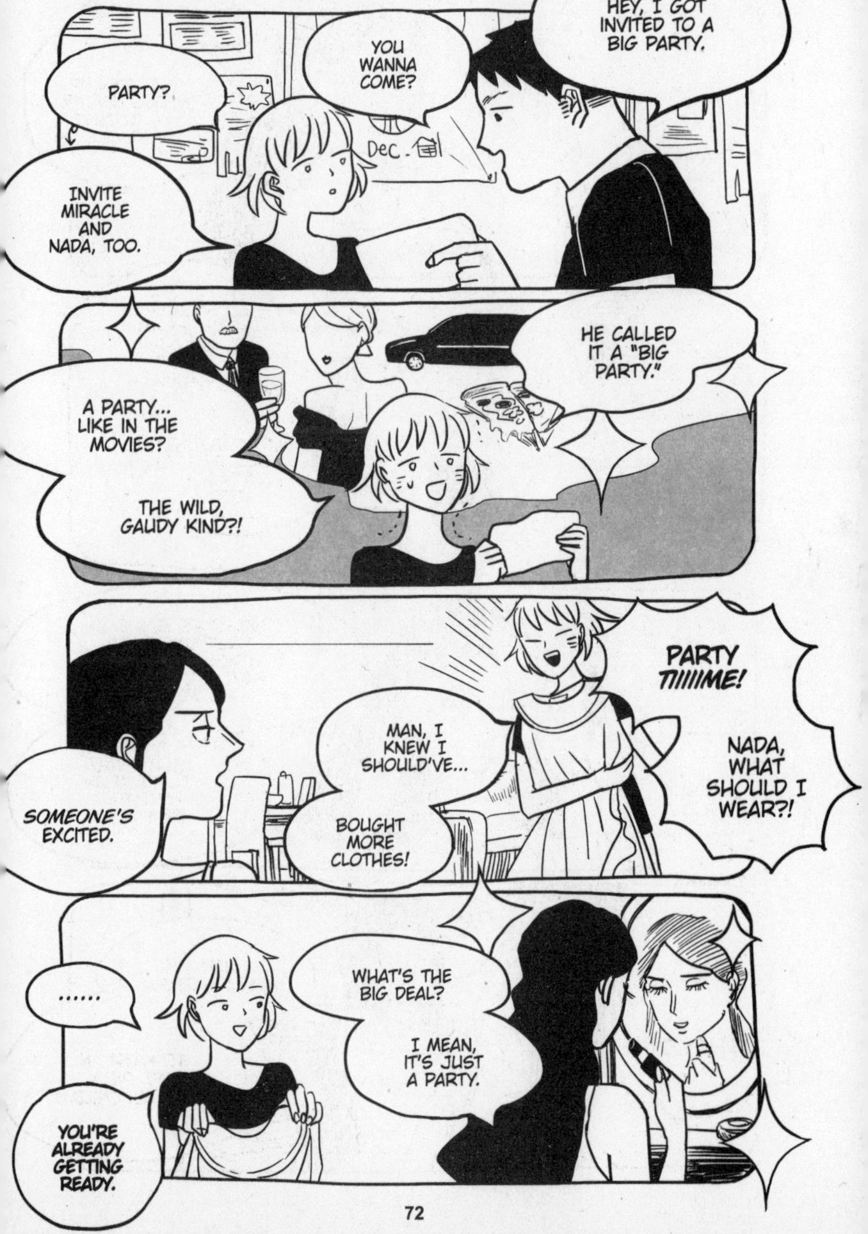
HEY, I GOT INVITED TO A BIG PARTY.
YOU WANNA COME?
PARTY?
Dec.
INVITE MIRACLE AND NADA, TOO.
HE CALLED IT A "BIG PARTY."
A PARTY... LIKE IN THE MOVIES?
THE WILD, GAUDY KIND?!
PARTY TIIIIME!
NADA, WHAT SHOULD I WEAR?!
MAN, I KNEW I SHOULD'VE...
BOUGHT MORE CLOTHES!
SOMEONE'S EXCITED.
WHAT'S THE BIG DEAL?
I MEAN, IT'S JUST A PARTY.
......
YOU'RE ALREADY GETTING READY.

PREPARATION

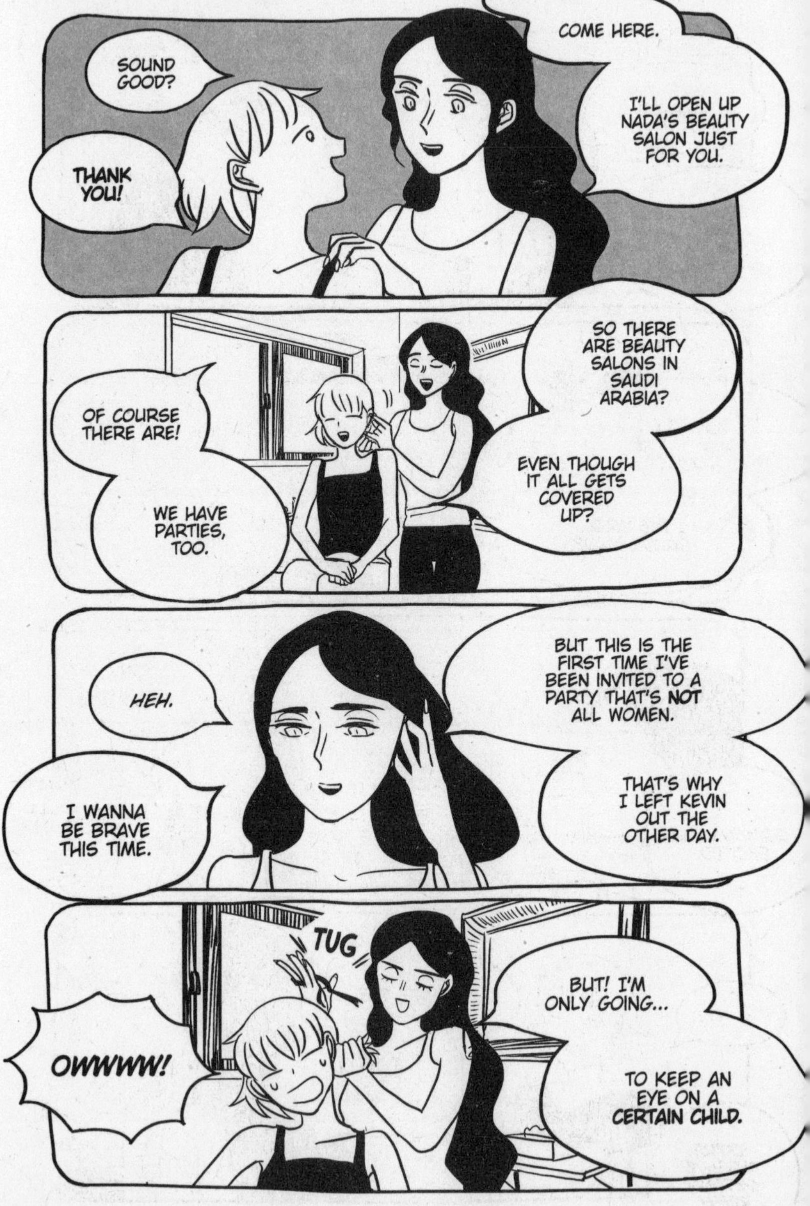
SATOKO...
COME HERE.
I'LL OPEN UP NADA'S BEAUTY SALON JUST FOR YOU.
SOUND GOOD?
THANK YOU!
SO THERE ARE BEAUTY SALONS IN SAUDI ARABIA?
EVEN THOUGH IT ALL GETS COVERED UP?
OF COURSE THERE ARE!
WE HAVE PARTIES, TOO.
BUT THIS IS THE FIRST TIME I'VE BEEN INVITED TO A PARTY THAT'S NOT ALL WOMEN.
THAT'S WHY I LEFT KEVIN OUT THE OTHER DAY.
HEH.
I WANNA BE BRAVE THIS TIME.
BUT! I'M ONLY GOING...
TO KEEP AN EYE ON A CERTAIN CHILD.
TUG
OWWWW!

FRATERNITIES AND SORORITIES

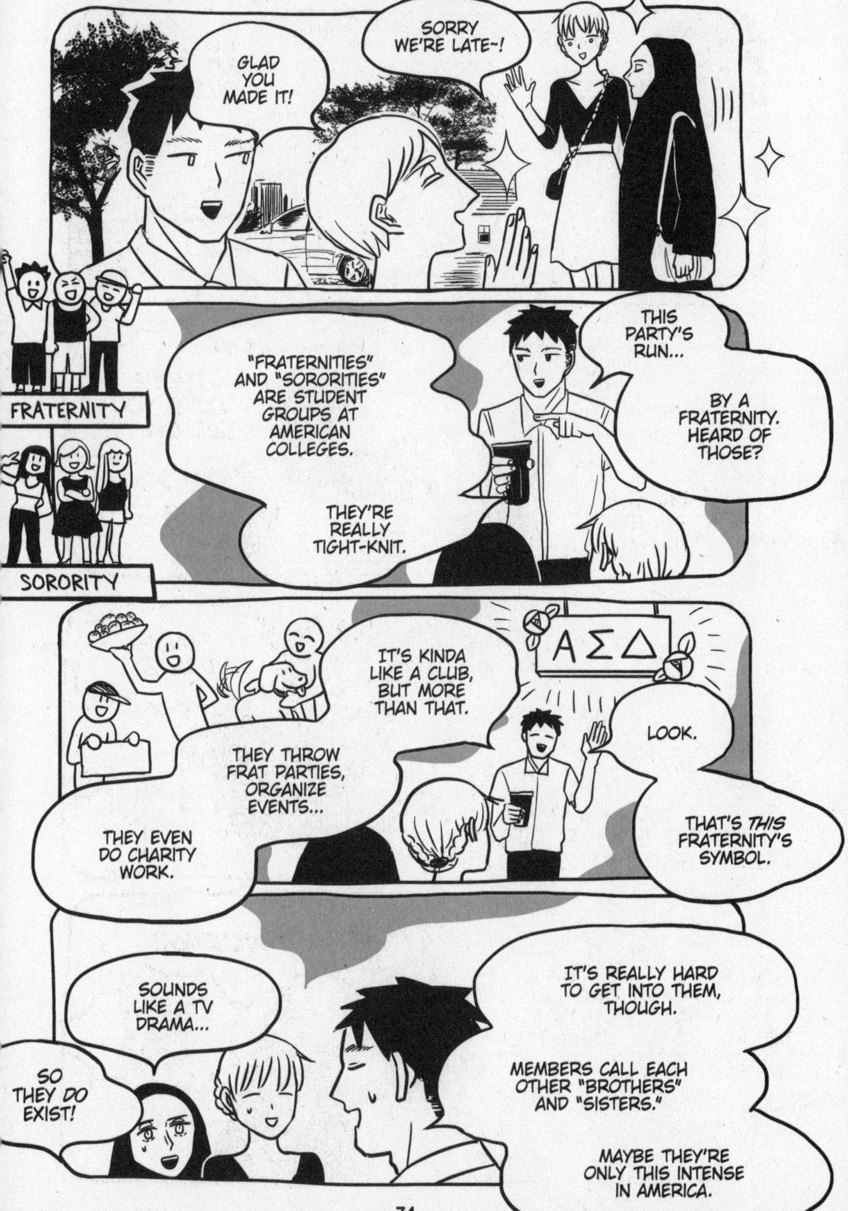
SORRY WE'RE LATE~!
GLAD YOU MADE IT!
THIS PARTY'S RUN...
BY A FRATERNITY. HEARD OF THOSE?
"FRATERNITIES" AND "SORORITIES" ARE STUDENT GROUPS AT AMERICAN COLLEGES.
THEY'RE REALLY TIGHT-KNIT.
FRATERNITY
SORORITY
LOOK.
THAT'S *THIS* FRATERNITY'S SYMBOL.
ΑΣΔ
IT'S KINDA LIKE A CLUB, BUT MORE THAN THAT.
THEY THROW FRAT PARTIES, ORGANIZE EVENTS...
THEY EVEN DO CHARITY WORK.
IT'S REALLY HARD TO GET INTO THEM, THOUGH.
MEMBERS CALL EACH OTHER "BROTHERS" AND "SISTERS."
MAYBE THEY'RE ONLY THIS INTENSE IN AMERICA.
SOUNDS LIKE A TV DRAMA...
SO THEY *DO* EXIST!

PARTY PEOPLE

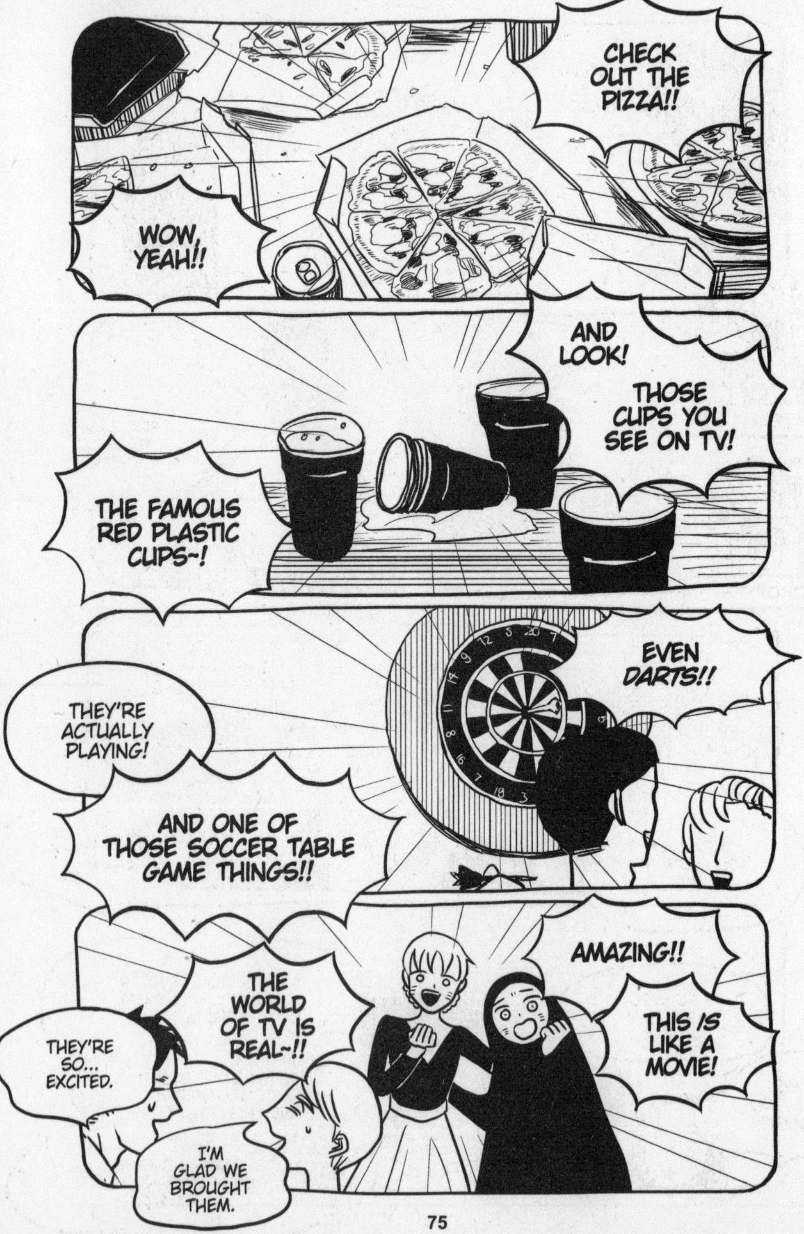

CHECK OUT THE PIZZA!!
WOW, YEAH!!
AND LOOK!
THOSE CUPS YOU SEE ON TV!
THE FAMOUS RED PLASTIC CUPS~!
EVEN DARTS!!
THEY'RE ACTUALLY PLAYING!
AND ONE OF THOSE SOCCER TABLE GAME THINGS!!
AMAZING!!
THIS *IS* LIKE A MOVIE!
THE WORLD OF TV IS REAL~!!
THEY'RE SO... EXCITED.
I'M GLAD WE BROUGHT THEM.

EXHAUSTED

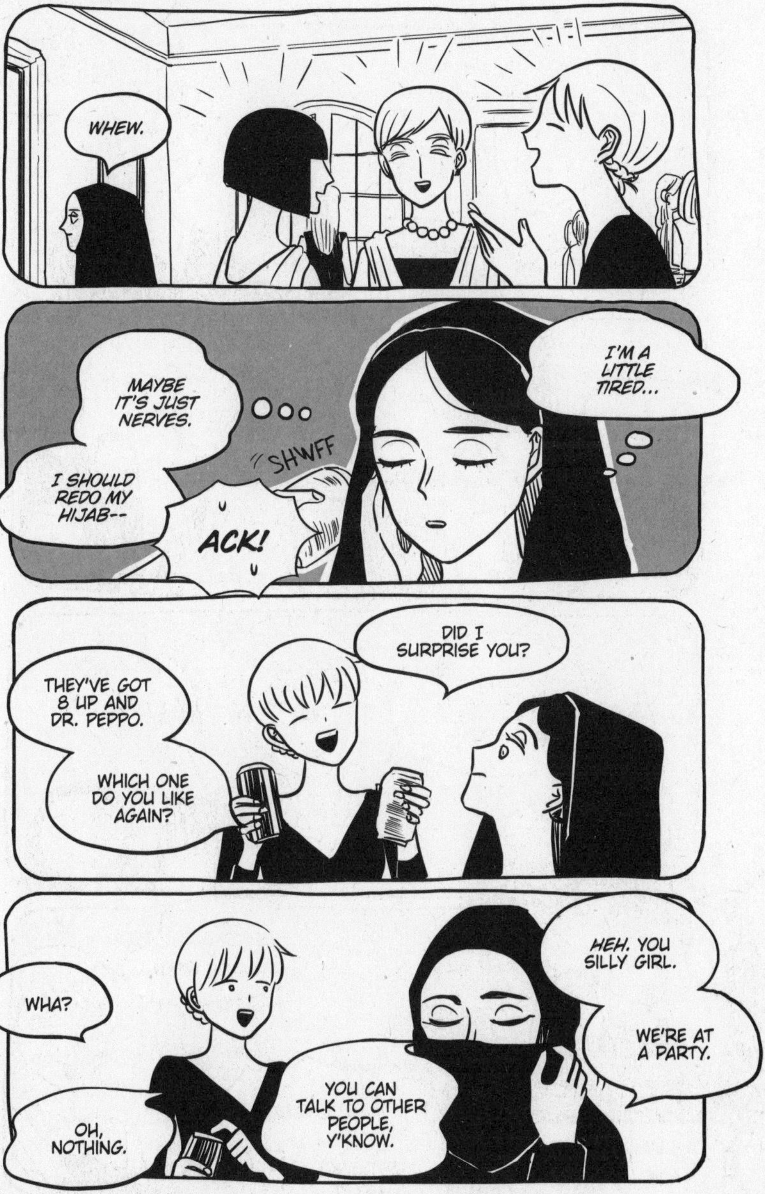
WHEW.
I'M A LITTLE TIRED...
MAYBE IT'S JUST NERVES.
SHWFF
I SHOULD REDO MY HIJAB--
ACK!
DID I SURPRISE YOU?
THEY'VE GOT 8 UP AND DR. PEPPO.
WHICH ONE DO YOU LIKE AGAIN?
HEH. YOU SILLY GIRL.
WHA?
WE'RE AT A PARTY.
YOU CAN TALK TO OTHER PEOPLE, Y'KNOW.
OH, NOTHING.

MARIJUANA

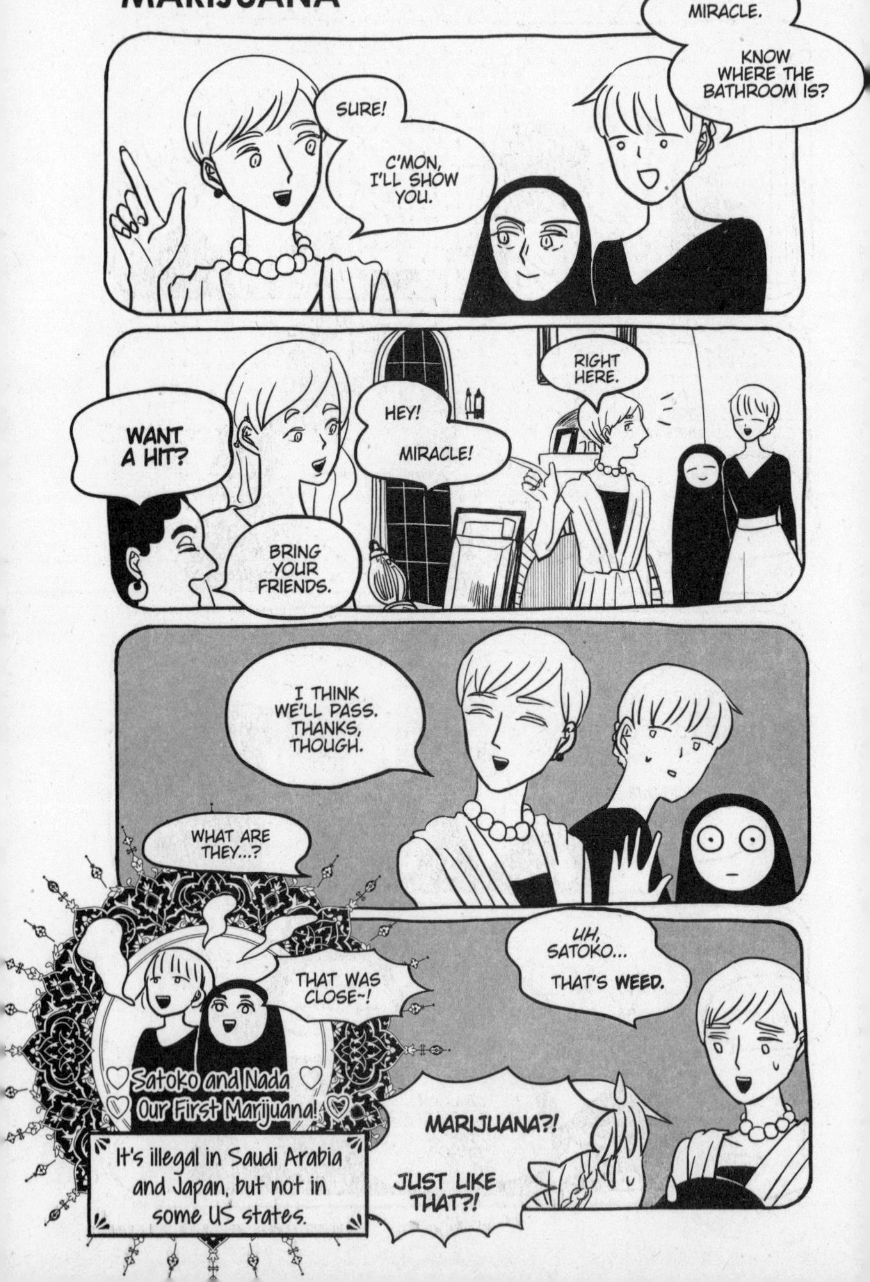
MIRACLE.
KNOW WHERE THE BATHROOM IS?
SURE!
C'MON, I'LL SHOW YOU.
RIGHT HERE.
HEY!
MIRACLE!
WANT A HIT?
BRING YOUR FRIENDS.
I THINK WE'LL PASS. THANKS, THOUGH.
WHAT ARE THEY...?
UH, SATOKO...
THAT'S WEED.
MARIJUANA?!
JUST LIKE THAT?!
THAT WAS CLOSE~!
Satoko and Nada Our First Marijuana!
It's illegal in Saudi Arabia and Japan, but not in some US states.

ANY AGE

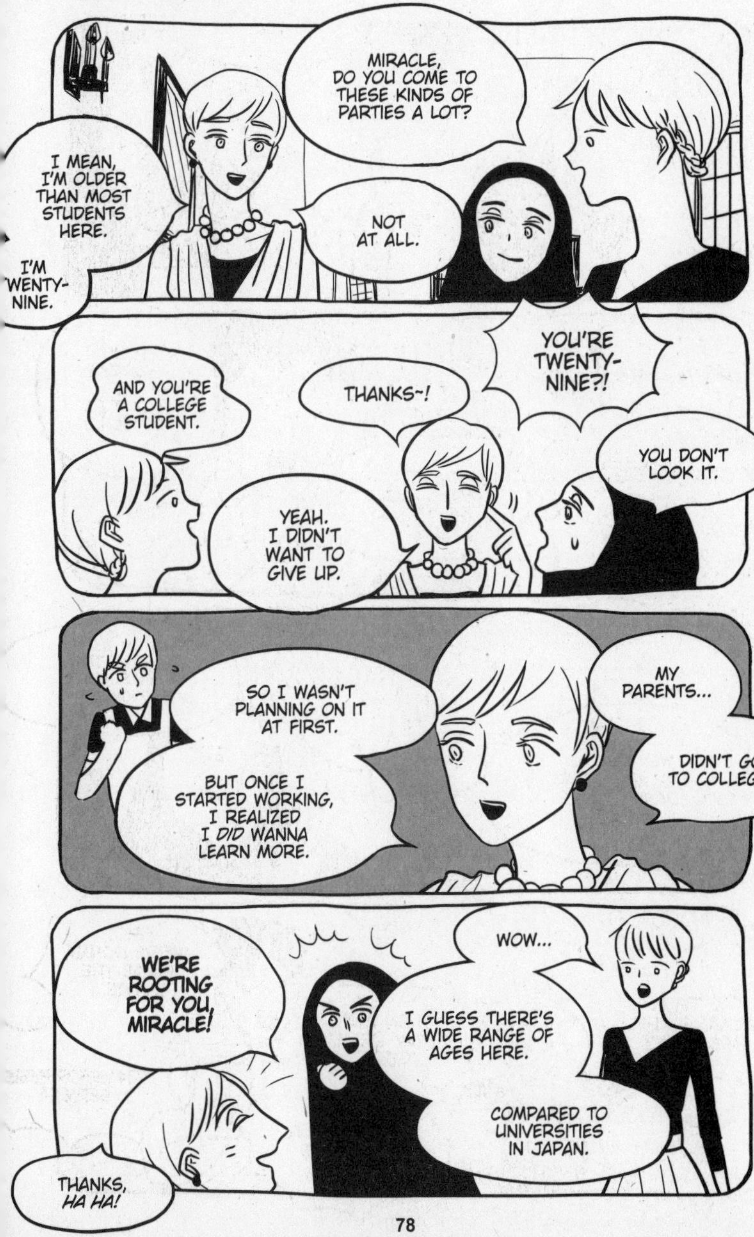
MIRACLE, DO YOU COME TO THESE KINDS OF PARTIES A LOT?
NOT AT ALL.
I MEAN, I'M OLDER THAN MOST STUDENTS HERE.
I'M WENTY-NINE.
YOU'RE TWENTY-NINE?!
THANKS~!
YOU DON'T LOOK IT.
AND YOU'RE A COLLEGE STUDENT.
YEAH. I DIDN'T WANT TO GIVE UP.
MY PARENTS...
DIDN'T GO TO COLLEGE.
SO I WASN'T PLANNING ON IT AT FIRST.
BUT ONCE I STARTED WORKING, I REALIZED I *DID* WANNA LEARN MORE.
WOW...
I GUESS THERE'S A WIDE RANGE OF AGES HERE.
COMPARED TO UNIVERSITIES IN JAPAN.
WE'RE ROOTING FOR YOU, MIRACLE!
THANKS, *HA HA!*

AFTERPARTY

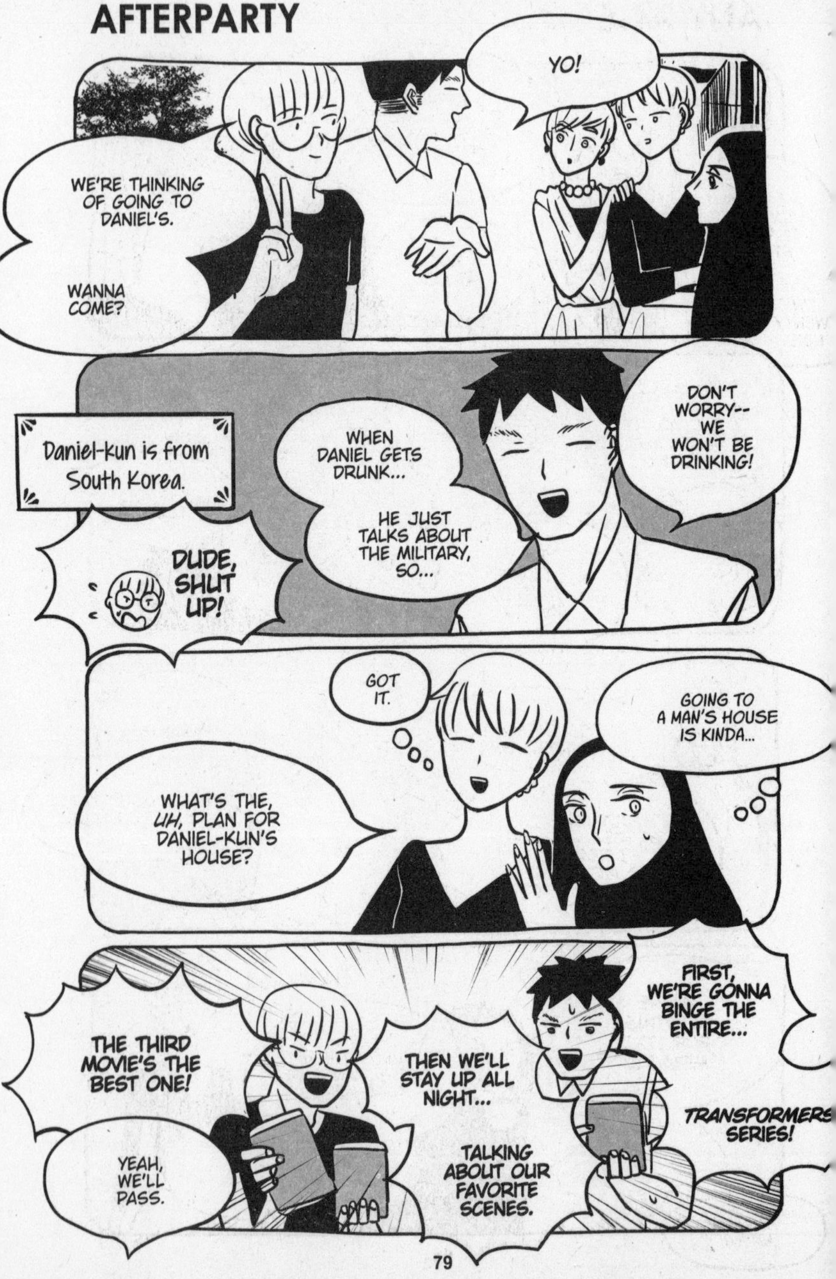

YO!
WE'RE THINKING OF GOING TO DANIEL'S.
WANNA COME?
DON'T WORRY-- WE WON'T BE DRINKING!
WHEN DANIEL GETS DRUNK...
HE JUST TALKS ABOUT THE MILITARY, SO...
Daniel-kun is from South Korea.
DUDE, SHUT UP!
GOING TO A MAN'S HOUSE IS KINDA...
GOT IT.
WHAT'S THE, UH, PLAN FOR DANIEL-KUN'S HOUSE?
FIRST, WE'RE GONNA BINGE THE ENTIRE...
TRANSFORMERS SERIES!
THEN WE'LL STAY UP ALL NIGHT...
TALKING ABOUT OUR FAVORITE SCENES.
THE THIRD MOVIE'S THE BEST ONE!
YEAH, WE'LL PASS.

SAMAR AND SAHAR

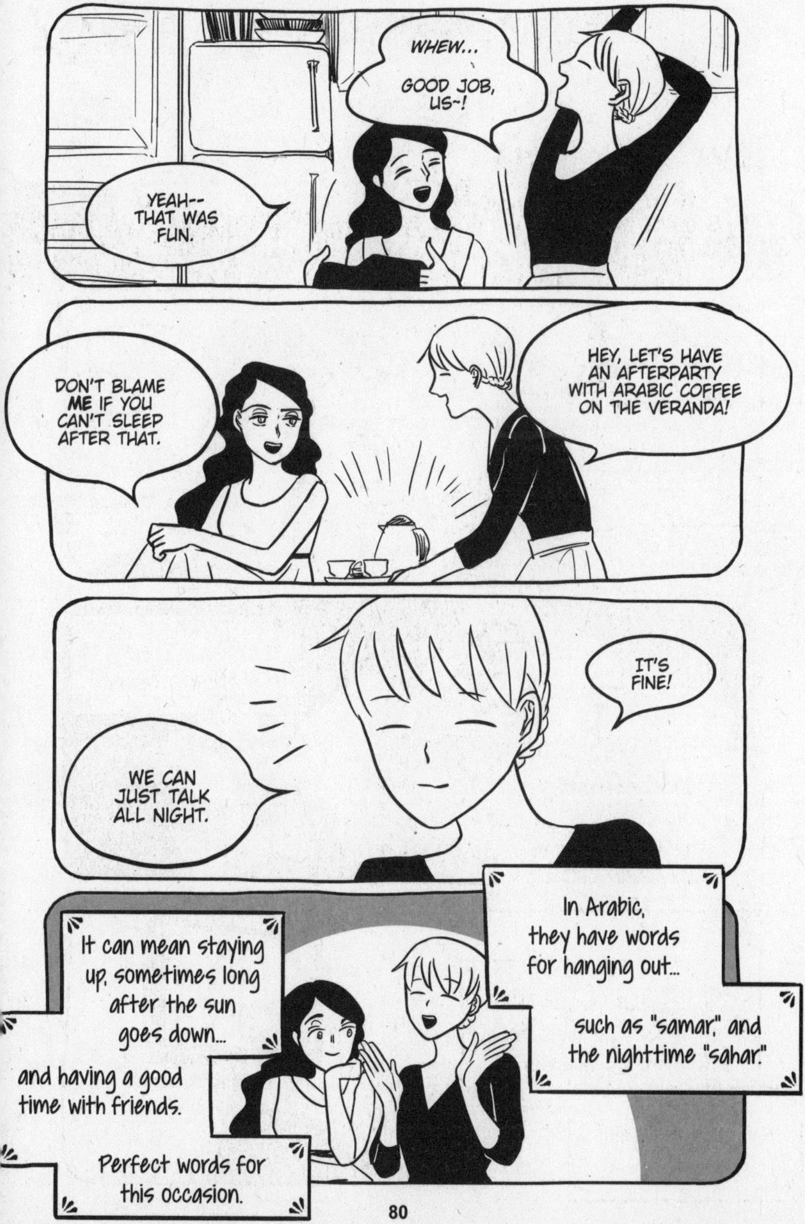
WHEW... GOOD JOB, US~!
YEAH-- THAT WAS FUN.
HEY, LET'S HAVE AN AFTERPARTY WITH ARABIC COFFEE ON THE VERANDA!
DON'T BLAME ME IF YOU CAN'T SLEEP AFTER THAT.
IT'S FINE!
WE CAN JUST TALK ALL NIGHT.
In Arabic, they have words for hanging out...
such as "samar," and the nighttime "sahar."
It can mean staying up, sometimes long after the sun goes down...
and having a good time with friends.
Perfect words for this occasion.

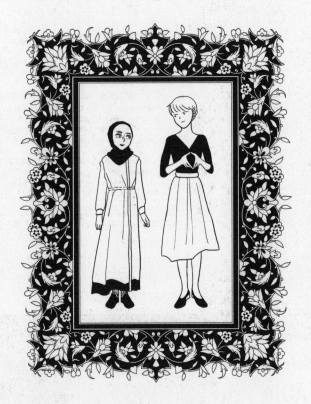

SATOKO AND NADA

Presented by Yupechika

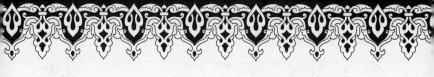

SATOKO AND NADA

Presented by Yupechika

GOTTA HURRY!

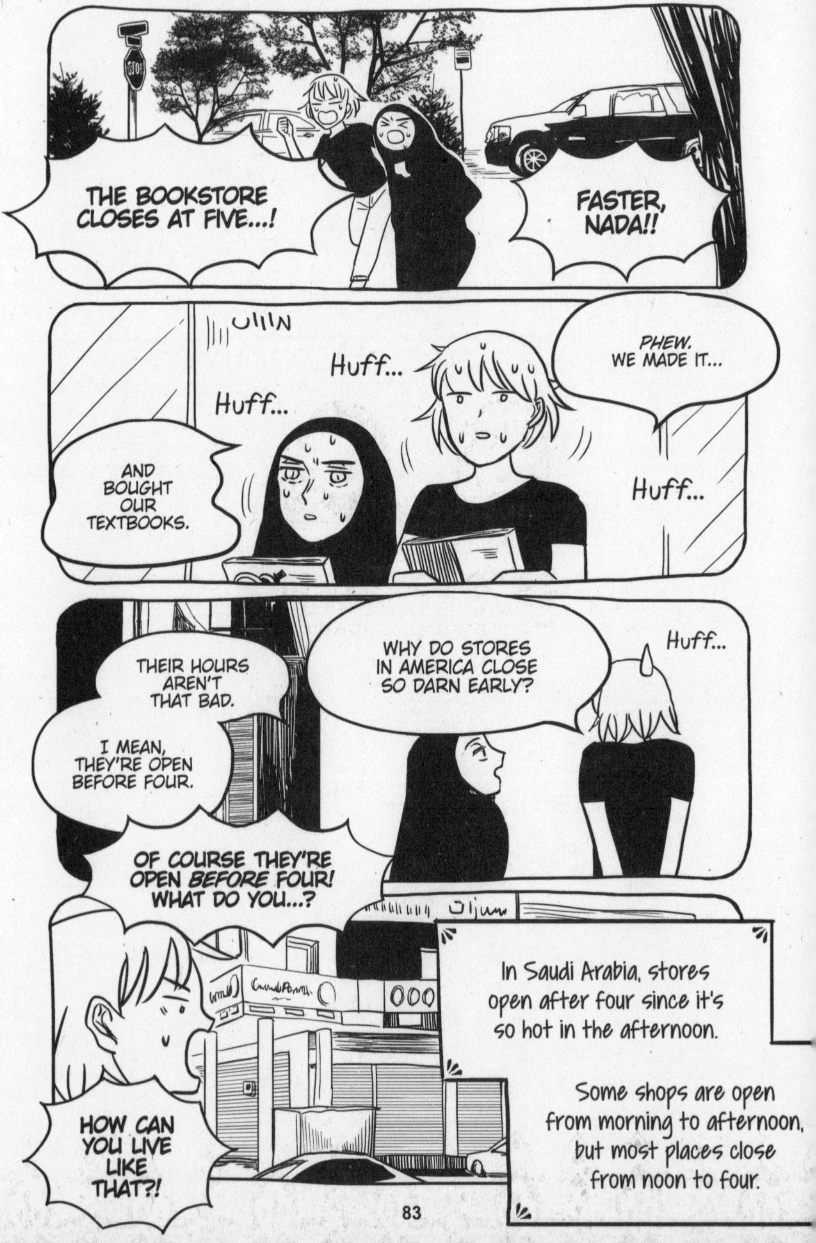
FASTER, NADA!!
THE BOOKSTORE CLOSES AT FIVE...!
PHEW. WE MADE IT...
Huff...
Huff...
Huff...
AND BOUGHT OUR TEXTBOOKS.
Huff...
WHY DO STORES IN AMERICA CLOSE SO DARN EARLY?
THEIR HOURS AREN'T THAT BAD.
I MEAN, THEY'RE OPEN BEFORE FOUR.
OF COURSE THEY'RE OPEN *BEFORE* FOUR! WHAT DO YOU...?
In Saudi Arabia, stores open after four since it's so hot in the afternoon.
Some shops are open from morning to afternoon, but most places close from noon to four.
HOW CAN YOU LIVE LIKE THAT?!

PRAYER TIME

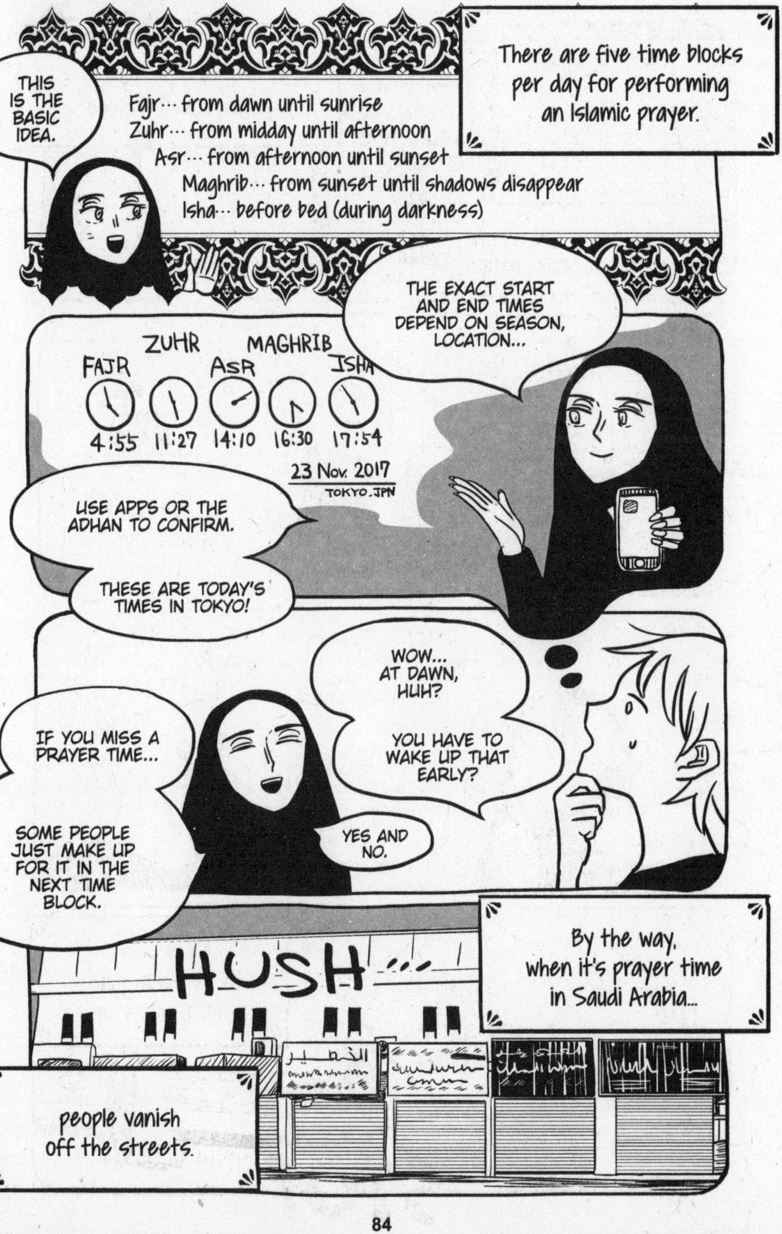
There are five time blocks per day for performing an Islamic prayer.
THIS IS THE BASIC IDEA.
Fajr… from dawn until sunrise
Zuhr… from midday until afternoon
Asr… from afternoon until sunset
Maghrib… from sunset until shadows disappear
Isha… before bed (during darkness)
THE EXACT START AND END TIMES DEPEND ON SEASON, LOCATION…
ZUHR
MAGHRIB
FAJR
ASR
ISHA
4:55
11:27
14:10
16:30
17:54
23 Nov. 2017
TOKYO.JPN
USE APPS OR THE ADHAN TO CONFIRM.
THESE ARE TODAY'S TIMES IN TOKYO!
WOW… AT DAWN, HUH?
YOU HAVE TO WAKE UP THAT EARLY?
YES AND NO.
IF YOU MISS A PRAYER TIME…
SOME PEOPLE JUST MAKE UP FOR IT IN THE NEXT TIME BLOCK.
By the way, when it's prayer time in Saudi Arabia…
HUSH…
people vanish off the streets.

STORES STOP FOR PRAYER?!

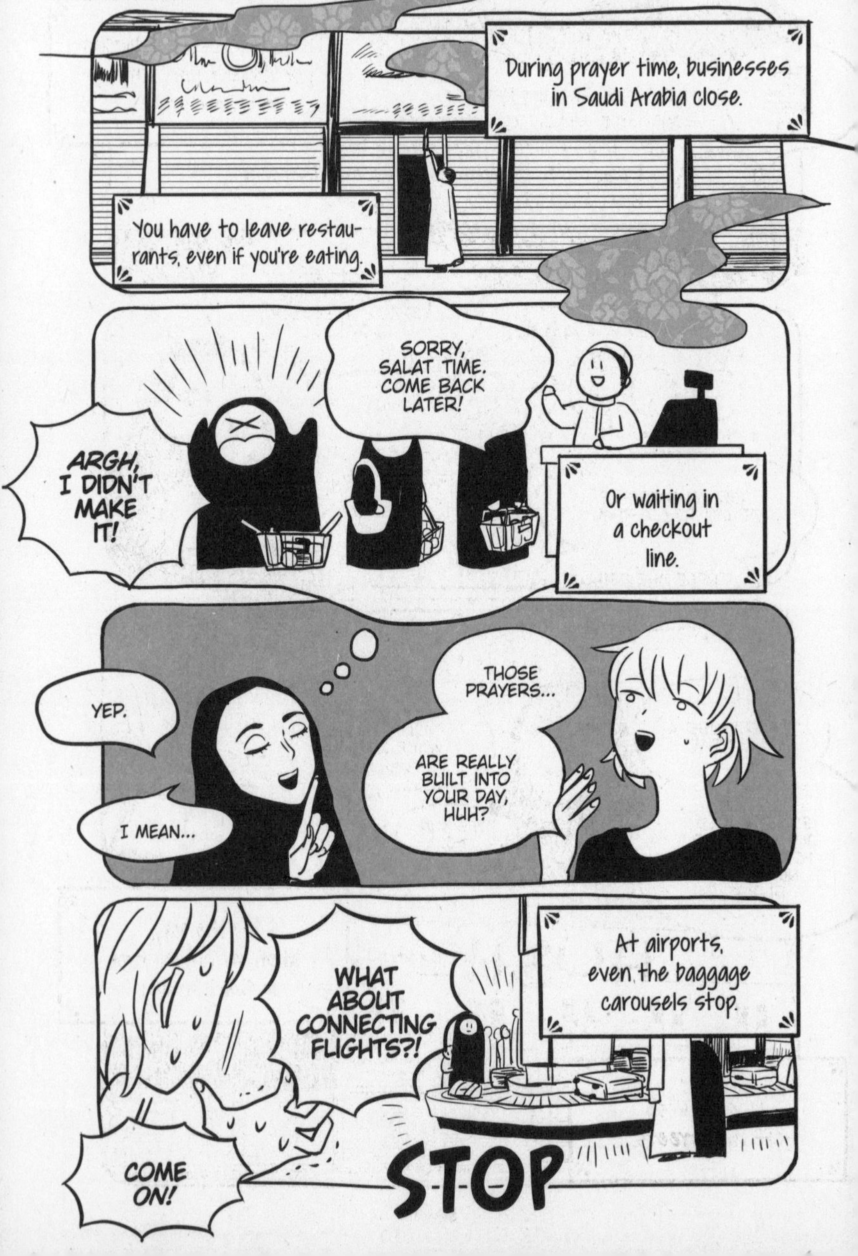
During prayer time, businesses in Saudi Arabia close.
You have to leave restaurants, even if you're eating.
SORRY, SALAT TIME. COME BACK LATER!
Or waiting in a checkout line.
ARGH, I DIDN'T MAKE IT!
THOSE PRAYERS...
ARE REALLY BUILT INTO YOUR DAY, HUH?
YEP.
I MEAN...
At airports, even the baggage carousels stop.
WHAT ABOUT CONNECTING FLIGHTS?!
STOP
COME ON!

DAY OFF

AND THEY DO! AT FIRST, I WAS SURPRISED TO SEE...

IF SHOPS CLOSE FOR PRAYER...

AMERICAN STORES **OPEN** IN THE AFTERNOON.

THEN THEY HAVE TO OPEN AND CLOSE SEVERAL TIMES A DAY.

AFTER PRAYER TIME...

LIKE AN IPHONE RELEASE?!

PEOPLE LINE UP OUTSIDE STORES TO WAIT FOR THEM TO OPEN.

MON	TUE	WED	THU

And in Saudi Arabia, the weekend is Friday and Saturday.

Friday is considered a holy day, so you have to participate in worship.

FRI OFF

SAT OFF

SUN WEEK-DAY.

Since weekends are on Friday and Saturday in Saudi Arabia...

but Saturday and Sunday in Japan...

it's common for local workers in a Japanese office to *really* only get Saturday off.

Hang in there, employees!

DORAYAKI

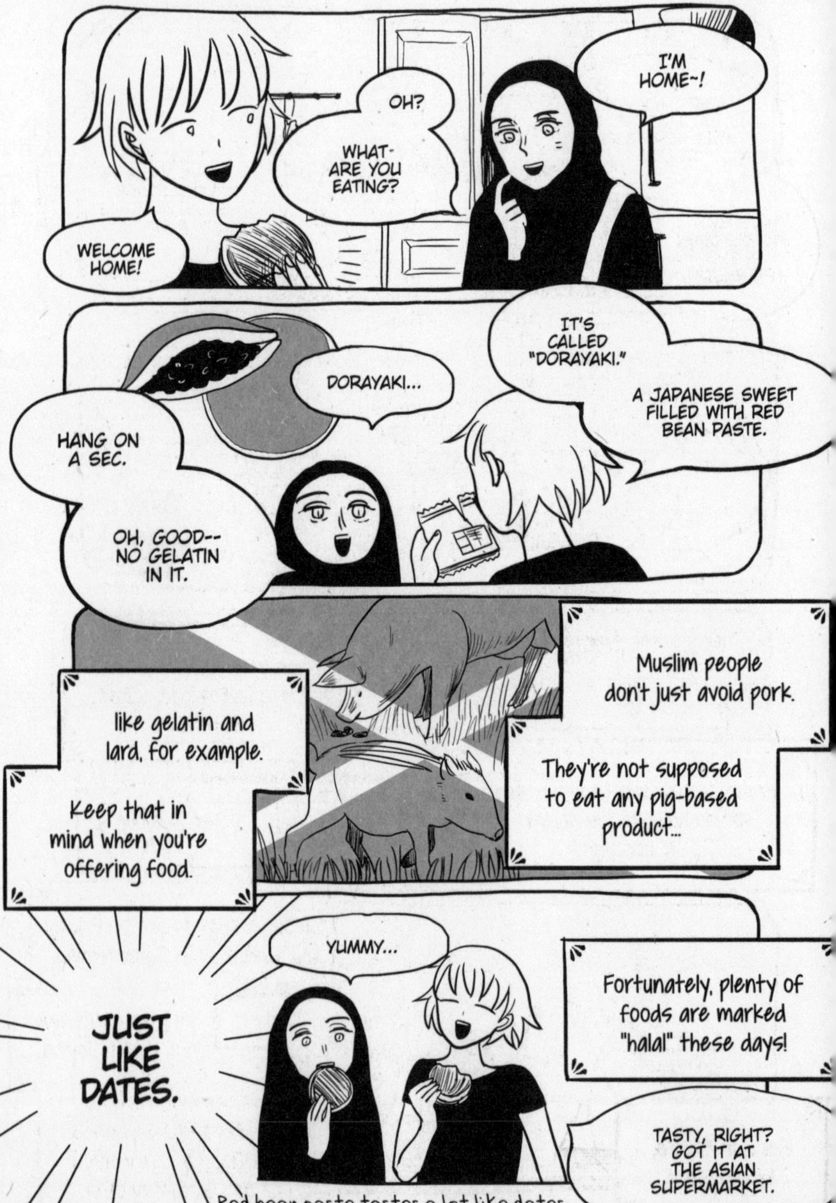
I'M HOME~!
OH?
WHAT- ARE YOU EATING?
WELCOME HOME!
IT'S CALLED "DORAYAKI."
A JAPANESE SWEET FILLED WITH RED BEAN PASTE.
DORAYAKI...
HANG ON A SEC.
OH, GOOD-- NO GELATIN IN IT.
Muslim people don't just avoid pork.
They're not supposed to eat any pig-based product...
like gelatin and lard, for example.
Keep that in mind when you're offering food.
Fortunately, plenty of foods are marked "halal" these days!
YUMMY...
TASTY, RIGHT? GOT IT AT THE ASIAN SUPERMARKET.
JUST LIKE DATES.
Red bean paste tastes a lot like dates.

THE FALL

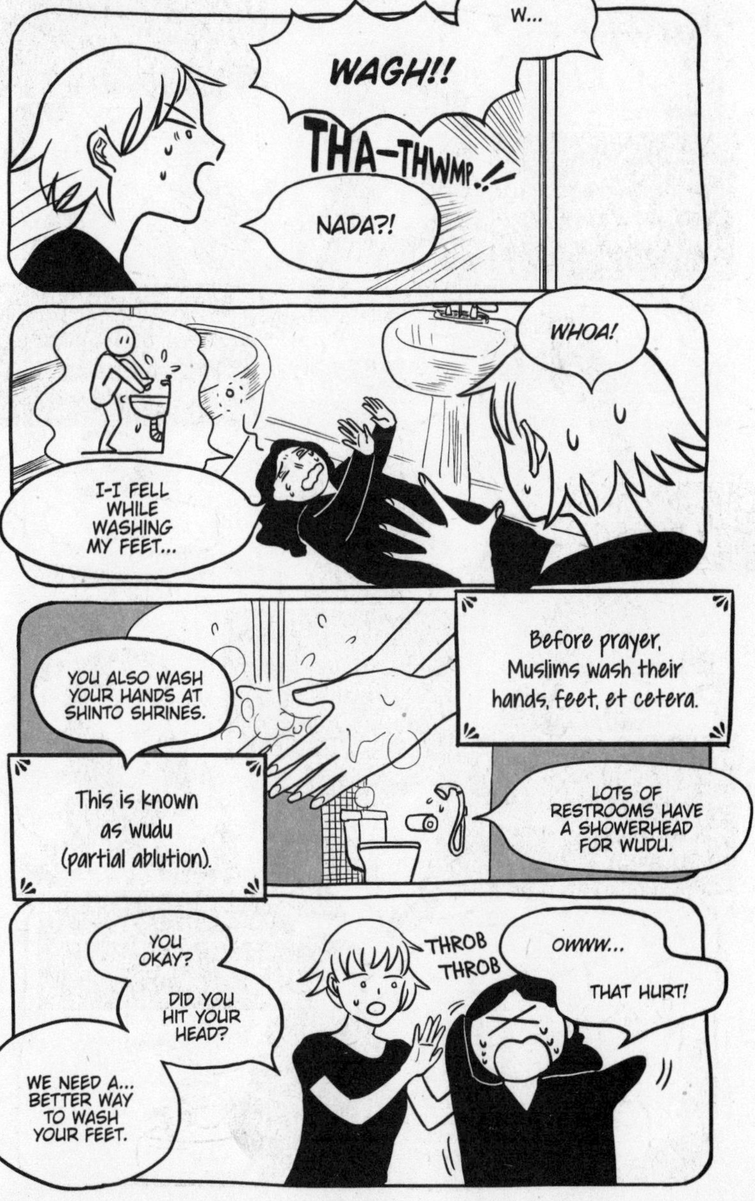
W...
WAGH!!
THA-THWMP.!
NADA?!
WHOA!
I-I FELL WHILE WASHING MY FEET...
Before prayer, Muslims wash their hands, feet, et cetera.
YOU ALSO WASH YOUR HANDS AT SHINTO SHRINES.
LOTS OF RESTROOMS HAVE A SHOWERHEAD FOR WUDU.
This is known as wudu (partial ablution).
OWWW...
THAT HURT!
THROB THROB
YOU OKAY?
DID YOU HIT YOUR HEAD?
WE NEED A... BETTER WAY TO WASH YOUR FEET.

WUDU

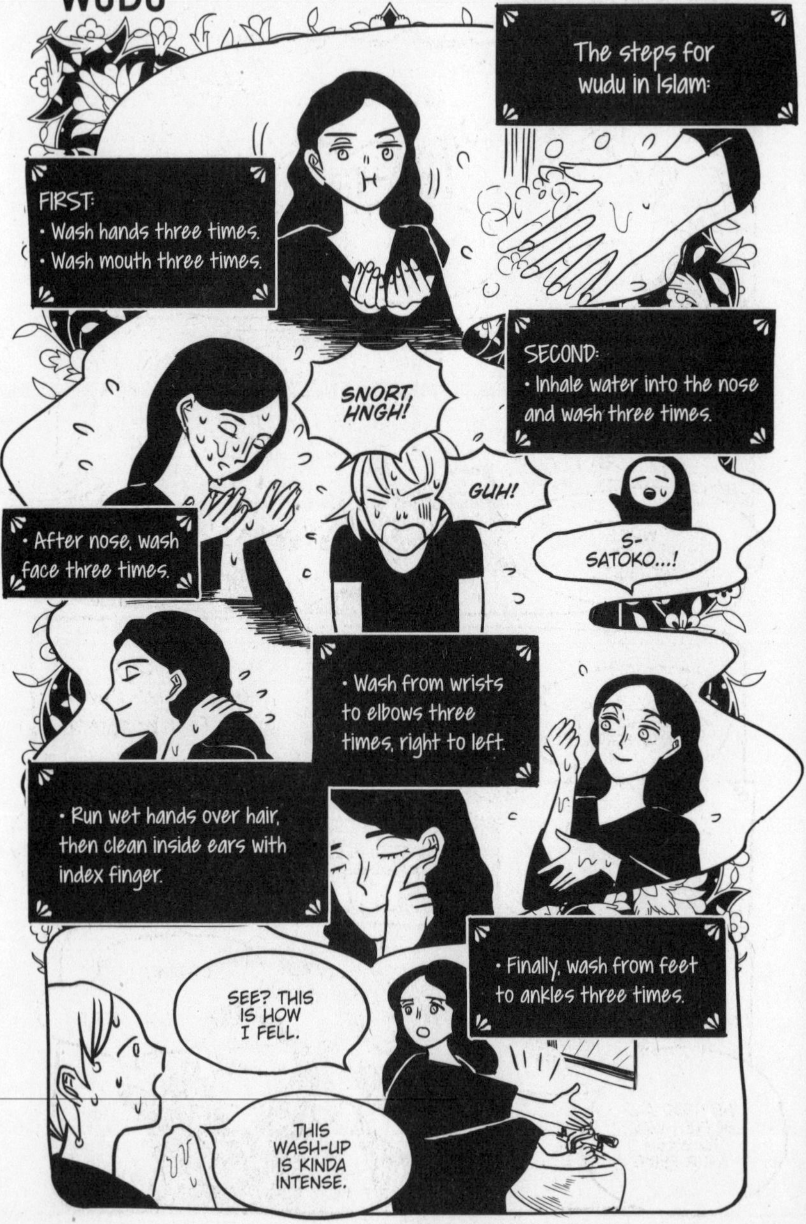

The steps for wudu in Islam:
FIRST: • Wash hands three times. • Wash mouth three times.
SECOND: • Inhale water into the nose and wash three times.
SNORT, HNGH!
S-SATOKO...!
GUH!
• After nose, wash face three times.
• Wash from wrists to elbows three times, right to left.
• Run wet hands over hair, then clean inside ears with index finger.
• Finally, wash from feet to ankles three times.
SEE? THIS IS HOW I FELL.
THIS WASH-UP IS KINDA INTENSE.

WASH BOWL

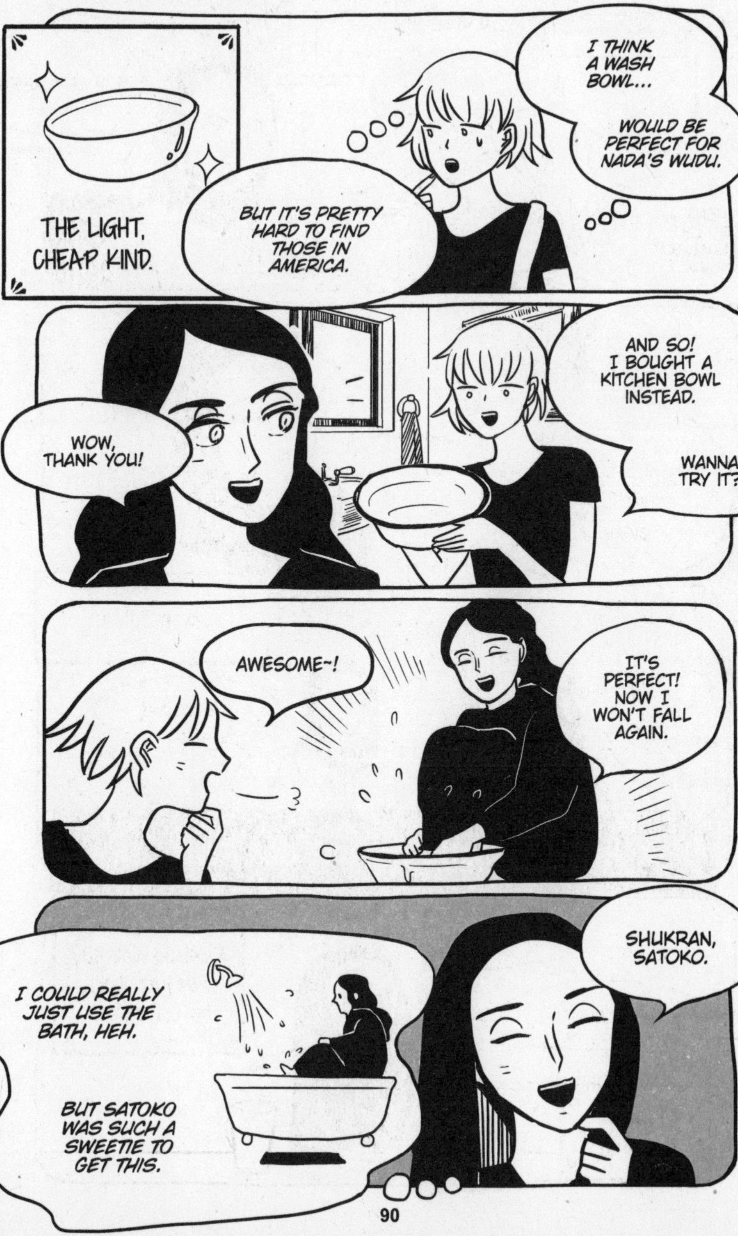
I THINK A WASH BOWL...
WOULD BE PERFECT FOR NADA'S WUDU.
BUT IT'S PRETTY HARD TO FIND THOSE IN AMERICA.
THE LIGHT, CHEAP KIND.
AND SO! I BOUGHT A KITCHEN BOWL INSTEAD.
WANNA TRY IT?
WOW, THANK YOU!
IT'S PERFECT! NOW I WON'T FALL AGAIN.
AWESOME~!
SHUKRAN, SATOKO.
I COULD REALLY JUST USE THE BATH, HEH.
BUT SATOKO WAS SUCH A SWEETIE TO GET THIS.

BISMILLAH

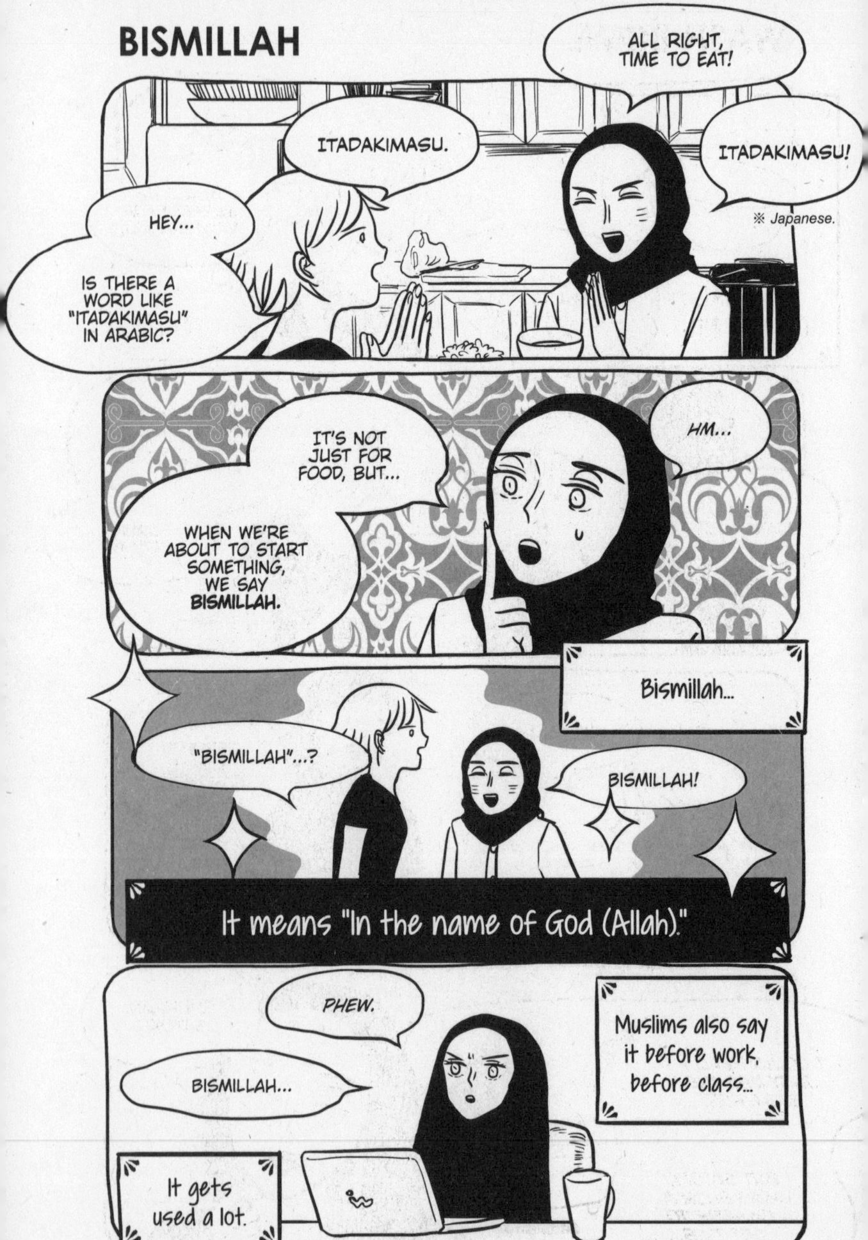
ALL RIGHT, TIME TO EAT!
ITADAKIMASU!
※ Japanese.
ITADAKIMASU.
HEY...
IS THERE A WORD LIKE "ITADAKIMASU" IN ARABIC?
HM...
IT'S NOT JUST FOR FOOD, BUT...
WHEN WE'RE ABOUT TO START SOMETHING, WE SAY BISMILLAH.
Bismillah...
BISMILLAH!
"BISMILLAH"...?
It means "In the name of God (Allah)."
Muslims also say it before work, before class...
PHEW.
BISMILLAH...
It gets used a lot.

DISTINCTION

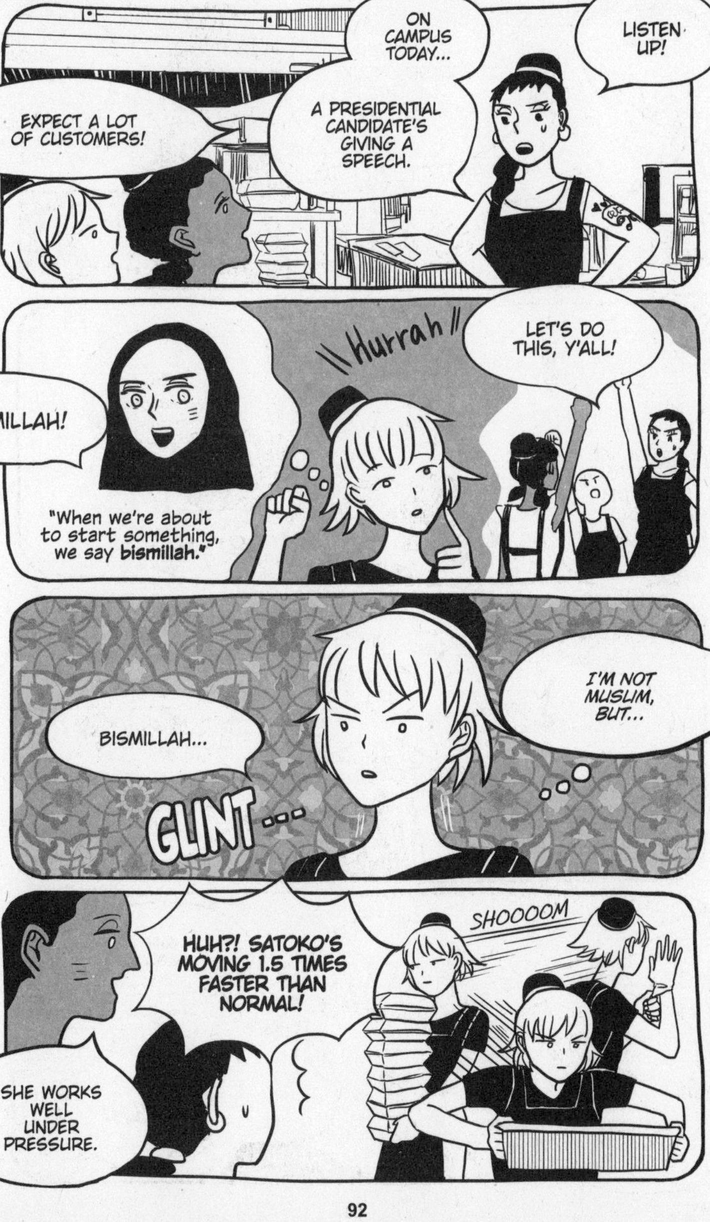

LISTEN UP!
ON CAMPUS TODAY...
A PRESIDENTIAL CANDIDATE'S GIVING A SPEECH.
EXPECT A LOT OF CUSTOMERS!
LET'S DO THIS, Y'ALL!
Hurrah
BISMILLAH!
"When we're about to start something, we say **bismillah**."
I'M NOT MUSLIM, BUT...
BISMILLAH...
GLINT...
SHOOOOM
HUH?! SATOKO'S MOVING 1.5 TIMES FASTER THAN NORMAL!
SHE WORKS WELL UNDER PRESSURE.

LEVEL OF INTEREST

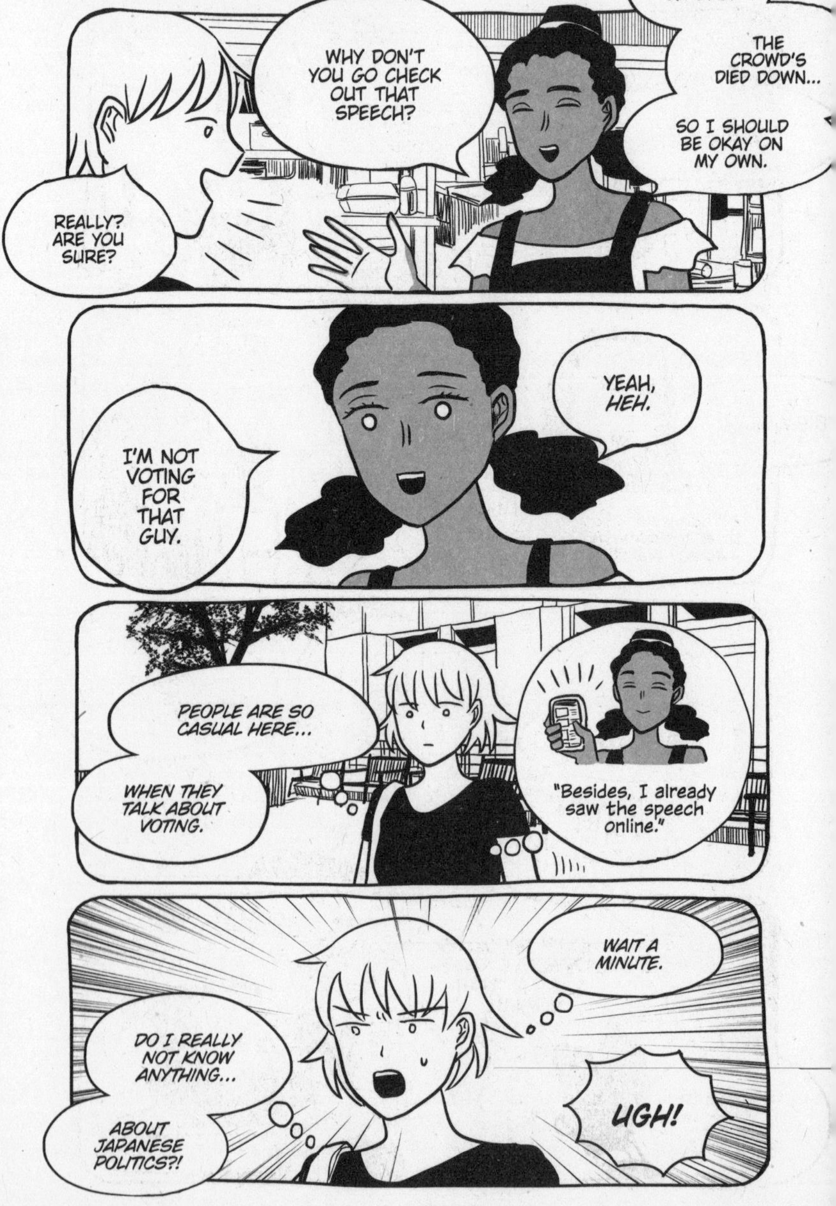
HEY, SATOKO!
THE CROWD'S DIED DOWN...
SO I SHOULD BE OKAY ON MY OWN.
WHY DON'T YOU GO CHECK OUT THAT SPEECH?
REALLY? ARE YOU SURE?
YEAH, HEH.
I'M NOT VOTING FOR THAT GUY.
"Besides, I already saw the speech online."
PEOPLE ARE SO CASUAL HERE...
WHEN THEY TALK ABOUT VOTING.
WAIT A MINUTE.
UGH!
DO I REALLY NOT KNOW ANYTHING...
ABOUT JAPANESE POLITICS?!

THE PRESIDENTIAL CANDIDATE'S SPEECH

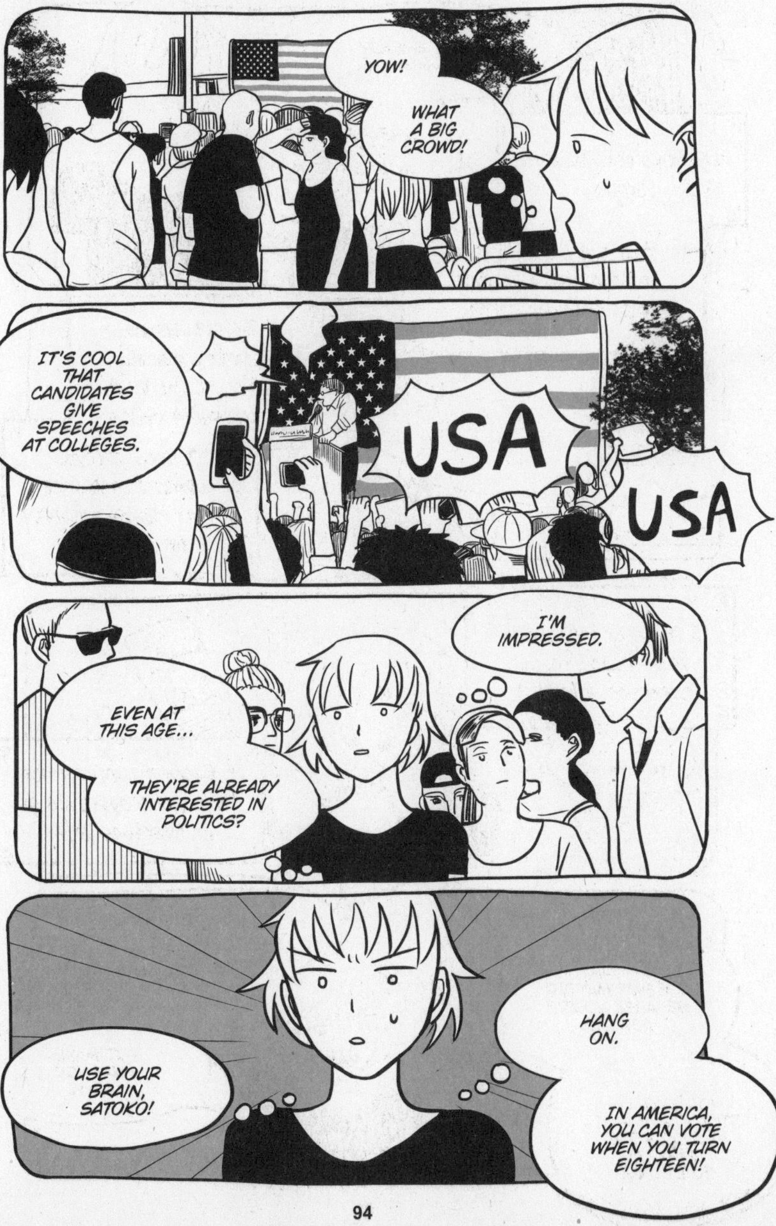
YOW!
WHAT A BIG CROWD!
USA
USA
IT'S COOL THAT CANDIDATES GIVE SPEECHES AT COLLEGES.
I'M IMPRESSED.
EVEN AT THIS AGE...
THEY'RE ALREADY INTERESTED IN POLITICS?
HANG ON.
IN AMERICA, YOU CAN VOTE WHEN YOU TURN EIGHTEEN!
USE YOUR BRAIN, SATOKO!

OVERSEAS VOTERS

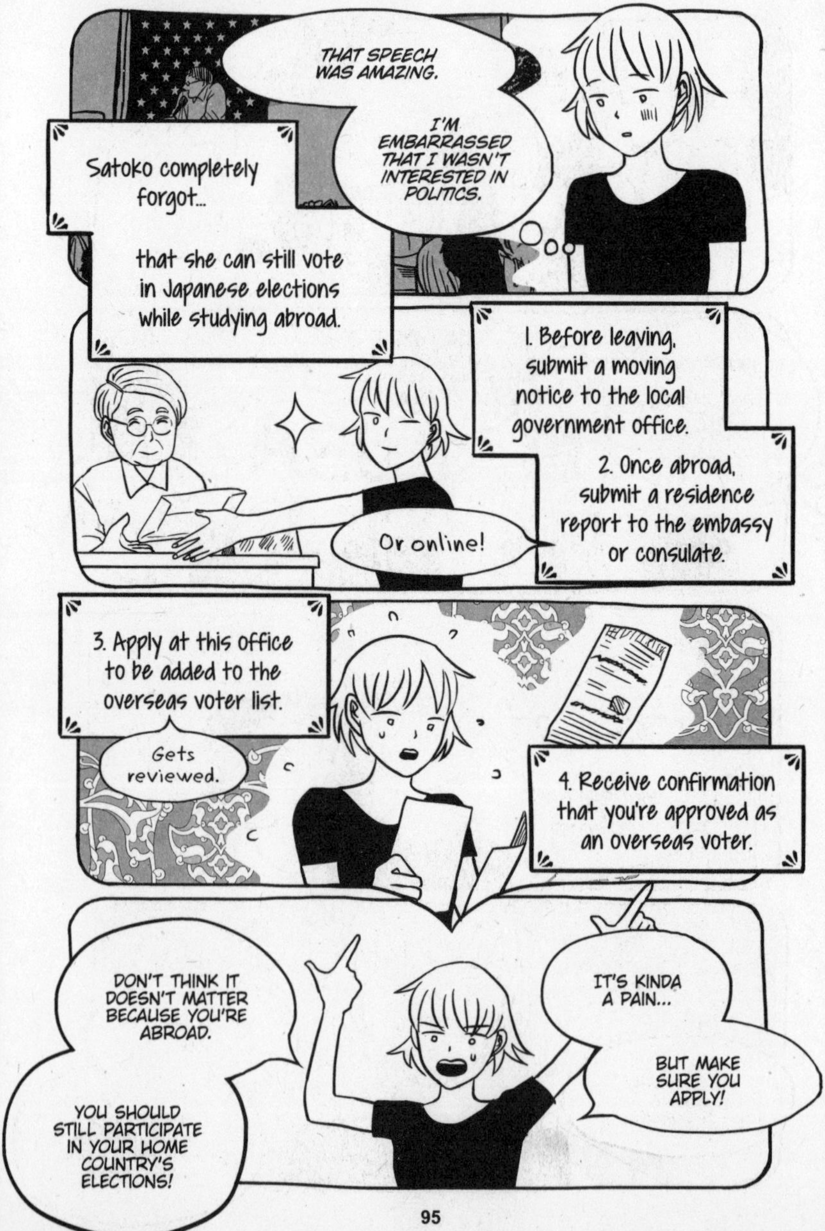

THAT SPEECH WAS AMAZING.
I'M EMBARRASSED THAT I WASN'T INTERESTED IN POLITICS.
Satoko completely forgot...
that she can still vote in Japanese elections while studying abroad.
1. Before leaving, submit a moving notice to the local government office.
2. Once abroad, submit a residence report to the embassy or consulate.
Or online!
3. Apply at this office to be added to the overseas voter list.
Gets reviewed.
4. Receive confirmation that you're approved as an overseas voter.
IT'S KINDA A PAIN...
BUT MAKE SURE YOU APPLY!
DON'T THINK IT DOESN'T MATTER BECAUSE YOU'RE ABROAD.
YOU SHOULD STILL PARTICIPATE IN YOUR HOME COUNTRY'S ELECTIONS!

WOMEN'S SUFFRAGE IN SAUDI ARABIA

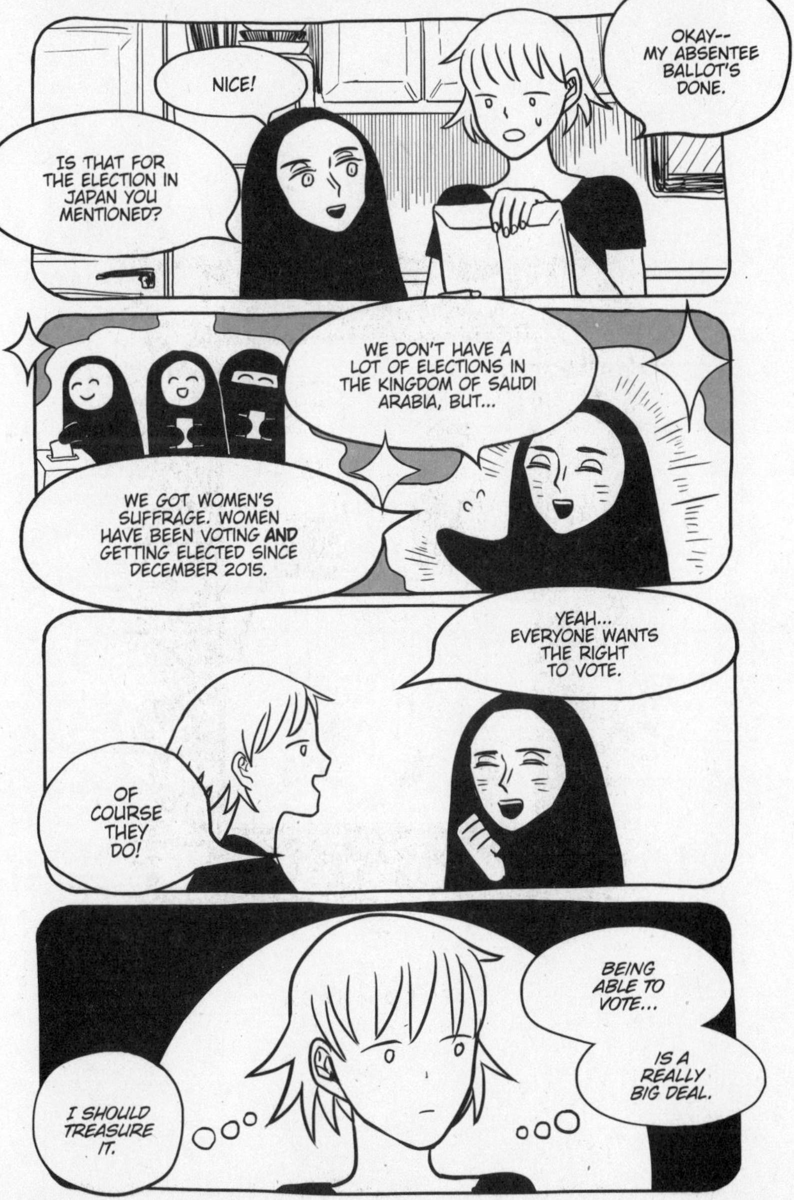
OKAY-- MY ABSENTEE BALLOT'S DONE.
NICE!
IS THAT FOR THE ELECTION IN JAPAN YOU MENTIONED?
WE DON'T HAVE A LOT OF ELECTIONS IN THE KINGDOM OF SAUDI ARABIA, BUT...
WE GOT WOMEN'S SUFFRAGE. WOMEN HAVE BEEN VOTING **AND** GETTING ELECTED SINCE DECEMBER 2015.
YEAH... EVERYONE WANTS THE RIGHT TO VOTE.
OF COURSE THEY DO!
BEING ABLE TO VOTE...
IS A REALLY BIG DEAL.
I SHOULD TREASURE IT.

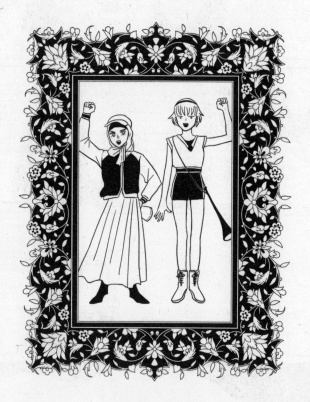

SATOKO AND NADA

Presented by Yupechika

FLAG

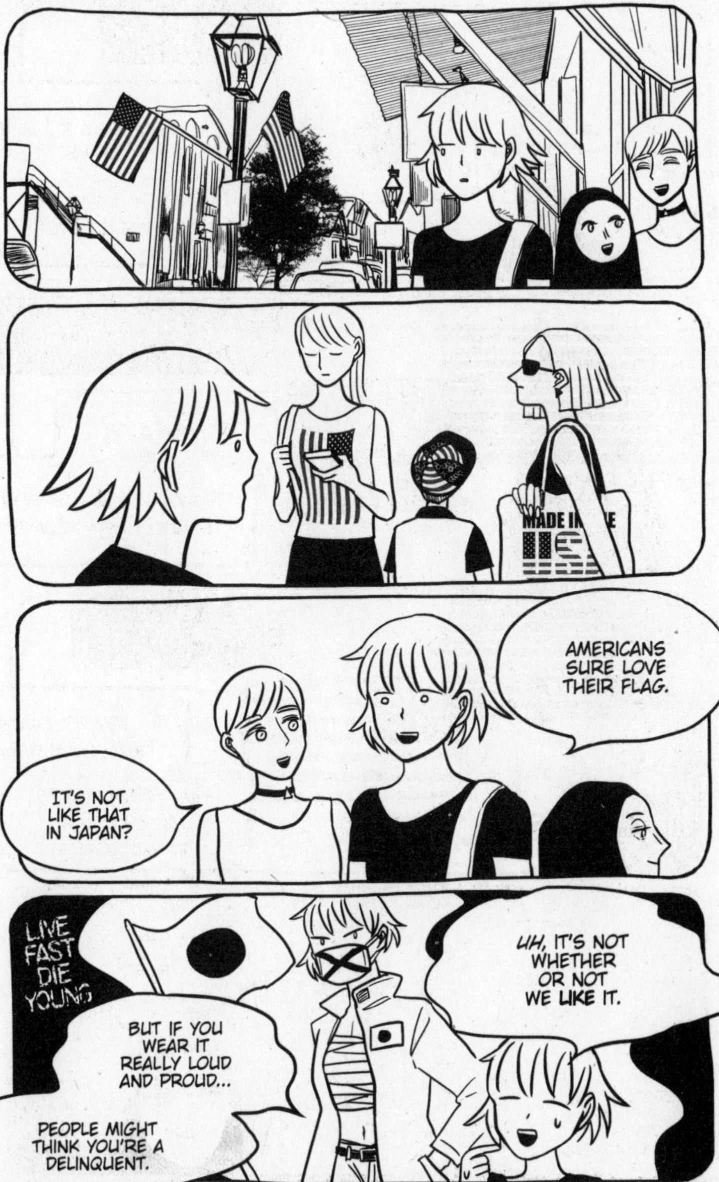
MADE IN
AMERICANS SURE LOVE THEIR FLAG.
IT'S NOT LIKE THAT IN JAPAN?
UH, IT'S NOT WHETHER OR NOT WE LIKE IT.
LIVE FAST DIE YOUNG
BUT IF YOU WEAR IT REALLY LOUD AND PROUD...
PEOPLE MIGHT THINK YOU'RE A DELINQUENT.

FLAGS AND THEIR MEANINGS

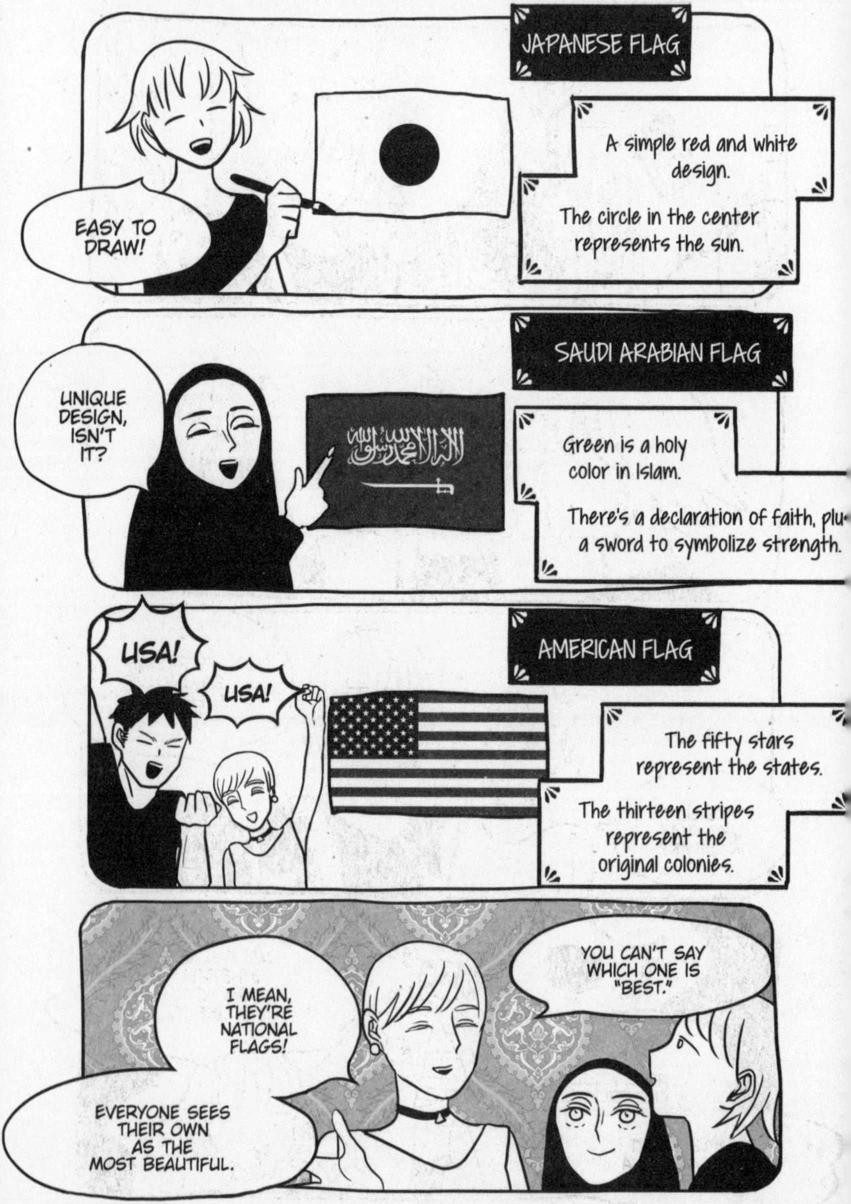

JAPANESE FLAG
A simple red and white design.
The circle in the center represents the sun.
EASY TO DRAW!
SAUDI ARABIAN FLAG
Green is a holy color in Islam.
There's a declaration of faith, plu
a sword to symbolize strength.
UNIQUE DESIGN, ISN'T IT?
AMERICAN FLAG
The fifty stars represent the states.
The thirteen stripes represent the original colonies.
USA!
USA!
YOU CAN'T SAY WHICH ONE IS "BEST."
I MEAN, THEY'RE NATIONAL FLAGS!
EVERYONE SEES THEIR OWN AS THE MOST BEAUTIFUL.

FLAG ETIQUETTE

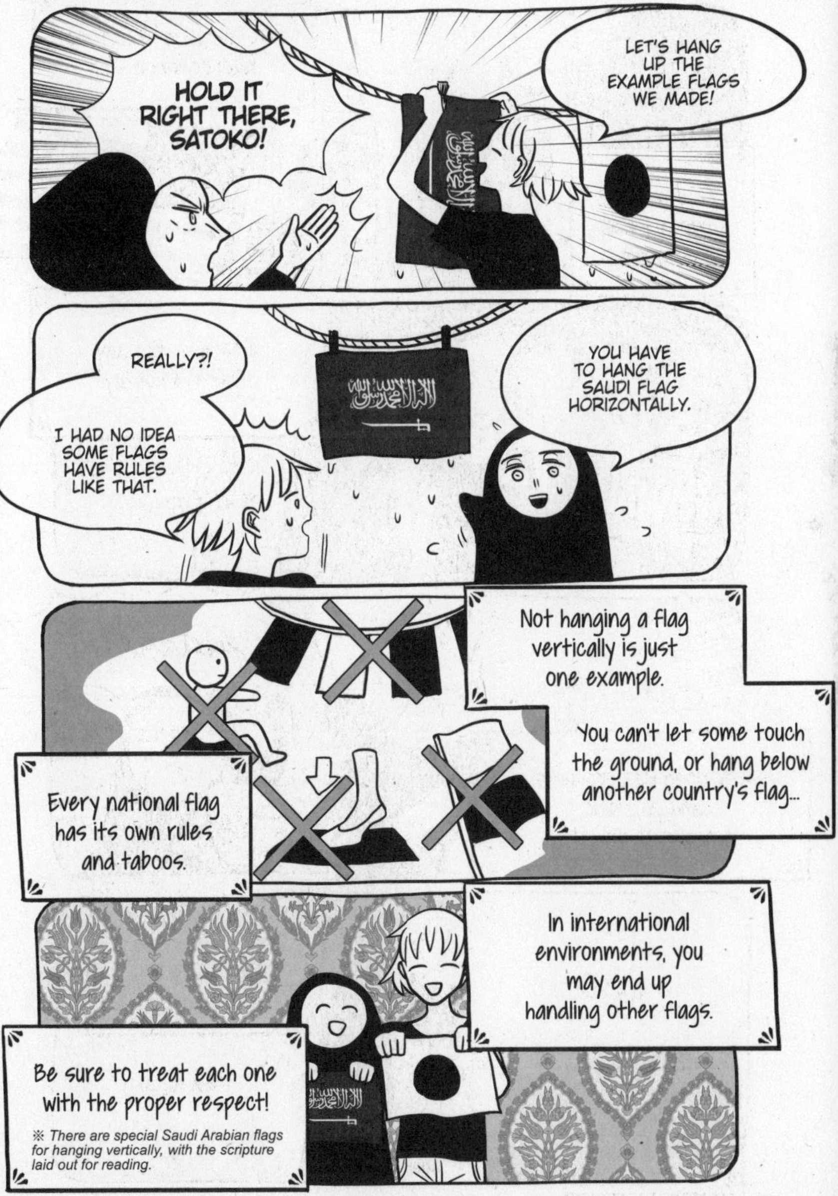
LET'S HANG UP THE EXAMPLE FLAGS WE MADE!
HOLD IT RIGHT THERE, SATOKO!
YOU HAVE TO HANG THE SAUDI FLAG HORIZONTALLY.
REALLY?!
I HAD NO IDEA SOME FLAGS HAVE RULES LIKE THAT.
Not hanging a flag vertically is just one example.
You can't let some touch the ground, or hang below another country's flag...
Every national flag has its own rules and taboos.
In international environments, you may end up handling other flags.
Be sure to treat each one with the proper respect!
※ There are special Saudi Arabian flags for hanging vertically, with the scripture laid out for reading.

SALE

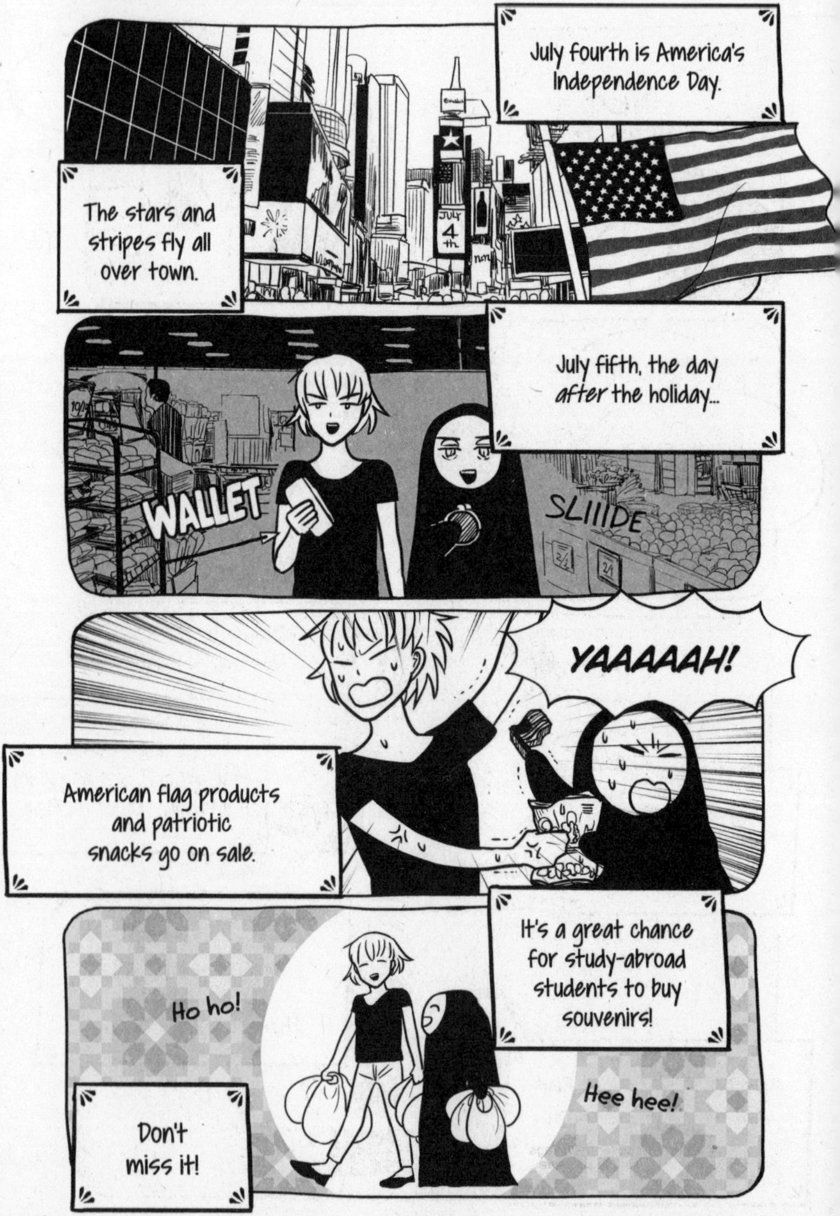
July fourth is America's Independence Day.
The stars and stripes fly all over town.
July fifth, the day after the holiday...
SLIIIDE
WALLET
YAAAAAH!
American flag products and patriotic snacks go on sale.
It's a great chance for study-abroad students to buy souvenirs!
Hee hee!
Ho ho!
Don't miss it!

HELL

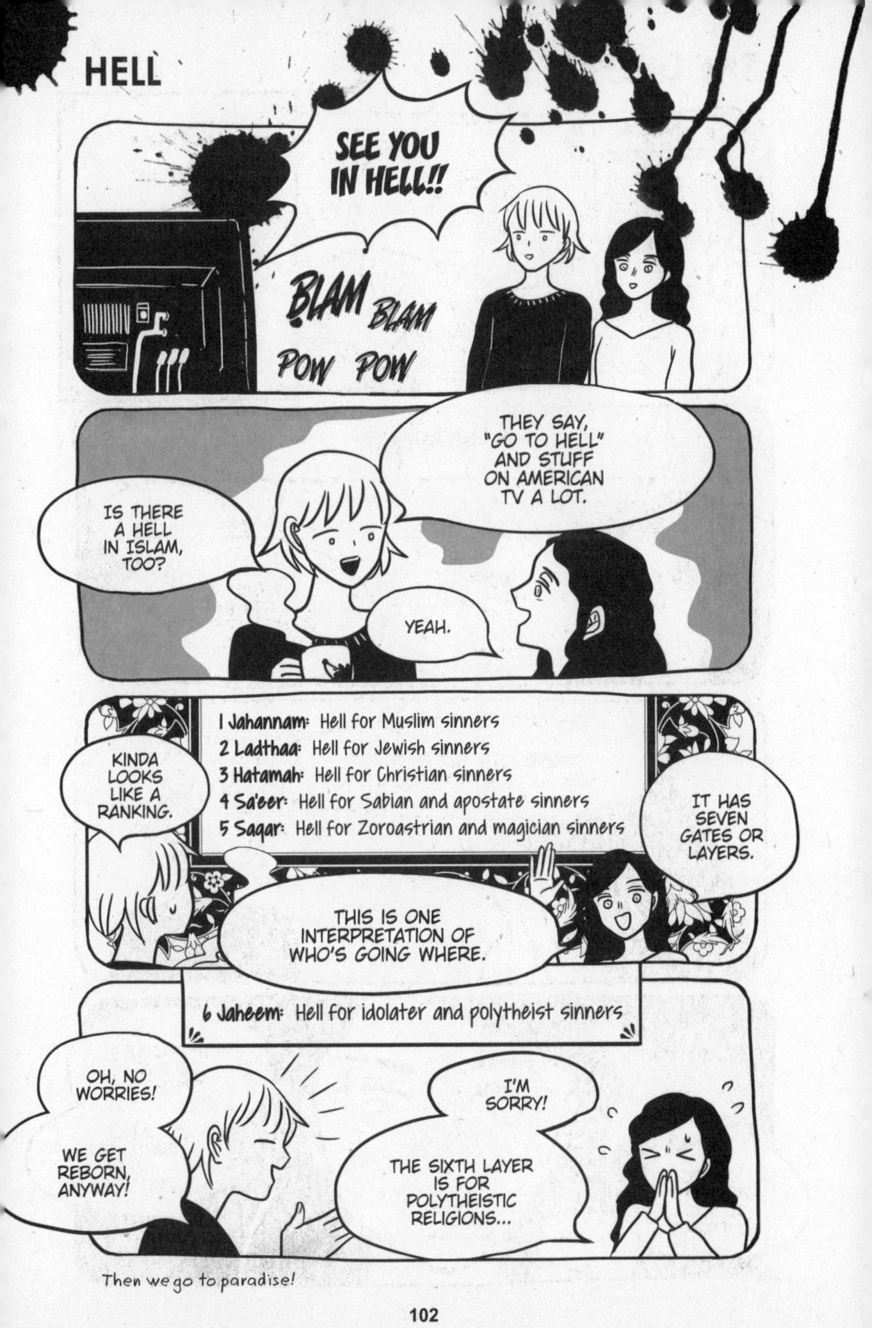
SEE YOU IN HELL!!
BLAM BLAM
POW POW
THEY SAY, "GO TO HELL" AND STUFF ON AMERICAN TV A LOT.
IS THERE A HELL IN ISLAM, TOO?
YEAH.
1 Jahannam: Hell for Muslim sinners
2 Ladthaa: Hell for Jewish sinners
3 Hatamah: Hell for Christian sinners
4 Sa'eer: Hell for Sabian and apostate sinners
5 Saqar: Hell for Zoroastrian and magician sinners
IT HAS SEVEN GATES OR LAYERS.
KINDA LOOKS LIKE A RANKING.
THIS IS ONE INTERPRETATION OF WHO'S GOING WHERE.
6 Jaheem: Hell for idolater and polytheist sinners
I'M SORRY!
THE SIXTH LAYER IS FOR POLYTHEISTIC RELIGIONS...
OH, NO WORRIES!
WE GET REBORN, ANYWAY!

Then we go to paradise!

THE DEEPEST PIT

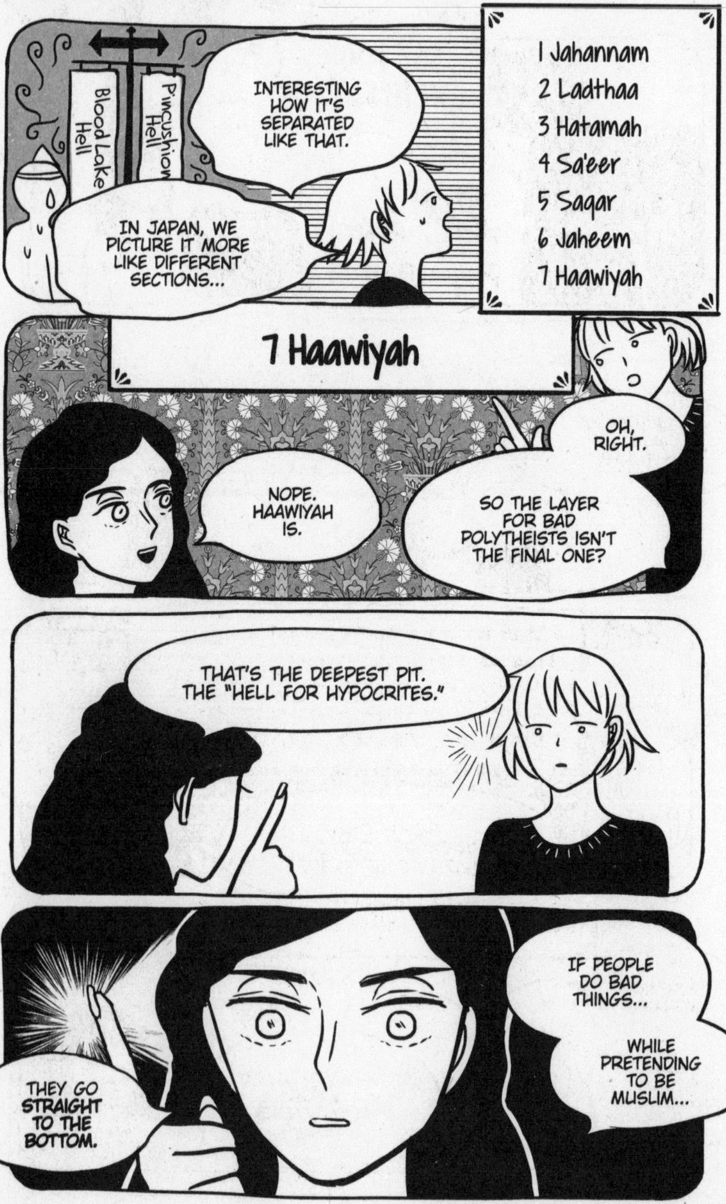
1 Jahannam
2 Ladthaa
3 Hatamah
4 Sa'eer
5 Saqar
6 Jaheem
7 Haawiyah
Pincushion Hell
Blood Lake Hell
INTERESTING HOW IT'S SEPARATED LIKE THAT.
IN JAPAN, WE PICTURE IT MORE LIKE DIFFERENT SECTIONS...
7 Haawiyah
OH, RIGHT.
SO THE LAYER FOR BAD POLYTHEISTS ISN'T THE FINAL ONE?
NOPE. HAAWIYAH IS.
THAT'S THE DEEPEST PIT. THE "HELL FOR HYPOCRITES."
IF PEOPLE DO BAD THINGS...
WHILE PRETENDING TO BE MUSLIM...
THEY GO STRAIGHT TO THE BOTTOM.

HOT CHOCOLATE

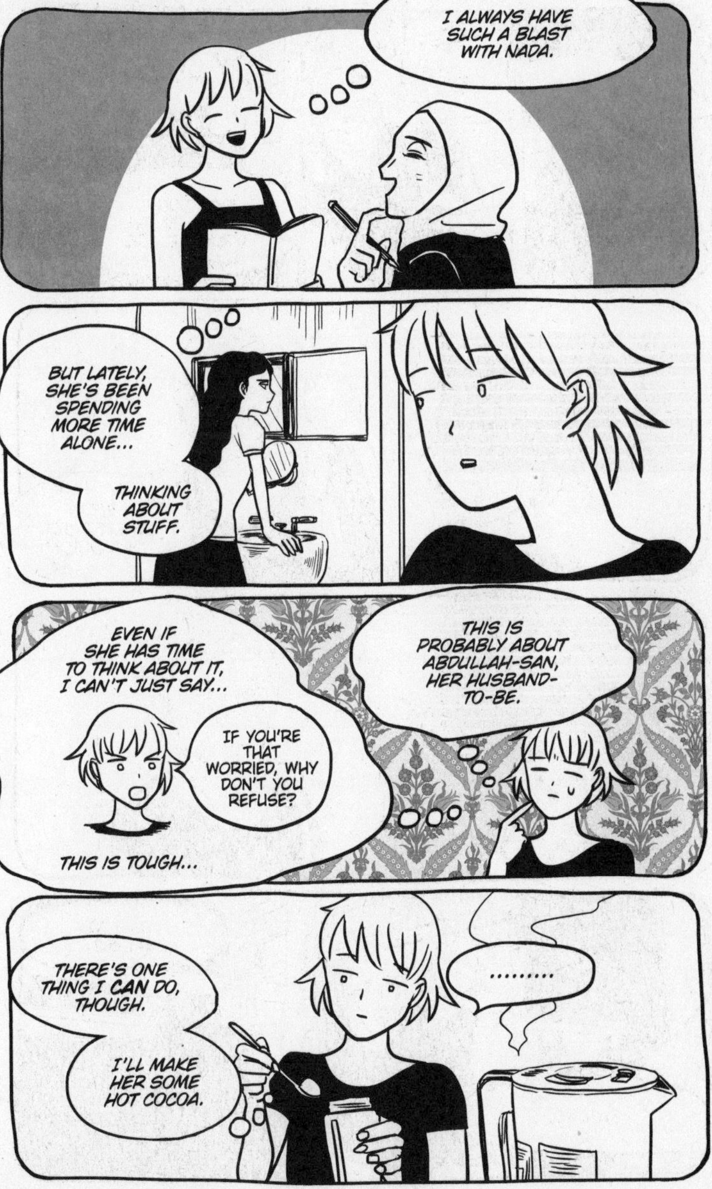
I ALWAYS HAVE SUCH A BLAST WITH NADA.
BUT LATELY, SHE'S BEEN SPENDING MORE TIME ALONE...
THINKING ABOUT STUFF.
THIS IS PROBABLY ABOUT ABDULLAH-SAN, HER HUSBAND-TO-BE.
EVEN IF SHE HAS TIME TO THINK ABOUT IT, I CAN'T JUST SAY...
IF YOU'RE THAT WORRIED, WHY DON'T YOU REFUSE?
THIS IS TOUGH...
....
THERE'S ONE THING I **CAN** DO, THOUGH.
I'LL MAKE HER SOME HOT COCOA.

WRONG DESTINATION

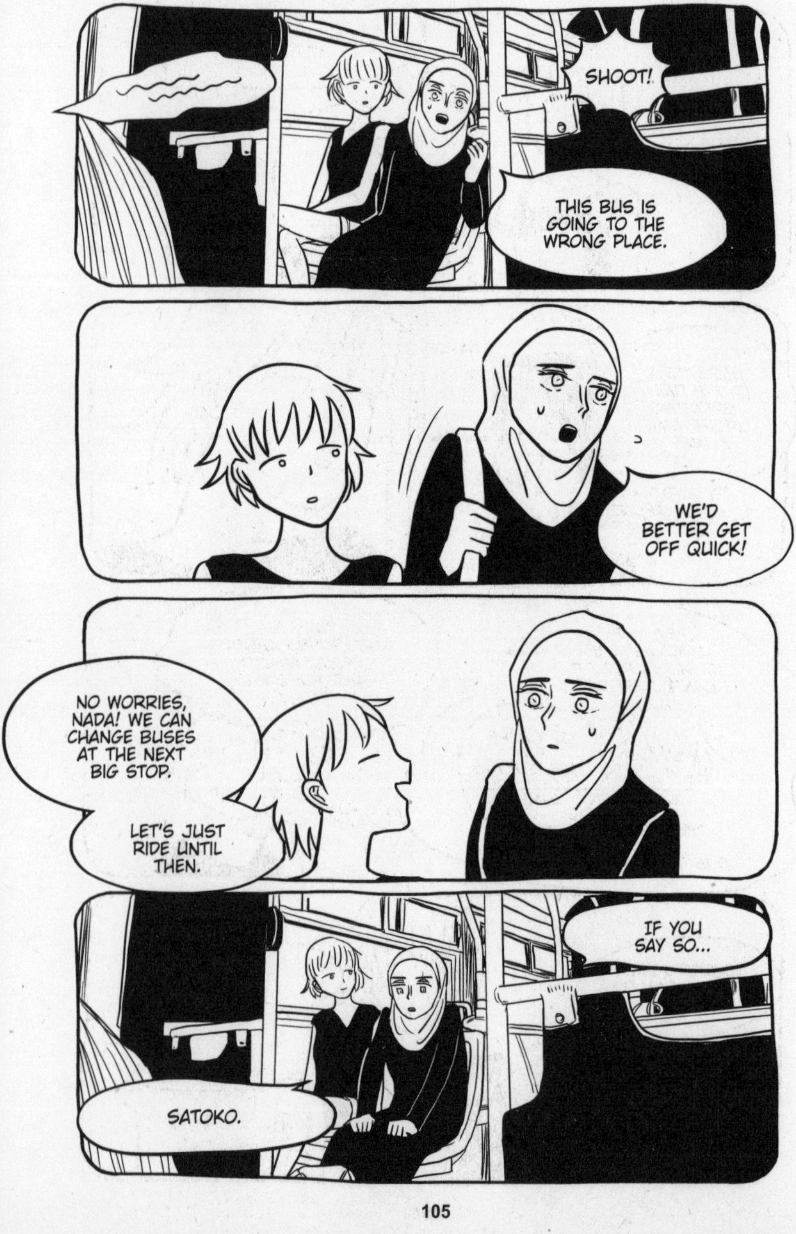
SHOOT!
THIS BUS IS GOING TO THE WRONG PLACE.
WE'D BETTER GET OFF QUICK!
NO WORRIES, NADA! WE CAN CHANGE BUSES AT THE NEXT BIG STOP.
LET'S JUST RIDE UNTIL THEN.
IF YOU SAY SO...
SATOKO.

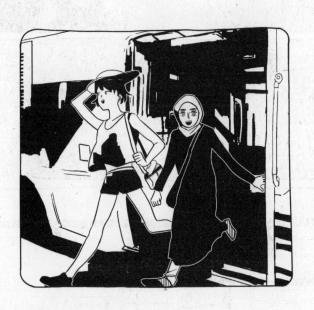

CORNFIELD

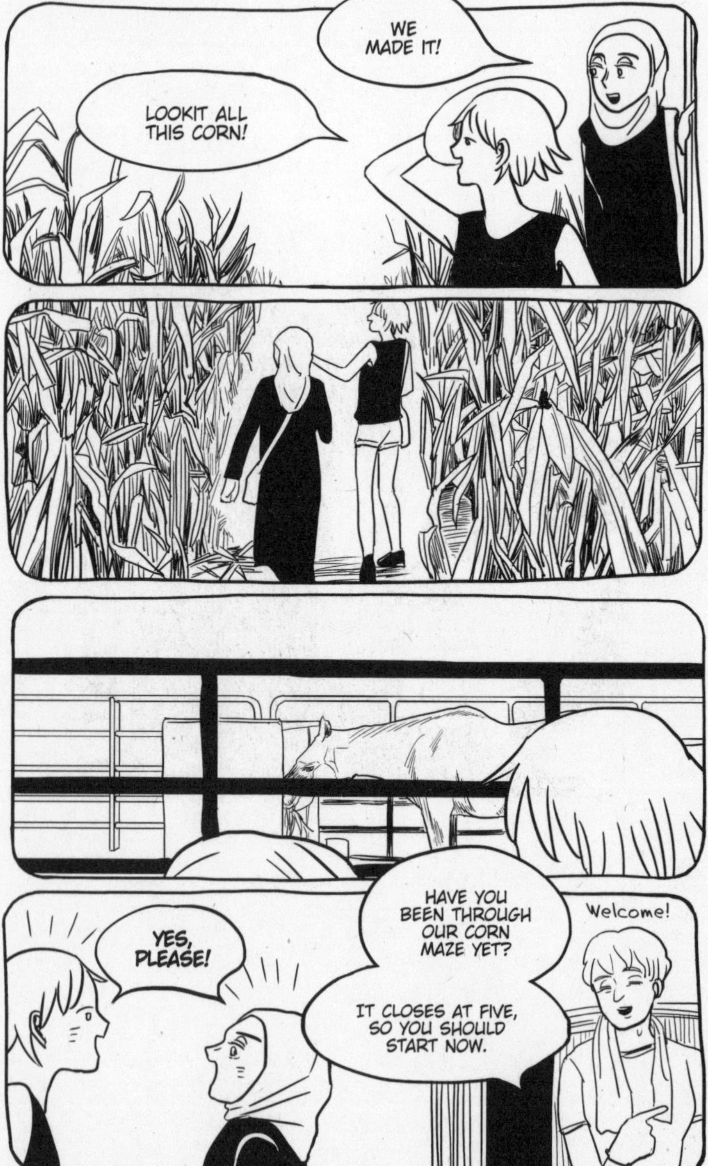
WE MADE IT!
LOOKIT ALL THIS CORN!
Welcome!
HAVE YOU BEEN THROUGH OUR CORN MAZE YET?
IT CLOSES AT FIVE, SO YOU SHOULD START NOW.
YES, PLEASE!

FAR AWAY

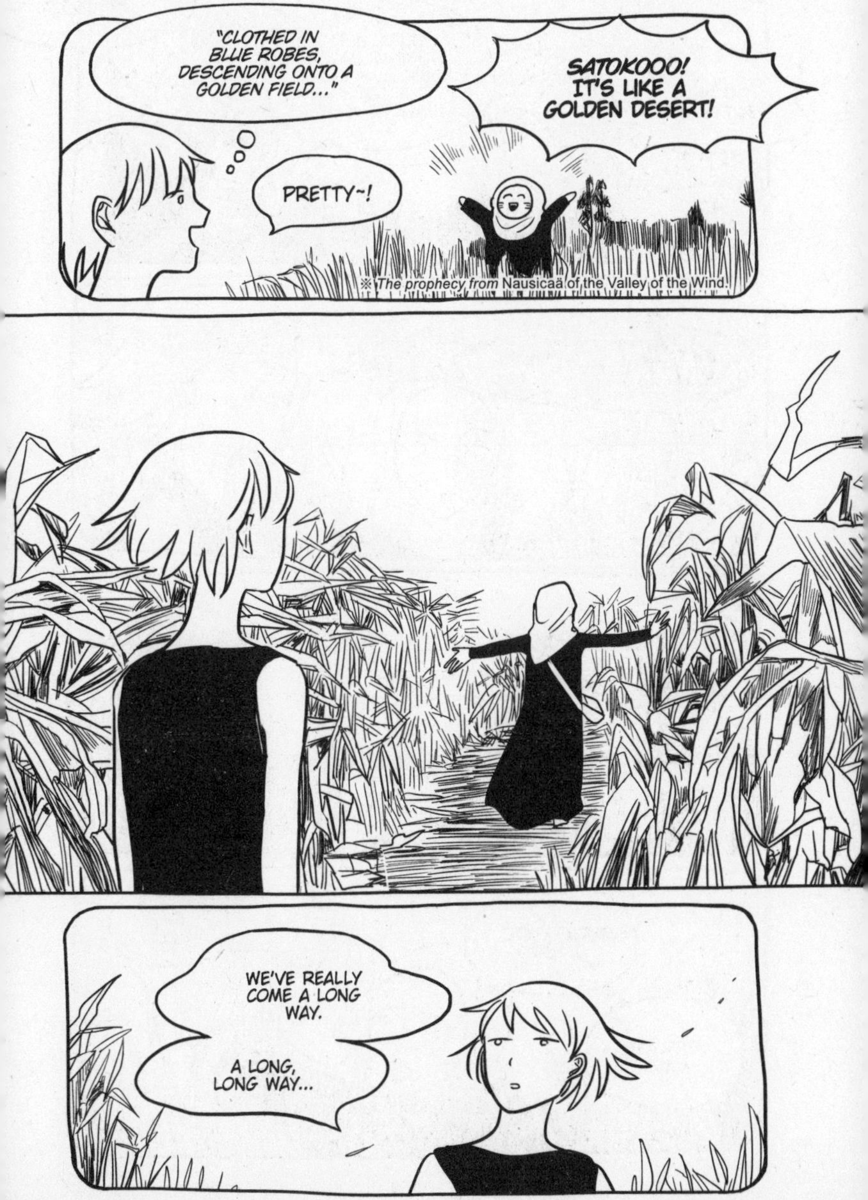
SATOKOOO! IT'S LIKE A GOLDEN DESERT!
"CLOTHED IN BLUE ROBES, DESCENDING ONTO A GOLDEN FIELD..."
PRETTY~!
※ The prophecy from Nausicaä of the Valley of the Wind.
WE'VE REALLY COME A LONG WAY.
A LONG, LONG WAY...

LIE DETECTOR

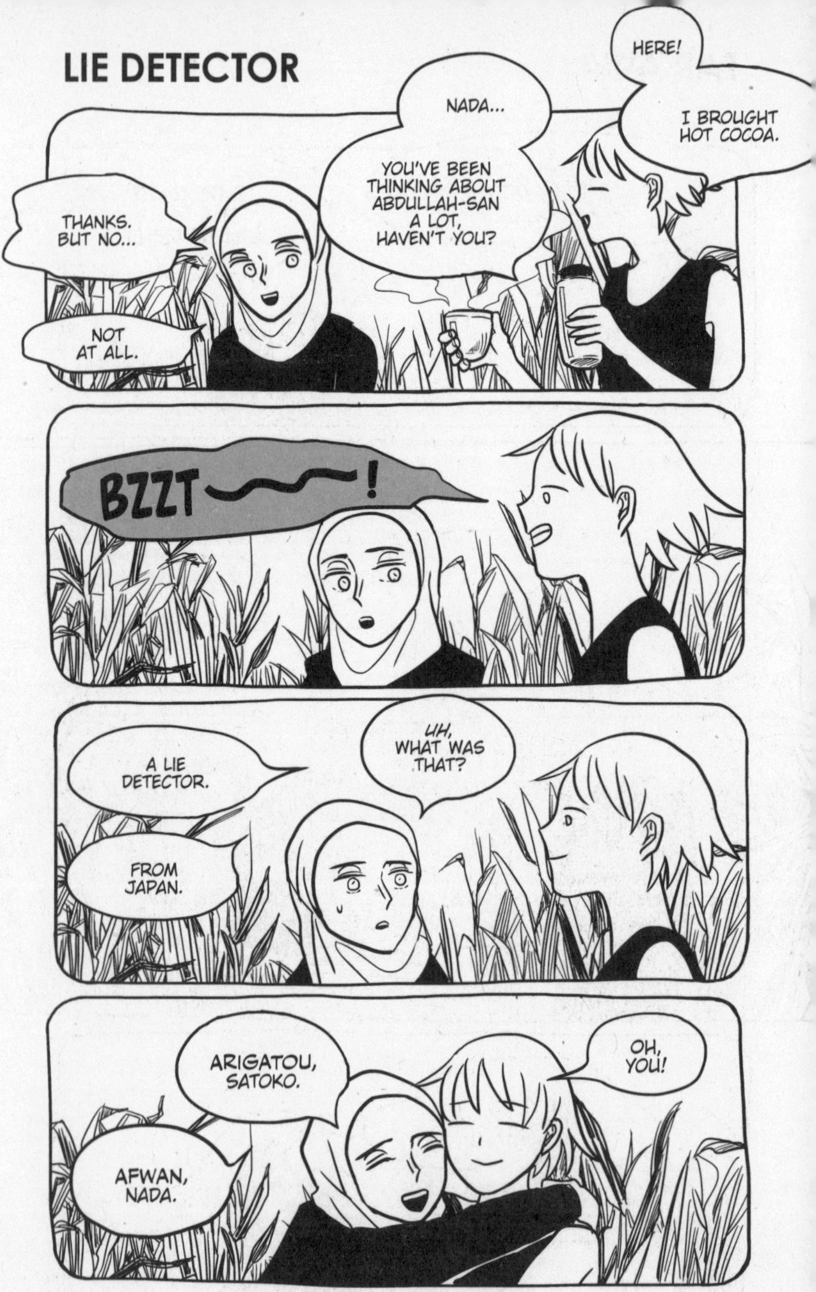
HERE!
I BROUGHT HOT COCOA.
NADA...
YOU'VE BEEN THINKING ABOUT ABDULLAH-SAN A LOT, HAVEN'T YOU?
THANKS. BUT NO...
NOT AT ALL.
BZZT~~!
UH, WHAT WAS THAT?
A LIE DETECTOR.
FROM JAPAN.
OH, YOU!
ARIGATOU, SATOKO.
AFWAN, NADA.

TALK TO ME

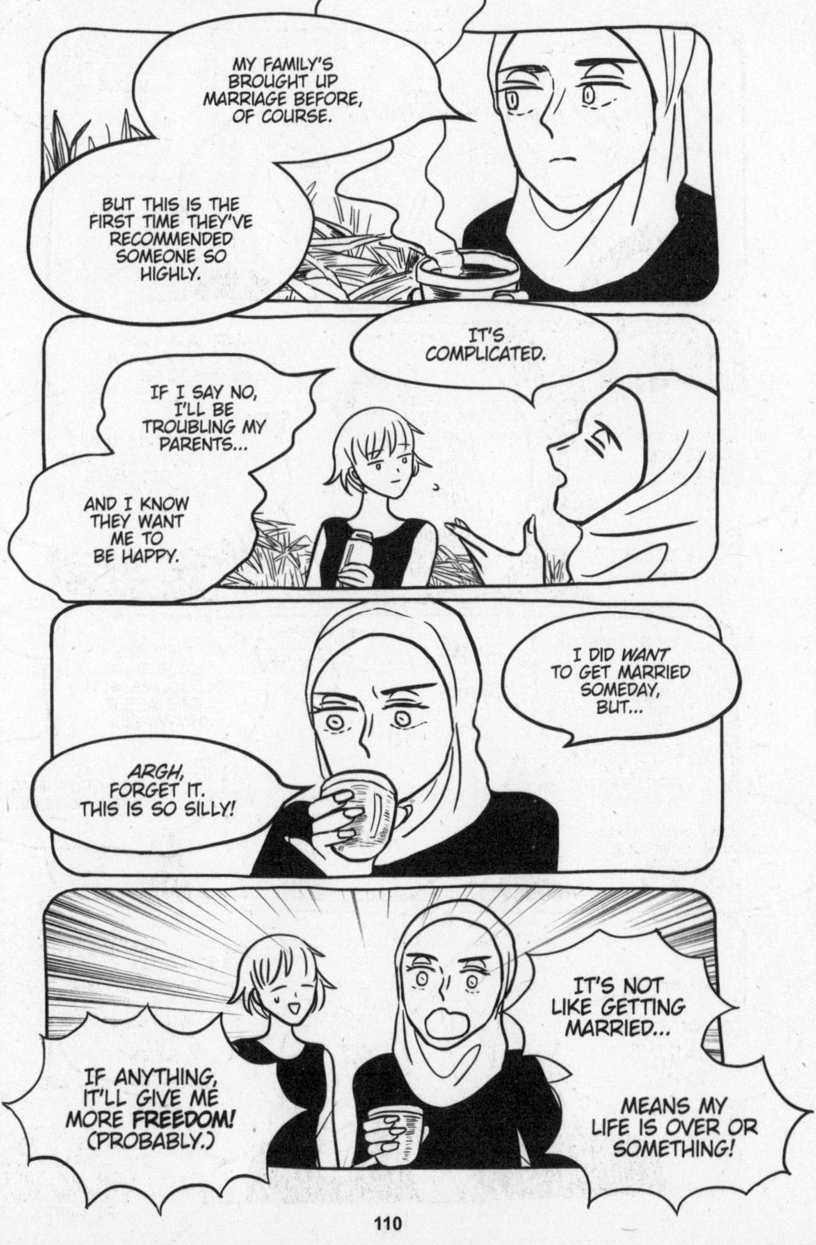
MY FAMILY'S BROUGHT UP MARRIAGE BEFORE, OF COURSE.
BUT THIS IS THE FIRST TIME THEY'VE RECOMMENDED SOMEONE SO HIGHLY.
IT'S COMPLICATED.
IF I SAY NO, I'LL BE TROUBLING MY PARENTS...
AND I KNOW THEY WANT ME TO BE HAPPY.
I DID *WANT* TO GET MARRIED SOMEDAY, BUT...
ARGH, FORGET IT. THIS IS SO SILLY!
IT'S NOT LIKE GETTING MARRIED...
MEANS MY LIFE IS OVER OR SOMETHING!
IF ANYTHING, IT'LL GIVE ME MORE **FREEDOM!** (PROBABLY.)

BEING WITH SOMEONE

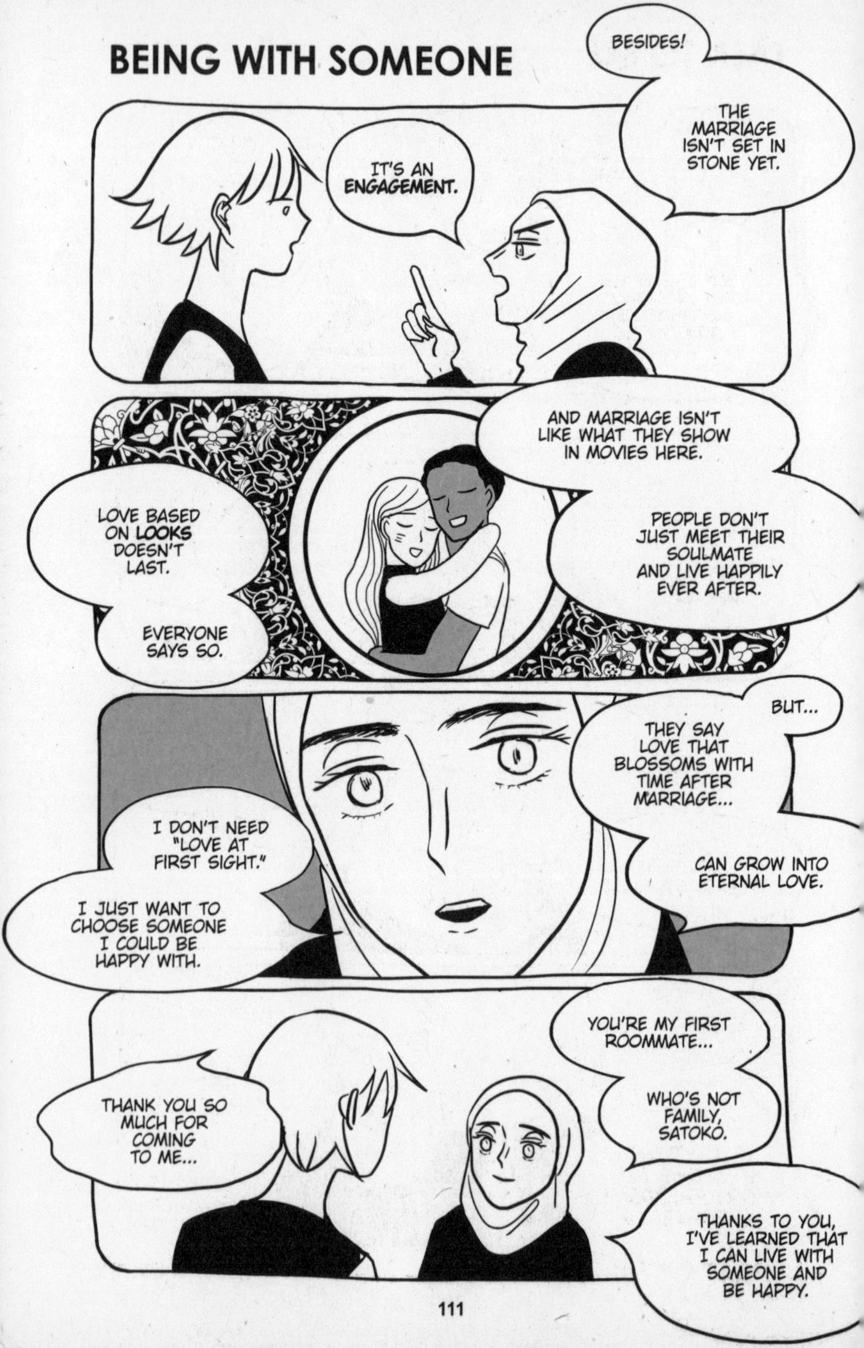
BESIDES!
THE MARRIAGE ISN'T SET IN STONE YET.
IT'S AN **ENGAGEMENT.**
AND MARRIAGE ISN'T LIKE WHAT THEY SHOW IN MOVIES HERE.
PEOPLE DON'T JUST MEET THEIR SOULMATE AND LIVE HAPPILY EVER AFTER.
LOVE BASED ON **LOOKS** DOESN'T LAST.
EVERYONE SAYS SO.
BUT...
THEY SAY LOVE THAT BLOSSOMS WITH TIME AFTER MARRIAGE...
CAN GROW INTO ETERNAL LOVE.
I DON'T NEED "LOVE AT FIRST SIGHT."
I JUST WANT TO CHOOSE SOMEONE I COULD BE HAPPY WITH.
YOU'RE MY FIRST ROOMMATE...
WHO'S NOT FAMILY, SATOKO.
THANKS TO YOU, I'VE LEARNED THAT I CAN LIVE WITH SOMEONE AND BE HAPPY.
THANK YOU SO MUCH FOR COMING TO ME...

LET'S GO HOME

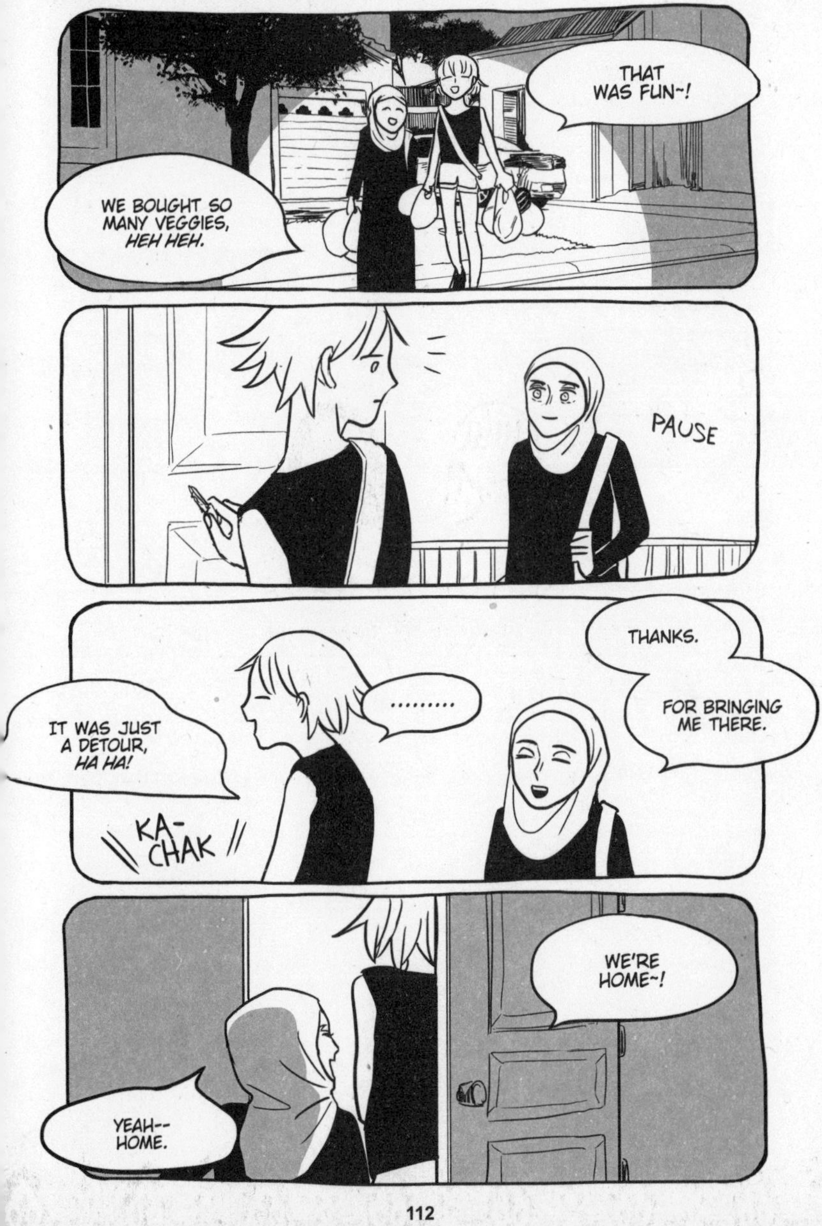
THAT WAS FUN~!
WE BOUGHT SO MANY VEGGIES, *HEH HEH.*
PAUSE
THANKS.
FOR BRINGING ME THERE.
....
IT WAS JUST A DETOUR, *HA HA!*
KA-CHAK
WE'RE HOME~!
YEAH-- HOME.

SATOKO AND NADA

Presented by Yupechika

Bonus track

SATOKO AND NADA

Presented by Yupechika

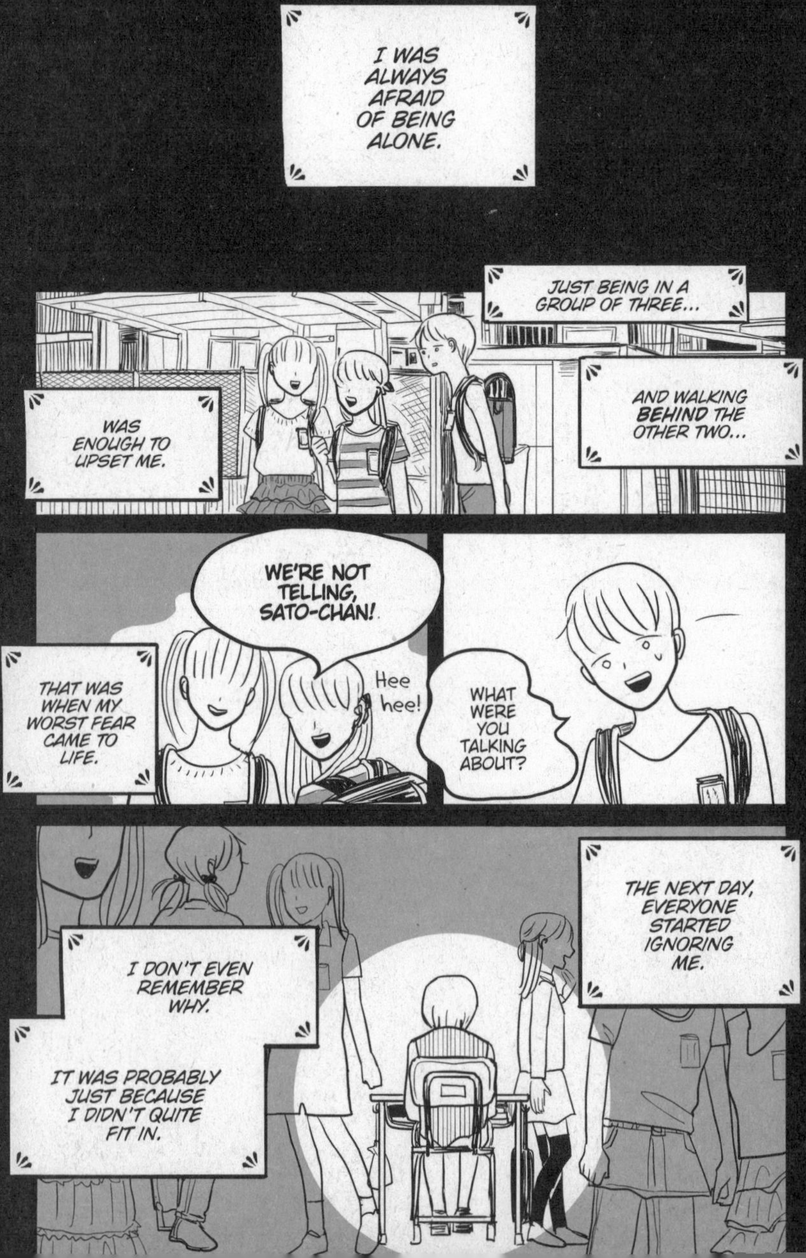
I WAS ALWAYS AFRAID OF BEING ALONE.
JUST BEING IN A GROUP OF THREE...
AND WALKING BEHIND THE OTHER TWO...
WAS ENOUGH TO UPSET ME.
WHAT WERE YOU TALKING ABOUT?
WE'RE NOT TELLING, SATO-CHAN!
Hee hee!
THAT WAS WHEN MY WORST FEAR CAME TO LIFE.
THE NEXT DAY, EVERYONE STARTED IGNORING ME.
I DON'T EVEN REMEMBER WHY.
IT WAS PROBABLY JUST BECAUSE I DIDN'T QUITE FIT IN.

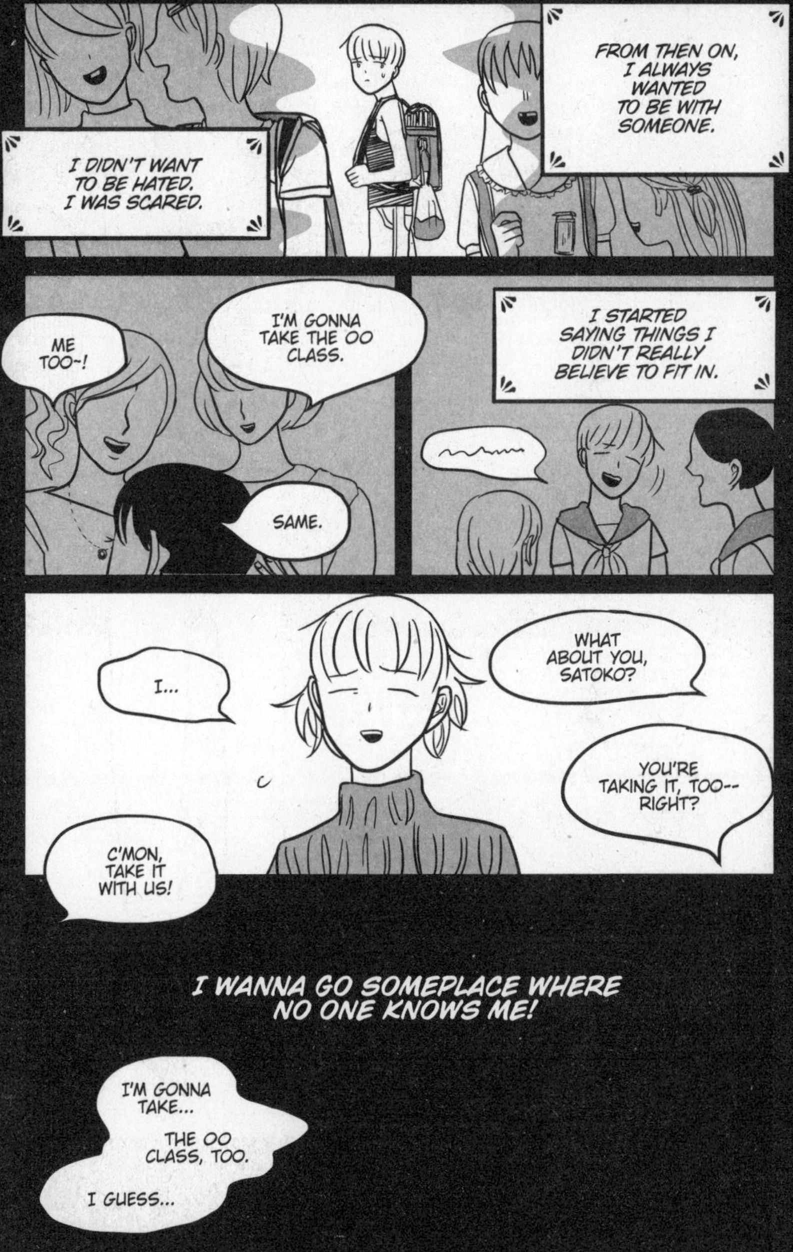
FROM THEN ON, I ALWAYS WANTED TO BE WITH SOMEONE.
I DIDN'T WANT TO BE HATED. I WAS SCARED.
I STARTED SAYING THINGS I DIDN'T REALLY BELIEVE TO FIT IN.
I'M GONNA TAKE THE OO CLASS.
ME TOO~!
SAME.
WHAT ABOUT YOU, SATOKO?
I...
YOU'RE TAKING IT, TOO-- RIGHT?
C'MON, TAKE IT WITH US!
I WANNA GO SOMEPLACE WHERE NO ONE KNOWS ME!
I'M GONNA TAKE...
THE OO CLASS, TOO.
I GUESS...

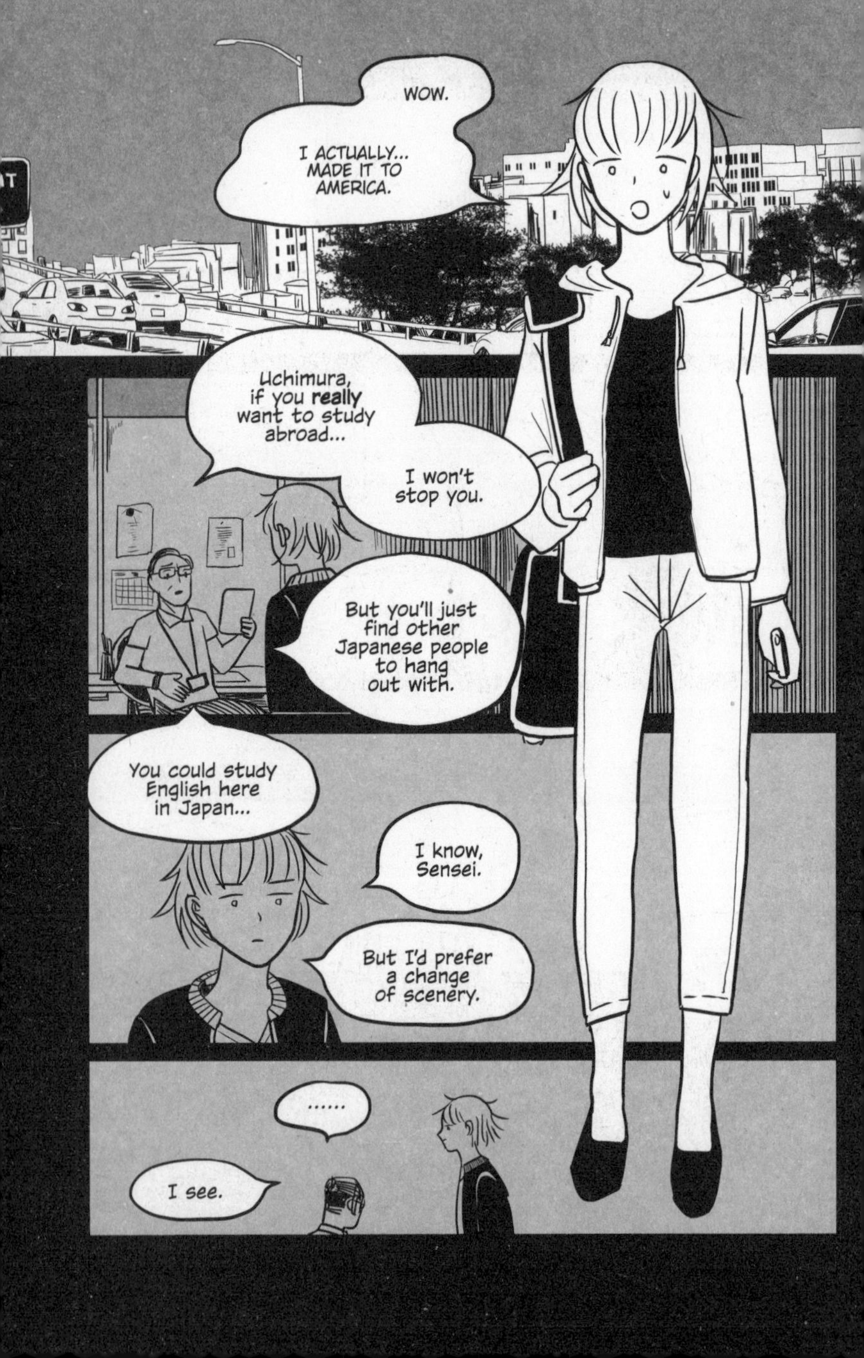
WOW.
I ACTUALLY... MADE IT TO AMERICA.
Uchimura, if you **really** want to study abroad...
I won't stop you.
But you'll just find other Japanese people to hang out with.
You could study English here in Japan...
I know, Sensei.
But I'd prefer a change of scenery.
......
I see.

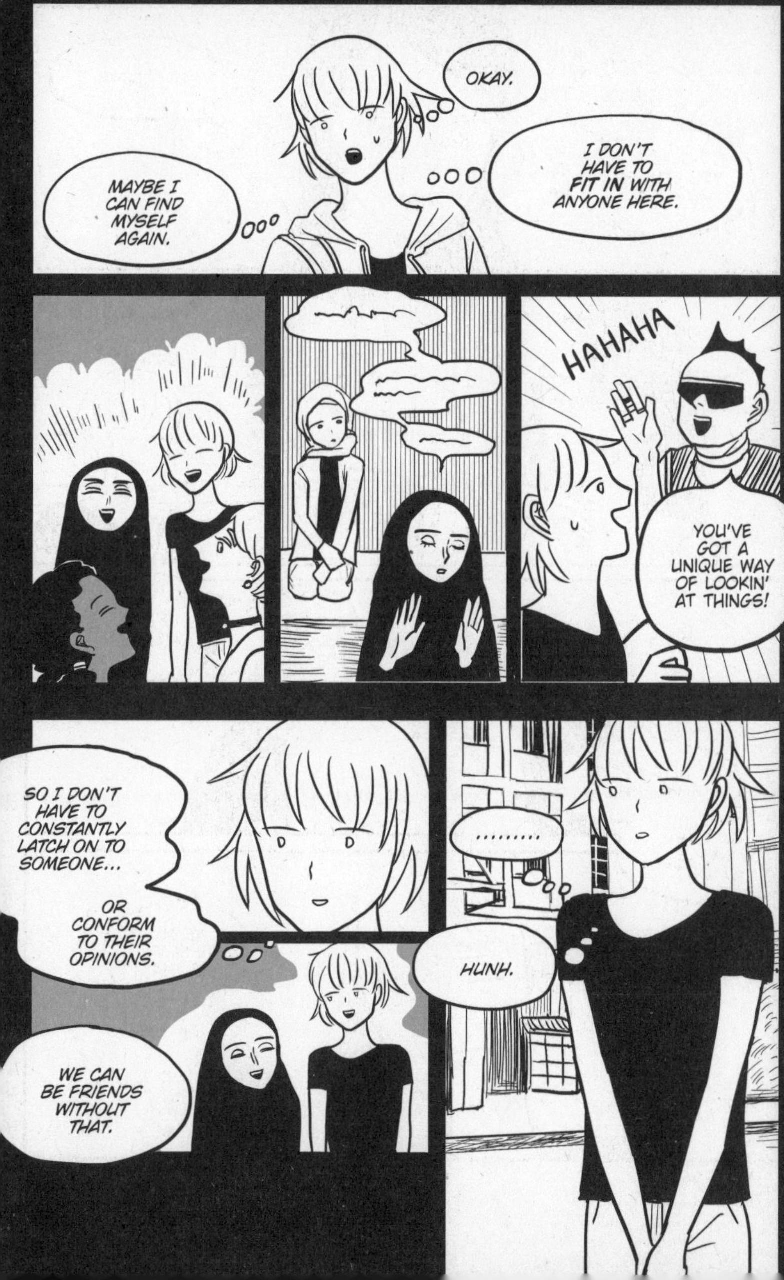
OKAY.
I DON'T HAVE TO FIT IN WITH ANYONE HERE.
MAYBE I CAN FIND MYSELF AGAIN.
HAHAHA
YOU'VE GOT A UNIQUE WAY OF LOOKIN' AT THINGS!
....
HUNH.
SO I DON'T HAVE TO CONSTANTLY LATCH ON TO SOMEONE...
OR CONFORM TO THEIR OPINIONS.
WE CAN BE FRIENDS WITHOUT THAT.

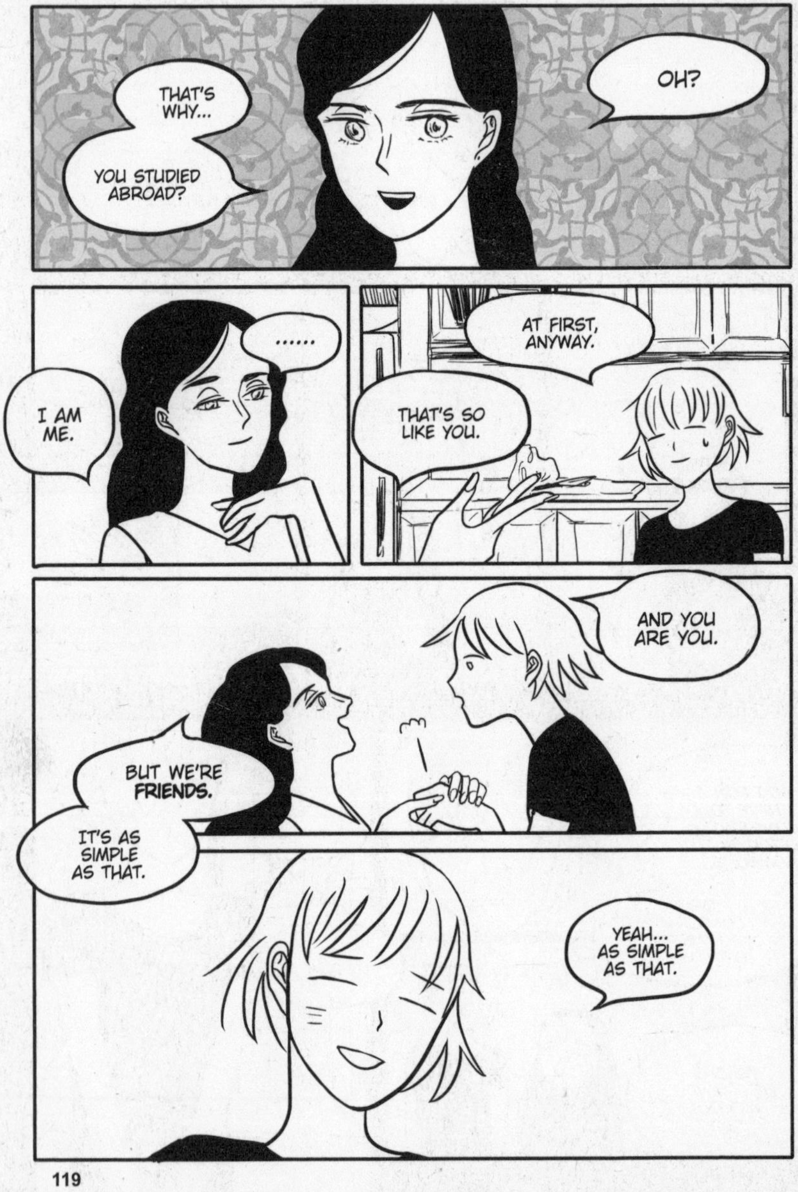
OH?
THAT'S WHY...
YOU STUDIED ABROAD?
AT FIRST, ANYWAY.
THAT'S SO LIKE YOU.
......
I AM ME.
AND YOU ARE YOU.
BUT WE'RE **FRIENDS.**
IT'S AS SIMPLE AS THAT.
YEAH... AS SIMPLE AS THAT.

Saudi Arabia

TRAVELOGUE

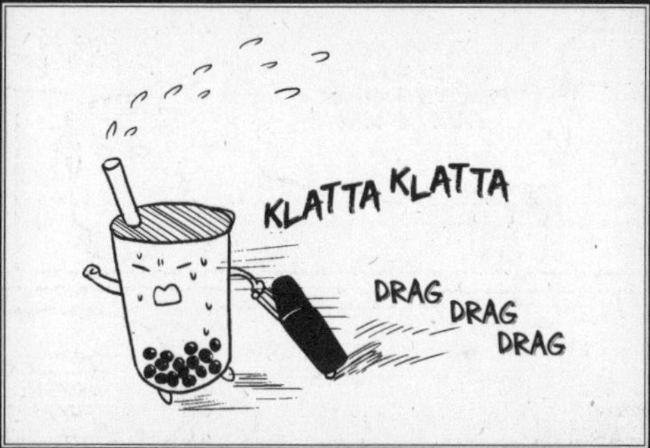
KLATTA KLATTA
DRAG DRAG DRAG

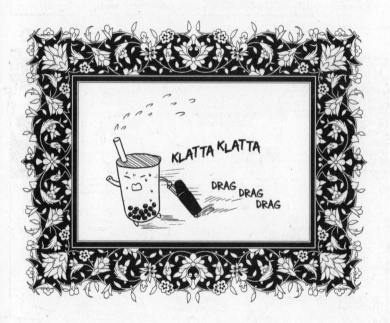

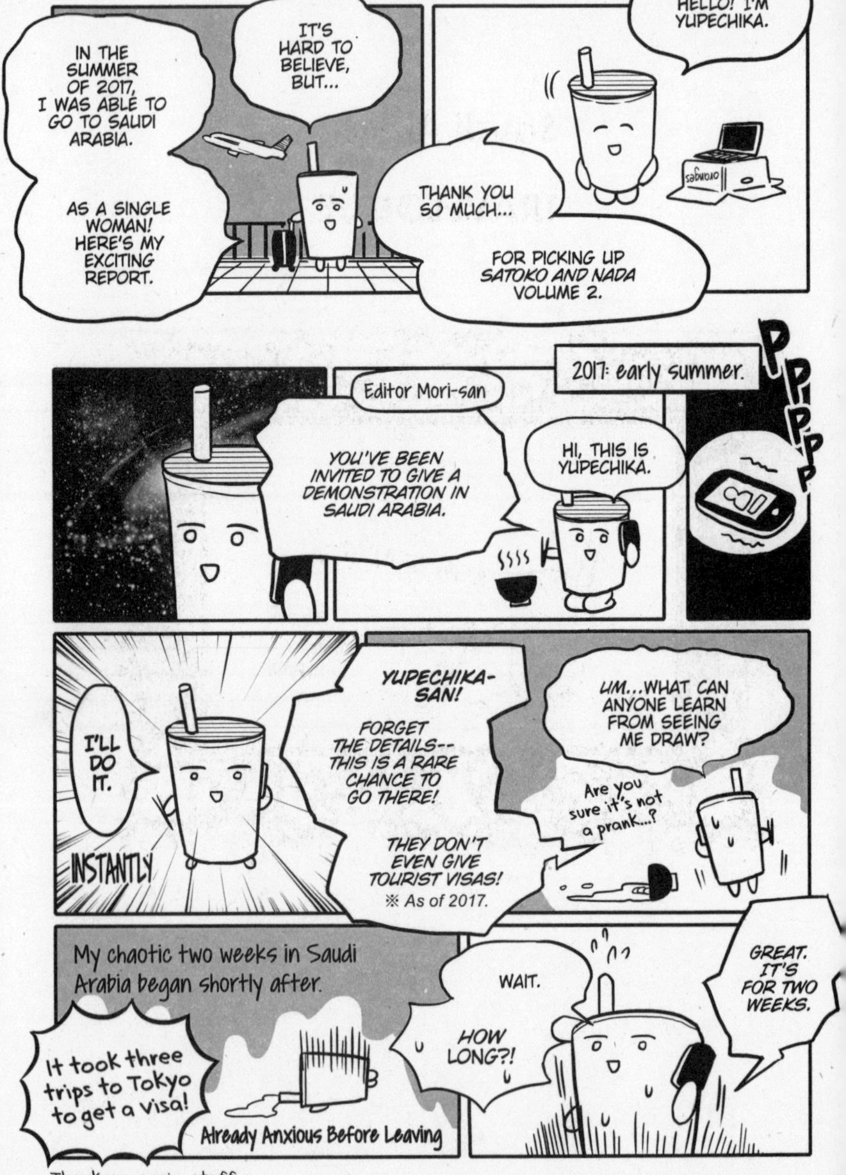
HELLO! I'M YUPECHIKA.
THANK YOU SO MUCH...
FOR PICKING UP SATOKO AND NADA VOLUME 2.
IT'S HARD TO BELIEVE, BUT...
IN THE SUMMER OF 2017, I WAS ABLE TO GO TO SAUDI ARABIA.
AS A SINGLE WOMAN! HERE'S MY EXCITING REPORT.
PPPPP
2017: early summer.
HI, THIS IS YUPECHIKA.
Editor Mori-san
YOU'VE BEEN INVITED TO GIVE A DEMONSTRATION IN SAUDI ARABIA.
UM...WHAT CAN ANYONE LEARN FROM SEEING ME DRAW?
Are you sure it's not a prank...?
YUPECHIKA-SAN!
FORGET THE DETAILS--THIS IS A RARE CHANCE TO GO THERE!
THEY DON'T EVEN GIVE TOURIST VISAS!
※ As of 2017.
I'LL DO IT.
INSTANTLY
GREAT. IT'S FOR TWO WEEKS.
WAIT.
HOW LONG?!
My chaotic two weeks in Saudi Arabia began shortly after.
It took three trips to Tokyo to get a visa!
Already Anxious Before Leaving

Thank you again, staff...

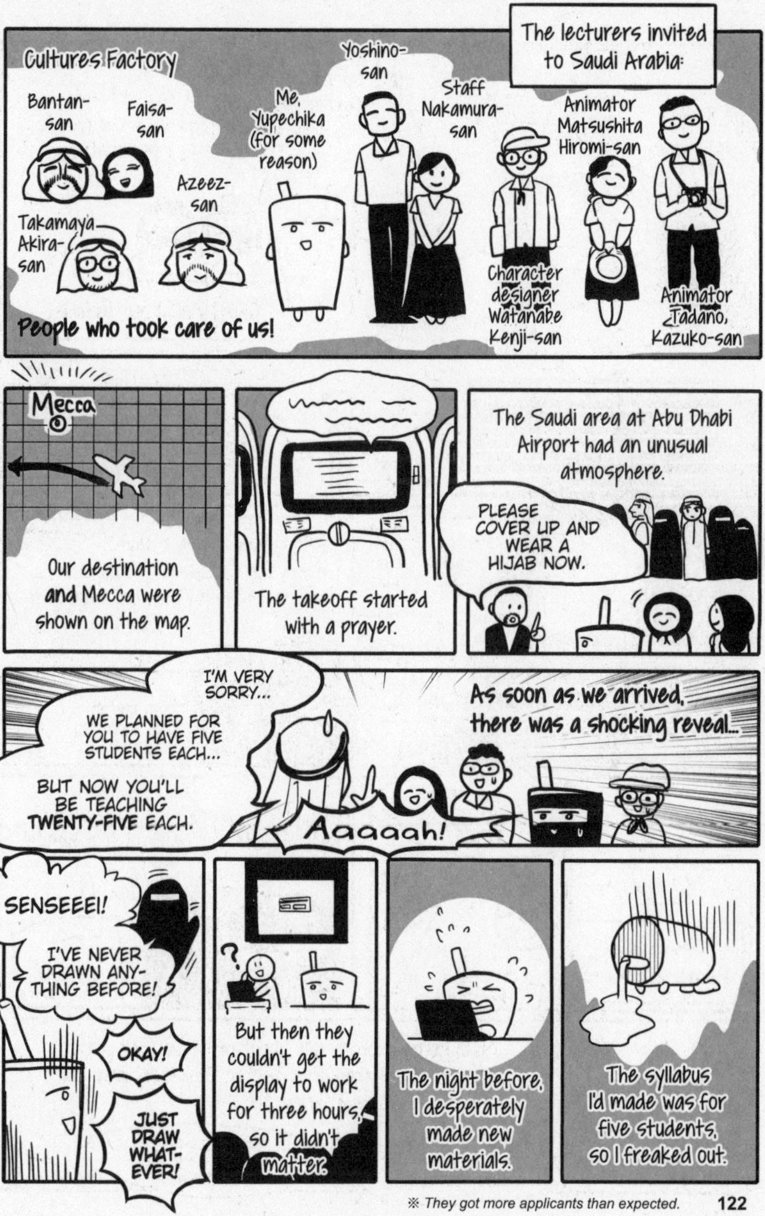
The lecturers invited to Saudi Arabia:
Animator Matsushita Hiromi-san
Staff Nakamura-san
Yoshino-san
Me, Yupechika (for some reason)
Animator Tadano, Kazuko-san
Character designer Watanabe Kenji-san
Cultures Factory
Faisa-san
Bantan-san
Azeez-san
Takamaya Akira-san
People who took care of us!
The Saudi area at Abu Dhabi Airport had an unusual atmosphere.
PLEASE COVER UP AND WEAR A HIJAB NOW.
The takeoff started with a prayer.
Mecca
Our destination and Mecca were shown on the map.
As soon as we arrived, there was a shocking reveal...
I'M VERY SORRY...
WE PLANNED FOR YOU TO HAVE FIVE STUDENTS EACH...
BUT NOW YOU'LL BE TEACHING TWENTY-FIVE EACH.
Aaaaah!
The syllabus I'd made was for five students, so I freaked out.
The night before, I desperately made new materials.
But then they couldn't get the display to work for three hours, so it didn't matter.
SENSEEEI!
I'VE NEVER DRAWN ANYTHING BEFORE!
OKAY!
JUST DRAW WHAT-EVER!

※ *They got more applicants than expected.*

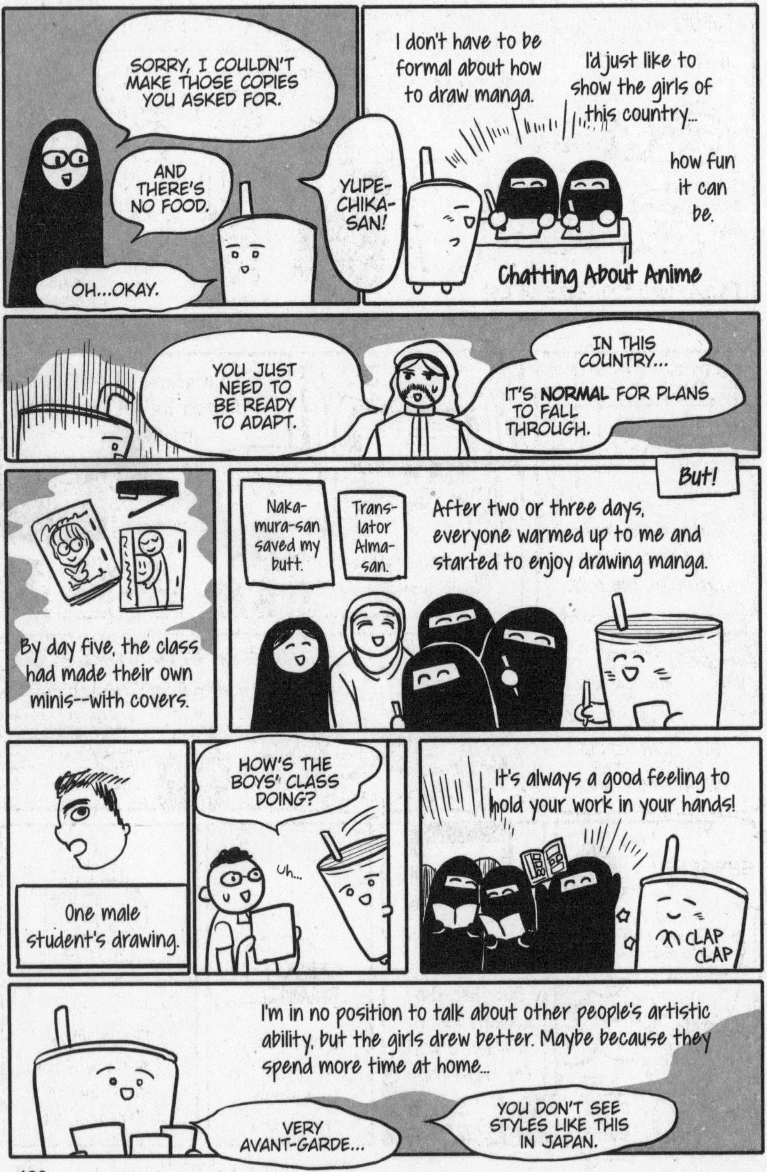

I don't have to be formal about how to draw manga.
I'd just like to show the girls of this country...
how fun it can be.
Chatting About Anime
SORRY, I COULDN'T MAKE THOSE COPIES YOU ASKED FOR.
YUPE-CHIKA-SAN!
AND THERE'S NO FOOD.
OH...OKAY.
IN THIS COUNTRY...
IT'S NORMAL FOR PLANS TO FALL THROUGH.
YOU JUST NEED TO BE READY TO ADAPT.
But!
After two or three days, everyone warmed up to me and started to enjoy drawing manga.
Trans-lator Alma-san.
Naka-mura-san saved my butt.
By day five, the class had made their own minis--with covers.
It's always a good feeling to hold your work in your hands!
CLAP CLAP
HOW'S THE BOYS' CLASS DOING?
Uh...
One male student's drawing.
I'm in no position to talk about other people's artistic ability, but the girls drew better. Maybe because they spend more time at home...
YOU DON'T SEE STYLES LIKE THIS IN JAPAN.
VERY AVANT-GARDE...

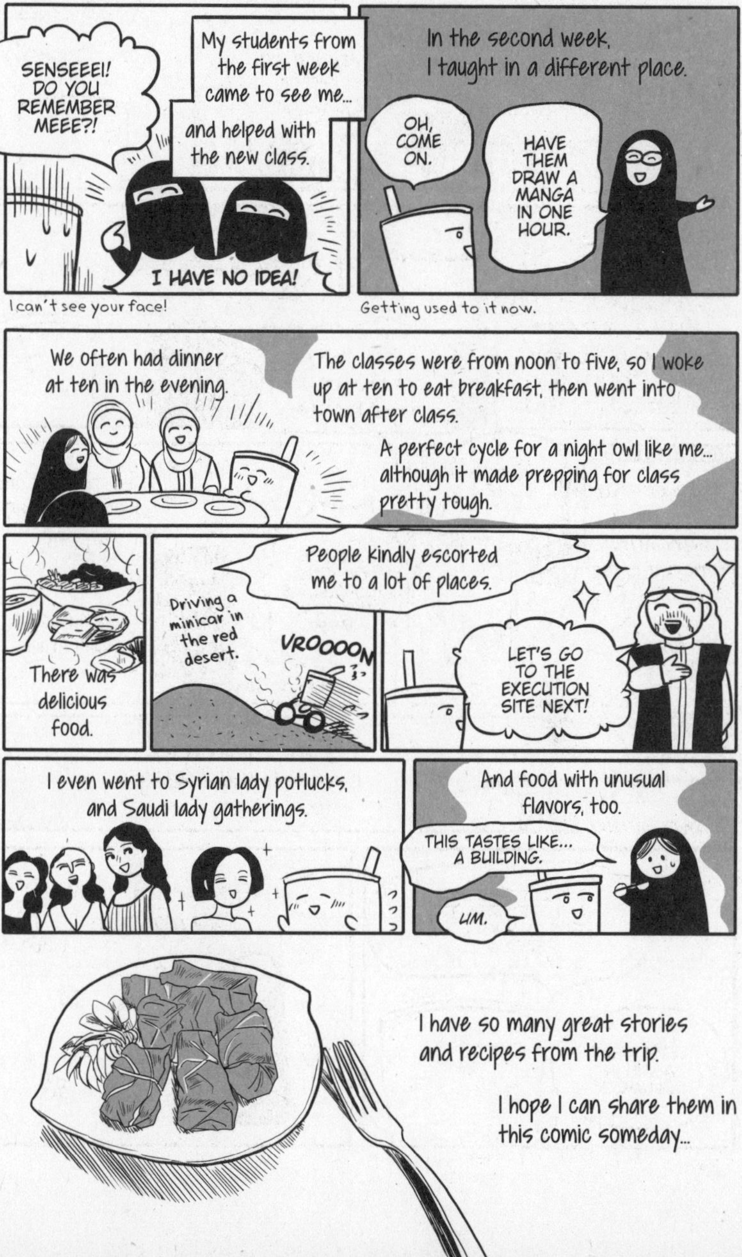
In the second week, I taught in a different place.
HAVE THEM DRAW A MANGA IN ONE HOUR.
OH, COME ON.
Getting used to it now.
My students from the first week came to see me...
and helped with the new class.
SENSEEEI! DO YOU REMEMBER MEEE?!
I HAVE NO IDEA!
I can't see your face!
The classes were from noon to five, so I woke up at ten to eat breakfast, then went into town after class.
We often had dinner at ten in the evening.
A perfect cycle for a night owl like me... although it made prepping for class pretty tough.
People kindly escorted me to a lot of places.
LET'S GO TO THE EXECUTION SITE NEXT!
Driving a minicar in the red desert.
VROOOON
There was delicious food.
And food with unusual flavors, too.
THIS TASTES LIKE... A BUILDING.
UM.
I even went to Syrian lady potlucks, and Saudi lady gatherings.
I have so many great stories and recipes from the trip.
I hope I can share them in this comic someday...

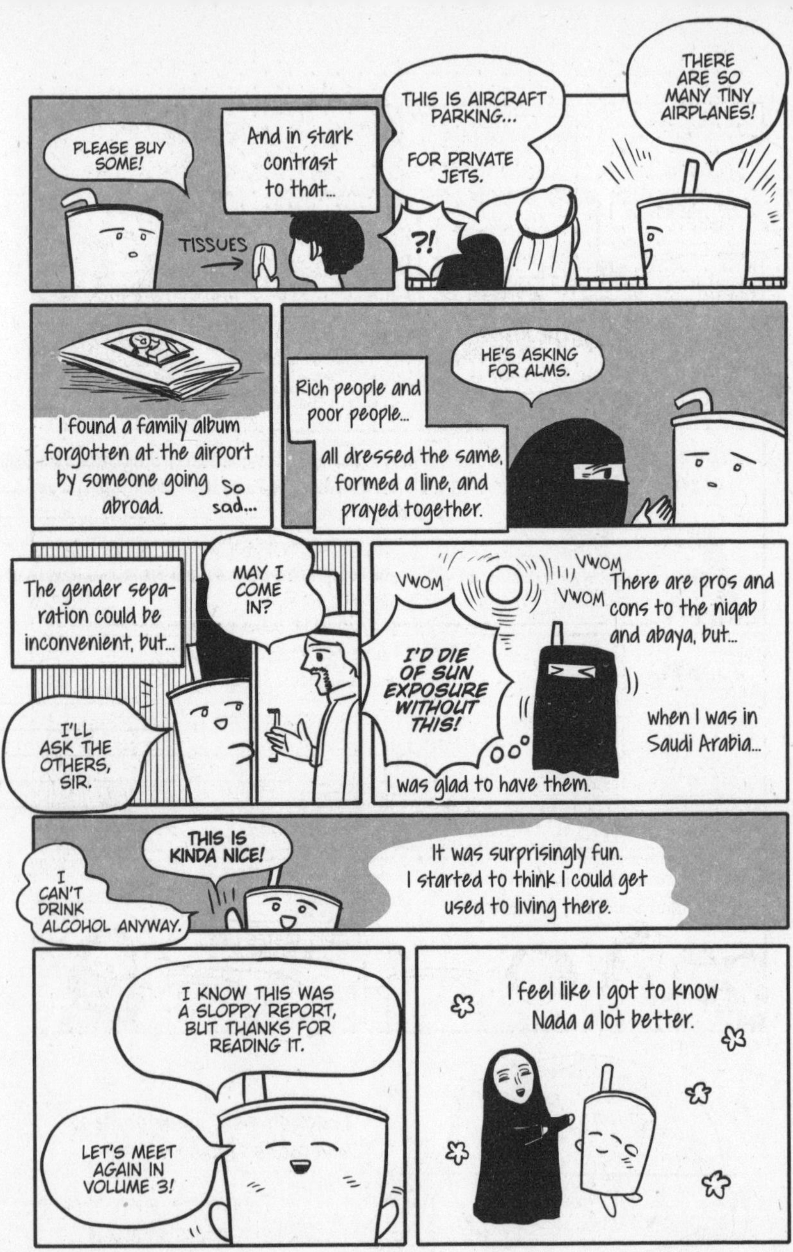
THERE ARE SO MANY TINY AIRPLANES!
THIS IS AIRCRAFT PARKING...
FOR PRIVATE JETS.
?!
And in stark contrast to that...
PLEASE BUY SOME!
TISSUES
HE'S ASKING FOR ALMS.
Rich people and poor people...
all dressed the same, formed a line, and prayed together.
I found a family album forgotten at the airport by someone going abroad.
So sad...
VWOM
There are pros and cons to the niqab and abaya, but...
VWOM
VWOM
I'D DIE OF SUN EXPOSURE WITHOUT THIS!
when I was in Saudi Arabia...
I was glad to have them.
MAY I COME IN?
The gender separation could be inconvenient, but...
I'LL ASK THE OTHERS, SIR.
It was surprisingly fun. I started to think I could get used to living there.
THIS IS KINDA NICE!
I CAN'T DRINK ALCOHOL ANYWAY.
I feel like I got to know Nada a lot better.
I KNOW THIS WAS A SLOPPY REPORT, BUT THANKS FOR READING IT.
LET'S MEET AGAIN IN VOLUME 3!

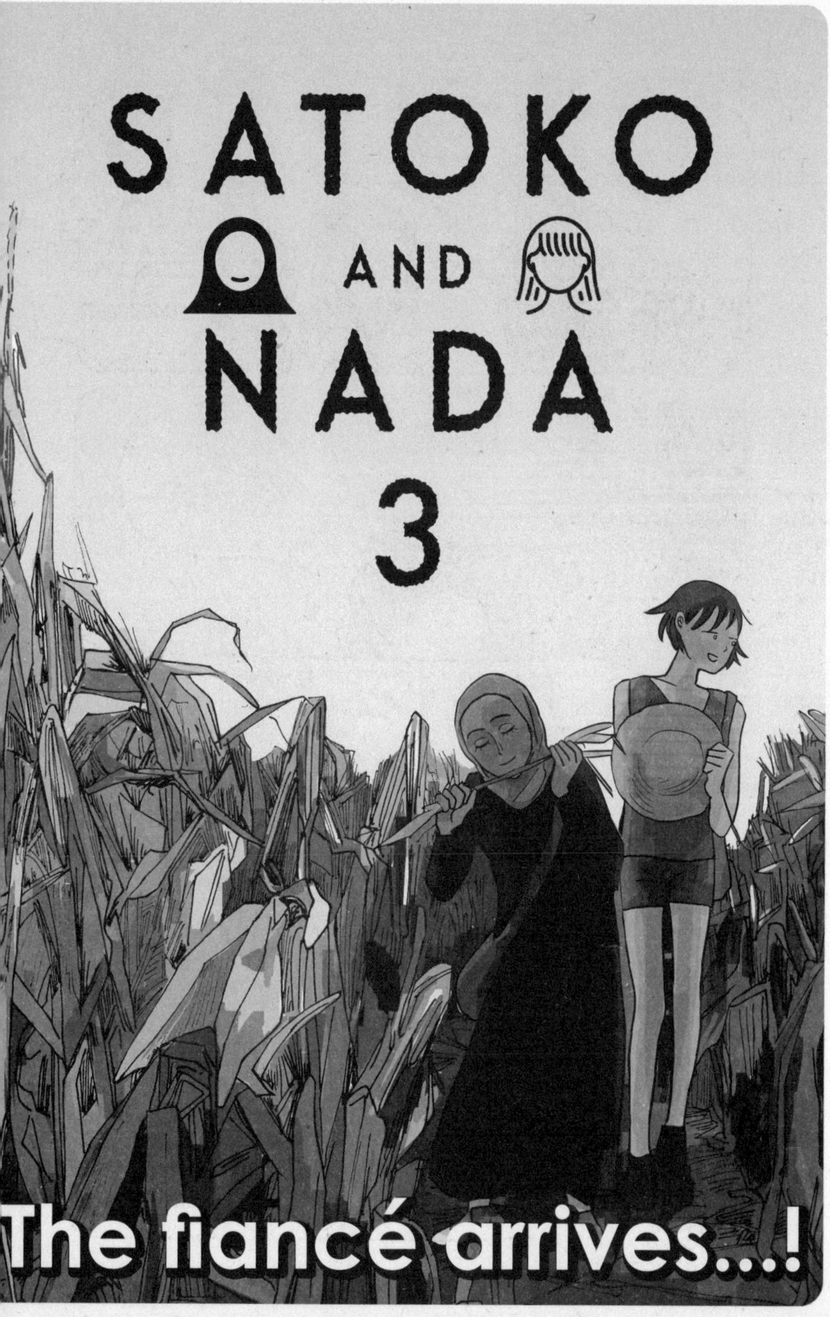
SATOKO AND NADA
3
The fiancé arrives...!

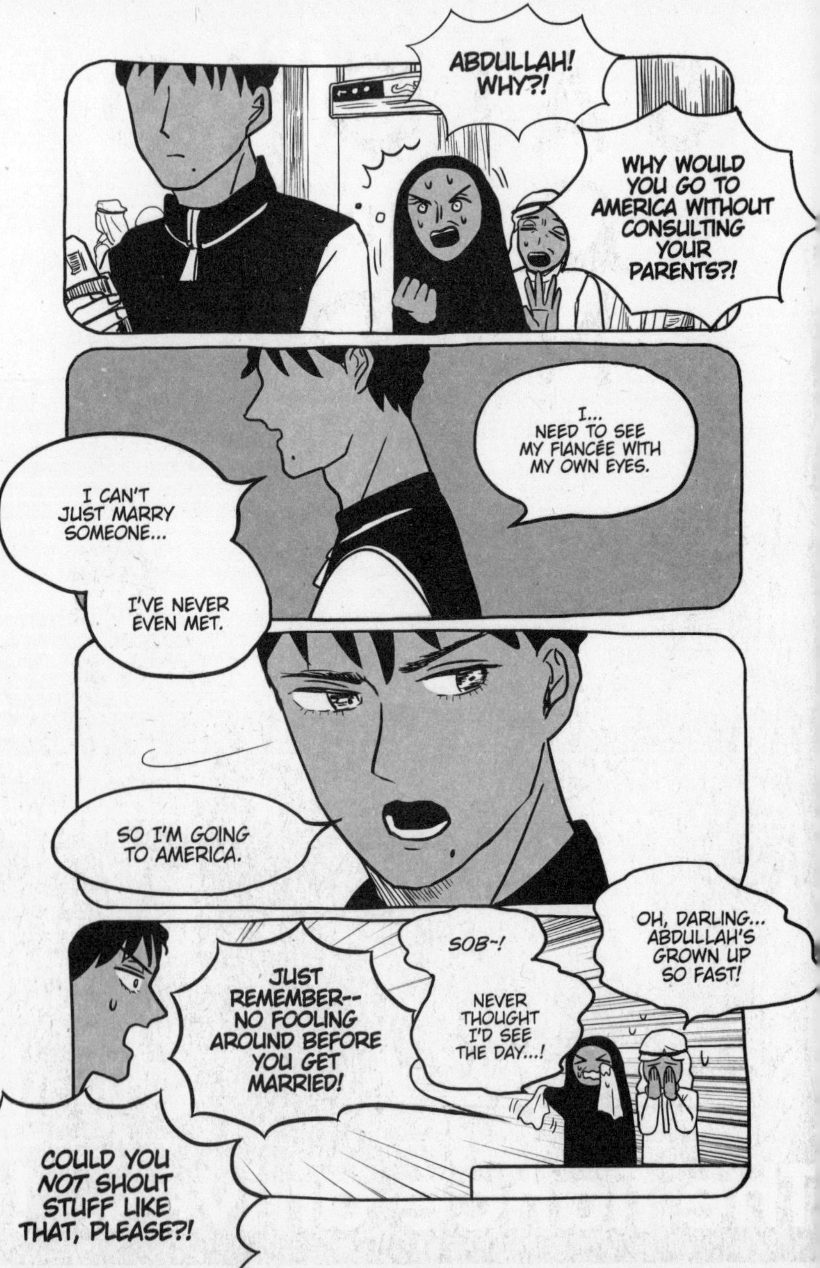
ABDULLAH! WHY?!
WHY WOULD YOU GO TO AMERICA WITHOUT CONSULTING YOUR PARENTS?!
I... NEED TO SEE MY FIANCÉE WITH MY OWN EYES.
I CAN'T JUST MARRY SOMEONE...
I'VE NEVER EVEN MET.
SO I'M GOING TO AMERICA.
OH, DARLING... ABDULLAH'S GROWN UP SO FAST!
SOB~!
NEVER THOUGHT I'D SEE THE DAY...!
JUST REMEMBER-- NO FOOLING AROUND BEFORE YOU GET MARRIED!
COULD YOU *NOT* SHOUT STUFF LIKE THAT, PLEASE?!

SEVEN SEAS ENTERTAINMENT PRESENTS

SATOKO AND NADA

story and art by YUPECHIKA script advis

TRANSLATION
Jenny McKeon

ADAPTATION
Lianne Sentar

LETTERING AND RETOUCH
Karis Page

COVER DESIGN
KC Fabellon

PROOFREADER
Danielle King
Shanti Whitesides

EDITOR
Jenn Grunigen

PRODUCTION MANAGER
Lissa Pattillo

MANAGING EDITOR
Julie Davis

EDITOR-IN-CHIEF
Adam Arnold

PUBLISHER
Jason DeAngelis

SATOKO TO NADA VOLUME 2

First published in Japan in 2017 by Star Seas Company.
Publication rights for this English edition arranged with Star Seas Company through Kodansha Ltd.,Tokyo.

Seven Seas press and purchase enquiries can be sent to Marketing Manager Lianne Sentar at press@gomanga.com. Information regarding the distribution and purchase of digital editions is available from Digital Manager CK Russell at digital@gomanga.com.

ISBN: 978-1-626929-85-2

Printed in Canada

First Printing: June 2019

10 9 8 7 6 5 4 3 2 1

FOLLOW US ONLINE: ***www.sevenseasentertainment.com***

READING DIRECTIONS

This book reads from ***right to left***, Japanese style. If this is your first time reading manga, you start reading from the top right panel on each page and take it from there. If you get lost, just follow the numbered diagram here. It may seem backwards at first, but you'll get the hang of it! Have fun!!

1
2
3
4
5
6
7
8
9

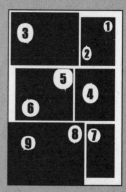